北大版海外汉语教材

初级中文：活学活用
ELEMENTARY CHINESE: LEARNING THROUGH PRACTICE

TEXTBOOK I

课本

第一册

张湘云　编著
Zhang, Xiangyun

图书在版编目（CIP）数据

初级中文：活学活用·课本·第一册/张湘云编著. —北京：北京大学出版社，2011.10
（北大版海外汉语教材）
ISBN 978-7-301-18167-6

I. 初… II. 张… III. 汉语—对外汉语教学—教材 IV. H195.4

中国版本图书馆CIP数据核字（2010）第243068号

书　　　　名：	初级中文：活学活用·课本·第一册
著作责任者：	张湘云　编著
责 任 编 辑：	邓晓霞 dxxvip@yahoo.com.cn
插画绘制：	张　晗　张婷婷
标 准 书 号：	ISBN 978-7-301-18167-6/H·2711
出版发行：	北京大学出版社
地　　　　址：	北京市海淀区成府路205号　100871
网　　　　址：	http://www.pup.cn
电子信箱：	zpup@pup.pku.edu.cn
电　　　　话：	邮购部 62752015　发行部 62750672　出版部 62754962　编辑部 62767349
印　刷　者：	北京中科印刷有限公司
经　销　者：	新华书店
	889毫米×1194毫米　　16开本　　24.75印张　　392千字
	2011年10月第1版　　2011年10月第1次印刷
定　　　价：	82.00元 (含一张CD)

未经许可，不得以任何方式复制或抄袭本书之部分或全部内容。
版权所有，侵权必究　举报电话：010-62752024
　　　　　　　　　　　电子信箱：fd@pup.pku.edu.cn

GENERAL INTRODUCTION

Overview

Elementary Chinese: Learning through Practice (初级中文：活学活用) is an introductory program that introduces Chinese language and culture to secondary school students in English-speaking countries and regions worldwide. It is intended to teach the basic grammar, vocabulary and overall structure of the contemporary written and spoken forms of the language as well as aspects of Chinese civilization and culture. The program is designed to best suit both students and instructors through newly developed methods of integrated approach and presentation that facilitate students' progress toward the goals of the National Standards for Foreign Language Education set by the American Council on the Teaching of Foreign Languages.

Guiding Principles

The design of the Five C standards established by the American Council for the Teaching of Foreign Languages.

Communication:

All exercises (dialogues, interviews, presentations, role-playing activities and games, etc.) in the program are designed to place students in a central role and are created to engage students in communication. Using this program, students will find themselves practicing more as language users than as language learners. They are directed to complete tasks in Chinese beginning in the very first chapter.

Culture:

Elementary Chinese: Learning through Practice emphasizes the teaching of culture through the vocabulary, grammar, and Culture Notes section of each chapter. Accurate and up-to-date information about Chinese culture is presented both directly and indirectly throughout examples, exercises and accompanying materials such as pictures, charts, and maps.

Connections:

This program also incorporates features in which the Chinese language is used as a medium for interdisciplinary presentations in the areas of the natural sciences, social sciences, arts and humanities. For instance, the Multiplication Table, introduced in Chapter Four to help practice numbers in Chinese, will help students to acquire and increase quantitative literacy in the language. In this way, students will constantly acquire new concepts and viewpoints that are available only through the learning of Chinese language and culture. For example, students will understand why the word '好' is composed of the two characters '女' and '子' and why "to plan" is "打算" in Chinese, etc.

Comparison:

The comparative grammar teaching method and the comparison questions for real situation and culture activities in each chapter will help students to develop insight into the nature of Chinese language and culture. It will also help them to gain a better understanding and appreciation of their own language and culture.

Communities:

In different parts of *Elementary Chinese: Learning through Practice* and with different kinds of exercises, students will be asked to communicate in Chinese not only with their instructors and peers in classroom but also with waiters, salespeople in Chinese communities and pen-friends and host family members through the Internet. This serves to help students better understand people of other ethnic groups and better prepare them to become participants of multilingual communities.

Organization of *Elementary Chinese: Learning through Practice*

This program consists of four main components: Textbook, Workbook, Lab Manual and Test Bank. Each component consists of eight chapters (ten including the two End-of-Unit Activities) that are subdivided into two theme-oriented units. At the end of each unit, there are cultural and task-based activities: oral presentations, interviews, learning of Chinese songs, and film screenings. For each activity, step-by-step directions are provided to lead both instructors and students.

Textbook:

Since each chapter is organized around a theme assigned to the chapter, all grammar, dialogues, exercises and vocabulary will be associated with that specific theme.

a) Instructional Text: Most of the instructional text are dialogues written in a natural conversational format that enables students to grasp how certain phrases and expressions may be used in today's real-life scenarios.

b) Vocabulary: Learning any language requires the mastery of new vocabulary. The main differences between Chinese and English require students to be able to relate words written in (at first glance) incomprehensible characters to words composed using the modern Western alphabet. The passage from one idiom to another is difficult, but *Elementary Chinese: Learning through Practice* strives to simplify and clarify that transition. For each chapter, the presentation of vocabulary is designed with two major considerations in mind: a gradually increasing amount of vocabulary from chapter to chapter and the reappearance of previously-studied vocabulary in subsequent chapters.

c) Grammar Explanation: A method of "simplifying" the "equations" of language transition and making the understanding of grammar easier for students underlies this section. In order to achieve this goal, several concrete measures are adopted: grammar explanations are given in English and in small steps; difficulties in grammar are stressed; "comparative grammar" is used in order to teach structure through an integrated approach; and "grammar shortcuts" are used as "catalysts" to speed the learning process.

Comparative

When learning Chinese grammar, students should look at how English and Chinese correspond as well as how they differ. For this reason, in addition to teaching the fundamental grammar rules of the language, references are also made to English structures whenever deemed necessary. For example, when presenting the conjunction "如果……, 就……," reference is made to the English-equivalent of the expression ("if... then..."), but emphasis is also placed on the fact that in English this expression is involved in both the indicative and subjunctive moods:

If the weather is nice, we will go to Beihai Park. **indicative**
If I were you, I would go study Chinese in China. **subjunctive**

In Chinese, there is no need to explain the differences that might occur between these moods because there is none; simply put, the subjunctive is understood rather than expressed. Being aware of these similarities and differences, students will be able to use the expression freely and accurately in communication.

Grammar "shortcuts"

Different ways of teaching grammar always leads to different results. *Elementary Chinese: Learning through Practice* provides a "shortcut" way for students to acquire the maximum amount of knowledge in the minimum amount of time. The shortcut method is effective, and despite its name, it does not leave out important details. The introduction of the verb "想" in Chapter Four is a relevant example. Instead of presenting the usages of this verb separately in different chapters as "想," "想家," "想念," etc., the multiple uses of the verb are presented in one chapter in this program:

想 + noun (person) to miss:
我想我的家人。 I miss my family.

想 + noun (not person) *to think about*
他想他的工作和将来。 He thinks about his work and future.

想 + verb *to want to do something*
我们想去长城。 We want to go to the Great Wall.

想 + clause *to think, or to believe*
　　　　　　　　　　　　　(to give one's opinion)
我想他是一个好老师。 I believe that he is a good teacher.

Presenting grammar in this way gives students one master key to open many different doors. Not only does this method make learning faster and more efficient, but it also improves the lasting impression that the material leaves on students' minds because it is easy to remember.

d) Exercises: There are two basic kinds of exercises in the Textbook: grammar and vocabulary. Being able to read, write, and speak the language requires that students know correct structure and grammar along with essential vocabulary. *Elementary Chinese: Learning through Practice* aims to make students' Chinese language skills well-rounded by providing practice in all areas. The objective of grammar exercises is to familiarize students with the structure covered in each chapter. Both kinds of exercises are designed to help students to understand the language input and to produce the language output: to be able to interact with other people in real-life situations.

e) Newspaper Reading: Another unique element of *Elementary Chinese: Learning through Practice* is the activity of "Newspaper Reading" designed for each lesson. Here, students are asked to find the characters and sentences they know from real newspaper articles carefully chosen according to students' vocabulary levels. In the first two to three lessons, they should be able to identify ten to fifteen characters in each article. This number will gradually increase as they progress, and the aim is to have students eventually able to recognize sentences and understand the meaning of entire paragraphs. The questions after the newspaper reading provide an opportunity for students to practice pronouncing the characters and reproduce sentences they have identified.

Field studies have shown that students have a strong preference for this activity because of the following reasons: 1) reading Chinese characters is a new experience, and they need the practice to get used to the reading of the target language; 2) as they find characters, words, expressions and eventually sentences that they can understand, they reap the rewards of learning; 3) in order to report the number of characters that they can recognize from the articles (an exercise that always follows each reading), students apply themselves to identify each character they know; 4) it may be the case that sometimes one or two characters prevent them from understanding an article title or sentence, but such situations often encourage them to ask for help from the instructor, generating a positive mood towards learning; 5) students find this activity the best way to not only review what they have previously studied but also learn new knowledge about Chinese society.

f) Culture Notes: Cultural information is embedded throughout Elementary Chinese: Learning through Practice. However, an additional section on culture is included to specifically introduce Chinese culture to students in order to promote more interest and active engagement with the chapter's cultural theme.

Most of the Culture Notes topics are directly related to the overall theme of the chapter. For instance, the theme of the very first chapter is self-introduction, and the title of the chapter is "I Am Your Teacher." In the Culture Notes of this chapter, students learn why Chinese people consider the respect for teachers as an example of moral excellence through the understanding of how characters are combined to form the word "teacher."

g) Self Assessment

Each chapter ends with a set of self-assessment questions designed again to engage students in active learning. By incorporating self-assessment into classroom activities, students are encouraged to be more reflective about their study of the language.

Workbook

The Workbook is an integral component of the program that students should use extensively in order to improve their skills. This part of the program is designed especially, but not exclusively, to emphasize students' writing skills. While the Textbook is the principal component of *Elementary Chinese: Learning through Practice*, the Workbook contains an abundance of exercises in many different forms that allow students to practice from all perspectives. The Workbook is also a continuation of the Textbook in two senses. First, it extends the learning of new vocabulary and characters by having an additional "Character Stroke" section not provided in the Textbook. The purpose of this section is to teach students the proper stroke order for writing Chinese characters through a step-by-step process that displays the addition of one stroke after another through separate but consecutive images. Another important feature of the Workbook is the introduction of radicals. Each chapter will introduce one radical. Over time, this approach will allow students to build a "database" of Chinese characters which will lead to quicker and more effective learning.

Lab Manual

Elementary Chinese: Learning through Practice is accompanied by a Lab Manual (in both hard copy and CD-ROM) that contains another set of exercises for each chapter different from those in the Textbook and Workbook. This Lab Manual serves as a resource for instructors. Designed using the maximum amount of vocabulary that students have learned up to that point, the exercises in the Lab Manual reflect much wider topics. Instructors may use the sentences (mostly mini-dialogues) in this portion of the program for listening comprehension exercises or as a means of communication: they may simply read the questions, leave the questions open-ended and encourage students to explore, experiment and use their language skills to independently discover meaningful answers in context.

Test Bank

The basic purpose of the Test Bank of *Elementary Chinese: Learning through Practice* is to provide instructors with a large resource of ideas and systematic questions to help assess students, learning processes and outcomes. The Test Bank is written in a flexible manner that allows instructors to directly use the questions provided for assessments in their courses, select only certain questions that they find suitable for quizzes or tests, or use the basic format of the questions provided but change vocabulary and expressions. It is entirely the instructor's choice whether or not to use specific items. Whatever the choice, the Test Bank is an immense resource for instructors to speed the preparation of tests, quizzes or other practice material with error-free questions and answers. The answer key for each test is provided to make grading more standardized and efficient.

Pedagogy

Elementary Chinese: Learning through Practice adopts a proficiency-based and student-centered pedagogical approach. That is to say, topics and vocabulary are of interest to students, activities are organized to increase responsibility and accountability, and exercises are designed based on meaningful activities in which students are fully engaged to attain a language learning objective. In this program, the emphasis of teaching is placed on the use of language in real-life situations. In the Textbook and Lab Manual especially, contextual exercises allow students to develop the ability to recognize when and where to use certain vocabulary, sentence structures and expressions that they have acquired from each chapter and to be a language user starting from the first day they learn Chinese with this program.

This program also uses innovative yet field-tested strategies to introduce vocabulary and grammar that improve the effectiveness of teaching. The way characters are taught is one difference between *Elementary Chinese: Learning through Practice* and other similar textbooks. While in almost all other textbooks, new characters are introduced in the form of words (composed of one, two, three or four characters：家 family, home、大家 everybody、家长制 patriarchal system、兄弟姐妹 siblings), the vocabulary, in this program is presented not only in words but also by its character components. For example, 学生 is introduced both as a word (student) and in its character components:

学 to study   生 life, fellow, to give birth to, etc.

星期天（日） as a word means "Sunday," but the meaning of each of the individual characters are also explained:

星 star   期 term
天 day   日 day, sun

What are the advantages of this teaching method? First of all, the explanation of each character helps students to better understand the meaning of the word: 学生 (student) is someone who is learning about life and 星期 (week) coincides with the seven-day system used for astrology in the ancient Chinese calendar. Secondly, it can improve the efficiency of learning. Once students remember the meaning of each character, they can easily understand:

星星 star
学期 semester
天天 every day, daily
天生 inborn, inherent, innate
生日 birthday

Therefore, students "harvest" five more words from the learning of just two. Thirdly, this informative or elicitation method of teaching allows them to become capable of understanding the formation of words and, eventually, of reading and comprehension. Finally, this method of teaching the vocabulary in the Textbook prepares students for a variety of exercises in other parts of the program.

In the Lab Manual exercises, students encounter words combined with a large number of the characters they have previously studied. For example, if students have learned "喝茶" (to drink tea) and if "买花" (to buy flowers) is also not unfamiliar to them, they will be encouraged to figure out the meaning of "花 (flower) 茶 (tea)" (jasmine tea) in a given context. In the Workbook exercises for each chapter, students will also encounter similar situations. *Elementary Chinese: Learning through Practice* takes advantage of this sort of situation and tries to motivate students' independent learning. If they are successful, the learning of new Chinese characters and words will not be a burden but rather a more enjoyable and satisfying experience.

Objective

Elementary Chinese: Learning through Practice is designed to teach the Chinese pronunciation system, characters production procedure, about 600 characters, basic sentence structures and variety of Chinese culture aspects. It intends to help students reach the Novice High or Intermediate-Low levels of listening, speaking, reading and writing on the measurement of "Proficiency Guidelines" identified by the American Council for the Teaching of Foreign Languages.

Zhang, Xiangyun
Emory & Henry College

Acknowledgments

I would like to thank my colleagues, especially the members of Academic Council at Emory & Henry College, for their help during the years I worked on Elementary Chinese: Learning through Practice. Their support allowed me to travel to China and collect first hand materials to use in the production of this program. Thank you very much.

I also would like to thank the artists and typesetting staff at Beijing Yue Er Culture & Art Inc. for their guidance, support and wonderful cooperation during the process of publishing Elementary Chinese: Learning through Practice. Please accept my gratitude and appreciation.

I am deeply indebted to Editor Qin Wuping for his permission to use articles from Xinmin Evening News. He has provided a wonderful opportunity for students to make real connections with Chinese communities and to learn Mandarin with authentic materials. I consider the editor's generosity as a significant contribution from the entire staff of Xinmin Evening News to the development of overseas education of Chinese language and culture. I send to you here my heartfelt thanks.

I am very grateful to my students (from The Westminster Schools in Atlanta, Georgia and Emory & Henry College in Emory, Virginia) and all other colleagues and friends for allowing me to use their writings and pictures in this program. Your enthusiasm and support was a constant inspiration during the years I worked on this program. Let me take a deep bow here to you all.

Finally, I thank foremost my husband and my son for believing in my ideas, encouraging my project and providing suggestions. I owe to them a great deal of gratitude for their love, support and understanding for the evenings and weekends when we should but could not be together. I love you both very much.

Zhang, Xiangyun

为什么要学中文

王亚丽(Wang Yali)13岁
亚特兰大现代中文学校八年级二班 老师 刘艳竹

　　我一开始要上中文学校是因为爸爸妈妈要我去。他们说我是中国人，应该学中文。他们也说学中文对我的脑子非常好。我一开始觉得特别难。但是爸爸妈妈坚持要我去，还不断的鼓励我，帮助我。

　　两年前，妈妈带我和佳佳去中国。那是我第一次去中国。我发现我在那儿可以看得懂电视，可以和人们用中文交流。人们都夸我中文说得好。我就感觉很自豪，也开始觉得学中文的好处了。

　　在看2004年奥运会时，我听到人们说2008年的奥运会是在中国，北京。我一听到就非常兴奋。我非常希望到中国去看奥运会。妈妈告诉我要是我的中文不好，就不能去中国。所以我想好好学中文。到时候，我不仅可以去看奥运会，而且还有可能可以给别人翻译挣点儿钱。

　　我小时候，听过好多中文故事、成语和传说。我觉得我从那些故事能学到很多东西。中文的神话非常精彩。我最喜欢哪吒闹海、西游记和宝莲灯。我希望我的中文再好一些，就可以读那些书了。

　　姥姥、姥爷、奶奶和爷爷年纪都大了，不能来美国了。我想去中国看望他们。我希望能够用中文跟他们交流。我希望能用中文给他们写信，发E-MAIL。我也想去中国看颐和园、长城、天安门等。

　　现在我上中学了。虽然我越来越忙，但是我还是不愿意放弃学中文。学中文使我了解到许多中国文化，我为有一个中国根而自豪。我现在觉得我也是中国人，应该知道我祖先说的语言。

怎么能学好中文

卢侯骏 (Jose Luna)

我知道你明年想学中文，我想告诉你怎样学好中文。你不可以在中文课上用电脑，我觉得练习写字是最重要的事。如果你用电脑，你就不能写得很好。你的发音也很重要，所以你得常常听中文录音，看中文报纸和电影。我知道你说英文，学中文的时候你得忘记英文后再开始学中文，我希望我的 suggestions 对你有用。

怎么做一个好中文学生

魏佩模 (Palmer Withers)

你好，我叫魏佩模，我想告诉你怎么做一个好中文学生：

一、你天天得听懂老师说的话，这样你的发音可以进步。

二、请你练习怎么写字，考试的时候就不会忘了。

三、不用电脑打字，只用手写字。

四、复习学过的字。

五、你得和朋友一起说中文。

目录 Table of CONTENTS

| 中文书写与发音入门
Introduction to the Chinese Writing System and Pronunciation | 1 |

| 第一单元：介绍与问候
Unit One: Introduction and Greetings | 9 |

| 第一课　我是你们的老师
Lesson 1　I Am Your Teacher | 11 |

| 第二课　李新，你好！
Lesson 2　Hello, Li Xin! | 39 |

| 第三课　我的家人
Lesson 3　My Family | 69 |

| 第四课　生日快乐！
Lesson 4　Happy Birthday! | 105 |

| 第一单元结尾活动
First Unit End Activities | 143 |

| 第二单元：学校生活
Unit Two: School Life | 153 |

| 第五课　今天你有几节课？
Lesson 5　How Many Classes Do You Have Today? | 155 |

i

目录 Table of CONTENTS

第六课　你们在中文课上做什么？ Lesson 6　What Do You Do in Chinese Class?	195

第七课　下课以后 Lesson 7　After Class	231

第八课　我的理想 Lesson 8　My Dream: What I Want to Become in the Future	269

第二单元结尾活动 Second Unit End Activities	317

生词索引 Index	331
Chinese - English	331
English - Chinese	352

中文书写与发音入门
Introduction to the Chinese Writing System and Pronunciation

Chinese Characters

What is the Meaning of "中文?"
"中文," or the Chinese language, is the short-form of "中国语言文字," or, more specifically, the Han people's language. Therefore, "汉语" (short-form of "汉族的语言") is a synonym of "中文." The term of "中国语言文字" can be divided into three parts: a) 中国: China or Chinese; b) 语言: spoken language (when used together with the word '文字' or spoken and written language when used alone); c) 文字: script or writing (namely written language). The combination of these three parts helps to understand why "学习中文" means to study the two forms of the Chinese language: spoken and written.

Evolution of the Chinese Characters
With over 4,000 years of history, the Chinese script is one of the oldest existing written languages in the world. However, the evolution of the Chinese language over such a long time period has been a relatively smooth one. It is generally acknowledged that Chinese came to its modern form through five major stages of evolution:

a) **Oracle Inscriptions (甲骨文 jiǎgǔwén),** characters carved on tortoise shells and animal bones during the Shang Dynasty (1600BC-1046BC) mostly for divination purpose, represent the earliest form of written Chinese. Although well-developed, these characters were more pictorial in form and thus much more complicated compared to the modern Chinese script.

b) **Bronze Inscriptions (金文 jīnwén),** characters etched on bronze vessels mostly for ceremonial occasions, are also called 钟鼎文 (Zhōngdǐngwén), meaning inscriptions on bronze bells and tripods. The Bronze Inscriptions were used from the late Shang Dynasty to the Western Zhou Dynasty (1046BC–771BC). Only parts of the characters had changed as Chinese writing evolved from Oracles to Bonze Inscriptions.

c) **Small Seal (小篆 xiǎozhuàn),** used in the Qin Dynasty (221BC-206 BC), marked an important stage in the evolution of the Chinese script because it simplified and unified different writing systems practiced across a China divided into several states during the Warring States Period (475BC–221BC). Compared to Oracle and Bronze Inscriptions, the Small Seal characters are more linear, lucid and distinct with respect to character strokes. It thus became a better standardized writing system.

d) **Official or Clerkly Script (隶书 lìshū),** used by government clerks and officials during the Han Dynasty (206 BC-220AD), is considered the beginning stage of the modern Chinese writing system. Composed of lesser strokes, the Li Shu characters became easier to read and write and remain to this day one of the favorite styles of Chinese calligraphy.

e) **Regular or Standard Script (楷书 kǎishū),** appearing towards the end of Han Dynasty, is the traditional writing system in contrast to the simplified characters (published in the 1950s and used now in Mainland China, Singapore and Malaysia). With the Regular Script, the strokes became straight and the characters took on a regular rectangular form.

Basic Rules for the Formation of the Chinese Characters

According to Xu Shen (许慎 **Xǔ Shèn**, 58AD-147AD), author of the first etymological Chinese characters dictionary 说文解字 (shuō wén jiě zì), Chinese characters can be classified into six categories based on the different ways they were composed. This theory is called Liu Shu (六书 **Liù Shū**). An introduction to the first four explanations of the theory will help beginning students to better understand and learn the Chinese language.

1) Pictographs 象形字 (xiàngxíngzì)

As the name of this type suggests, some Chinese characters were pictures (or, rather, rough sketches) of the objects they represented. It is therefore the most basic method of character formation. The following examples respectively represent 人 (man, person), 日 (sun), 月 (moon), 山 (mountain), and 水 (water, river).

2) Indicatives 指事字 (zhǐshìzì)

In this category, the characters are composed either of only indicative signs such as 一 (yī: one), 二 (èr: two), 三 (sān: three), 上 (shàng: upper), and 下 (xià: below) or of a pictograph and an abstract sign such as 刃 (rèn: blade = a dot on the edge of a knife) and 旦 (dàn: dawn = the sun rises from the horizon), etc.

3) Ideographs 会意字 (huìyìzì)

Composed of two or more characters, the characters in this category combine the meanings of each character in order to create a new meaningful and phonetic unit. For example, the combination of two people in '从' (cóng) is "to follow," and when three people are put together in '众' (zhòng), the new character means "mass." When '小' (xiǎo: small) is placed on top of '大' (dà: big), the meaning of the combined character '尖' (jiān) is "sharp." Here are some more examples from this category:

女 (nǚ: womam)	子 (zǐ: child)	好 (hǎo: good)
亻 (human)	言 (yán: word, speech)	信 (xìn: to trust, letter)
竹 (zhú: bamboo)	毛 (máo: hair)	笔 (bǐ: pen)

4) Phonetic-semantic compounds 形声字 (xíngshēngzì)

Characters composed of one element to signify the meaning (the radical of the character) and another to indicate the pronunciation belong to this category. The character '令' (lìng: command, order) is a perfect example. As the phonetic element, '令' combined with different radicals may compose many other characters:

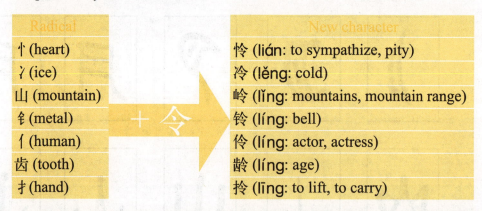

Radical		New character
忄 (heart)		怜 (lián: to sympathize, pity)
冫 (ice)		冷 (lěng: cold)
山 (mountain)	+ 令	岭 (lǐng: mountains, mountain range)
钅 (metal)		铃 (líng: bell)
亻 (human)		伶 (líng: actor, actress)
齿 (tooth)		龄 (líng: age)
扌 (hand)		拎 (līng: to lift, to carry)

The Basic Stroke Orders for the Writing of Chinese Characters

A single unbroken movement of writing is a stroke. There are 33 different kinds of strokes in the Chinese writing systems. However, 17 of the most commonly used ones are introduced here. They are classified into the following categories:

Name of the stroke	Stroke	Examples
1. horizontal	一	一 二 干
2. vertical	丨	十 中 川
3. upward	ノ	打 地 理

Downward stokes

4. downward left	ノ	八 分 千
5. vertical downward left	丿	月 用 周

6. downward right	㇏	八 大 又

Dots

7. left to right dot	丶	文 河 杰
8. right to left dot	ノ	前 办 半

Turning strokes

9. turning from horizontal to vertical	ㄱ	口 围 国
10. turning from vertical to horizontal	ㄴ	山 母 互
11. turning from downward to horizontal	㇌	去 参 红
12. turning from horizontal to downward	㇉	水 多 双

Strokes with a hook

13. horizontal hook	㇐	你 买 官
14. vertical hook	亅	水 小 寸
15. horizontal to vertical hook	㇆	刀 力 月
16. vertical to horizontal hook	㇄	儿 包 扎
17. downward hook	㇁	我 找 式

Basic rules for the order of the strokes

'From left to right and from top to down' are rules that can be applied to the writing of most Chinese characters. For example:

From left to right: 人 儿 川

From top to bottom: 三 言 主 吕

However, the middle vertical stroke precedes the side ones in the case of '小' and '水,' and it is written last when the middle vertical stroke crosses others.

Middle before sides: 小 水

Middle after other strokes: 串 甲 干 丰

In the case of an enclosure, the outside strokes precede the inside ones for an open enclosure, and the inside strokes precede the final closing stroke for a closed enclosure:

Enclosure before inside strokes: 同 网 周

Inside strokes before the closing of the enclosure: 因 囚 回 国

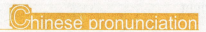
Chinese pronunciation

What is Pinyin (拼音 pīnyīn)?

Pinyin is the Romanization system, recognized by the International Organization for Standardization, used to teach standard Mandarin pronunciation. It is therefore the pronunciation system used in *Elementary Chinese: Learning through Practice*.

Chinese pronunciation is composed of three parts:

1. Twenty-three initials:

b	p	m	f	d	t	n	l	g	k	h	z
c	s	zh	ch	sh	r	j	q	x	y	w	

2. Thirty-five finals:

a	ai	an	ang	ao	e	ei	en	eng
er	i	ia	ian	iang	iao	ie	in	ing
iong	iu	o	ong	ou	u	ua	uai	uan
uang	ui	un	uo	ü	üan	üe	ün	

3. Tones:

In Chinese, most of the syllables can be pronounced in four different tones. Each tone of the same syllable represents a different character and thus indicates a different meaning:

bā
八 eight

bá
拔 to pull out

bǎ
把 to hold, to grasp, or to grip

bà
爸 father, dad

The four tones are represented by the following four tone-marks:

first tone: ―

second tone: /

third tone: ∨

fourth tone: \

The tone marks are placed over the vowel when the syllable contains a single vowel: **lǔ, mò**, and over the vowel that comes first in alphabetical order when the final is composed of two vowels: **lái, móu**. The only exception is when **i** and **u** are combined into one syllable. In this case, the tone mark falls on the second vowel: **liú, shuì**.

mā	jiá	lǒu	huāng
妈 (mother)	夹 (lined)	篓 (basket)	荒 (waste)
niǔ	kuí		
纽 (button)	葵 (certain herbaceous plants with big flowers)		

Neutral-Tone: if a syllable is not marked with a tone mark, it should be pronounced short and soft. It is a so called neutral-tone syllable:

ne	ma	xuésheng	nǐmen
呢	吗	学生 (student)	你们 (you)

Note that when a word's pronunciation is composed of two identical syllables, the repeated syllable normally remains neutral:

bàba	māma	gēge	jiějie
爸爸 (dad)	妈妈 (mom)	哥哥 (elder brother)	姐姐 (elder sister)

Tone changes may occur under certain conditions even though the marker is not changed in appearance. For example:

A: the third tone moves to the second when it is followed by another third tone:

你好 "nǐhǎo" (hello) → "níhǎo"
五百 "wǔ bǎi" (five hundred) → "wú bǎi"

B. the negation word "不" is pronounced in the second tone in front of another fourth tone:

不是 "bù shì" (not to be) → "bú shì"
不累 "bù lèi" (not to be tired) → "bú lèi"

C. The numeral "一" retains its original first tone pronunciation "yī" in counting, reading of numbers, when followed by another "一," or when coming at the end of a word, expression and sentence.

一，二，三，四，五…… (one, two, three, four, five, ...) → yī, èr, sān, sì, wǔ, ...
一九八八年 (the year of 1988) → yī jiǔ bā bā nián
一一得一 (one times one is one) → yī yī dé yī

However, when the numeral "一" precedes a first-, second- or third-tone syllable, its first tone changes to the fourth;

一天 "yī tiān" (one day) → "yì tiān"
一年 "yī nián" (one year) → "yì nián"
一百 "yī bǎi" (one hundred) → "yì bǎi"

and it changes to the second tone when "一" is followed by a fourth-tone syllable.

一个学生 "yī gè xuésheng" (one student) → "yí gè xuésheng"
一半 "yī bàn" (half) → "yí bàn"

Note that the letters "j, q, x, y" never combine with the letter "u" in a syllable. So whenever "u" follows these letters, it must be recognized as "ü" even if the umlaut is not present.

第一单元
Unit One

介绍与问候
Introduction and Greetings

第一课
LESSON ONE

我是你们的老师
I Am Your Teacher

学习目的
Learning Objectives

自我介绍	To introduce oneself
问好	To greet people
问别人与介绍自己的姓名	To ask and tell names
中国人姓名的顺序	To understand Chinese names
问问题	To ask questions

本课学习内容
CONTENTS of the chapter

一	学习发音 Pronunciation
	■ 声母 consonants：b, p, m, f, d, t, n, l, w, y
	■ 韵母 vowels：a, o, e, i, u, ü
二	课文：我是你们的老师 Text: I Am Your Teacher
三	生词 Vocabulary
	■ 名词 nouns：老师、同学、学生、中文、王、姓、名字、李同文、刘小明
	■ 代词 pronouns：你，你们、我、您、什么
	■ 动词 verbs：姓、是、叫
	■ 形容词 adjectives：好、小
	■ 副词 adverbs：不、也
	■ 助词 particles：的、呢、吗
	■ 词句 expressions：请问
四	语法 Grammar
	■ 形容词做谓语　　　Adjectives used as predicates
	■ "你"和"您"的区别　Difference between 你 and 您
	■ 动词"是"　　　　　The verb "to be"
	■ 否定词"不"　　　　The negation word "not"
	■ "好"加动词　　　　好 + verb
	■ 如何问问题　　　　How to ask questions
	■ 单数和复数　　　　Singular and plural forms
五	练习 Exercises
六	读报 Newspaper Reading
七	文化点滴 Culture Notes
八	自我测试 Self Assessment

第一课 我是你们的老师
I Am Your Teacher

一、学习发音 Pronunciation

b	d	
p	t	w
m	n	y
f	l	

+ a o e i u ü

Drill 1

bā (八)	bá (拔)	bǎ (把)	bà (爸)
bō (波)	bó (博)	bǒ (跛)	bò (簸)
bī (逼)	bí (鼻)	bǐ (笔)	bì (必)
		bǔ (补)	bù (不)

Drill 2

pā (趴)	pá (爬)		pà (怕)
pō (坡)	pó (婆)	pǒ (笸)	pò (破)
pī (批)	pí (皮)	pǐ (匹)	pì (僻)
pū (扑)	pú (菩)	pǔ (普)	pù (铺)

Drill 3

mā (妈)	má (麻)	mǎ (马)	mà (骂)	ma (吗)
				me (么)
mō (摸)	mó (磨)	mǒ (抹)	mò (末)	
mī (咪)	mí (迷)	mǐ (米)	mì (秘)	
	mú (模子)	mǔ (母)	mù (木)	

Drill 4

fā (出发)	fá (乏)	fǎ (法)	fà (发型)
	fó (佛)		
fū (夫)	fú (服)	fǔ (甫)	fù (富)

Drill 5

dā (搭)	dá (达)	dǎ (打)	dà (大)	
	dé (德)			de (的)
dī (低)	dí (敌)	dǐ (底)	dì (弟)	
dū (首都)	dú (独)	dǔ (堵)	dù (度)	

Drill 6

tā (他)		tǎ (塔)	tà (踏)
			tè (特)
tī (踢)	tí (提)	tǐ (体)	tì (替)
tū (突)	tú (图)	tǔ (土)	tù (兔)

Drill 7

	ná (拿)	nǎ (哪)	nà (那)	
				ne (呢)
nī (妮)	ní (泥)	nǐ (你)	nì (逆)	
	nú (奴)	nǔ (努)	nù (怒)	
		nǚ (女)		

Drill 8

lā (拉)	lá (旯)	lǎ (喇嘛)	là (辣)	
			lè (快乐)	le (了)
	lí (离)	lǐ (里)	lì (力)	
lū (撸)	lú (卢)	lǔ (鲁)	lù (路)	
	lǘ (驴)	lǚ (旅)	lǜ (绿)	

第一课 我是你们的老师
I Am Your Teacher

Drill 9

wā (挖)	wá (娃)	wǎ (瓦)	wà (袜)
wō (窝)		wǒ (我)	wò (握)
wū (屋)	wú (无)	wǔ (五)	wù (务)

Drill 10

yā (鸭)	yá (牙)	yǎ (雅)	yà (亚)
yē (耶)	yé (爷)	yě (也)	yè (业)
yī (一)	yí (移)	yǐ (已)	yì (义)
yū (迂)	yú (于)	yǔ (雨)	yù (育)

Drill 11

m		má (麻)		d		dù (杜)
n		ná (拿)		t		tù (兔)
l		lá (旯)		l		lù (路)
d	+ á →	dá (达)		m	+ ù →	mù (木)
f		fá (乏)		b		bù (不)
b		bá (拔)		p		pù (瀑)
p		pá (爬)		w		wù (务)
w		wá (娃)

Drill 12

b		bǐ (比)				
n		nǐ (你)		m		mō (摸)
m	+ ǐ →	mǐ (米)			+ ō →	
l		lǐ (里)		p		pō (坡)
y		yǐ (已)

二、课文 Text

同学们好！老师好！

老　　师：同学们，你们好！
学生们：老师好！
老　　师：我姓王，是你们的中文老师。
学生们：王老师，您好！

你姓什么？你叫什么名字？

老　师：请问，你姓什么？叫什么名字？
学　生：我姓李，叫李同文。

我不姓李，我姓刘。

老　师：你呢？你也姓李吗？
学　生：我不姓李，我姓刘。
老　师：你叫什么名字？
学　生：我叫刘小明。

第一課 我是你们的老师
I Am Your Teacher

課文

同學們好！老師好！

老　　師：同學們，你們好！
學生們：老師好！
老　　師：我姓王，是你們的中文老師。
學生們：王老師，您好！

你姓什麼？你叫什麼名字？

老　　師：請問，你姓什麼？叫什麼名字？
學　　生：我姓李，叫李同文。

我不姓李，我姓劉。

老　　師：你呢？你也姓李嗎？
學　　生：我不姓李，我姓劉。
老　　師：你叫什麼名字？
學　　生：我叫劉小明。

三、生词 Vocabulary

NOUNS

lǎoshī 老师 (老師) teacher	lǎo 老：old, aged
	shī 师 (師)：model, teacher, a skilled person in a certain profession
tóngxué 同学 (同學) schoolmate, classmate	tóng 同：same, alike, together
xuésheng 学生 (學生) student	xué 学 (學)：to study, to learn
	shēng 生：life, to give birth
Zhōngwén 中文 (中文) Chinese	zhōng 中：center, middle
	wén 文：character, script, writing, language
Wáng 王 (王) a surname, king	xìng 姓 surname
míngzi 名字 (名字) name	míng 名：name, given name, fame
	zì 字：word, character
Lǐ Tóngwén 李同文 (李同文) a person's name	lǐ 李：a Chinese surname
Liú Xiǎomíng 刘小明 (劉小明) a person's name	liú 刘 (劉)：a Chinese surname
	xiǎo 小：small, little
	míng 明：bright, brilliant

LESSON 1

第一课 我是你们的老师
I Am Your Teacher

PRONOUNS

nǐ
你/你 you (singular)

nǐmen
你们/你們 you (plural)

wǒ
我/我 I, me

nín
您/您 you (formal and polite form)

shénme
什么/什麼 what

VERBS

xìng
姓/姓 to be surnamed

shì
是/是 to be

jiào
叫/叫 to be called, to call

ADJECTIVES

hǎo
好/好 good, well, nice, fine

xiǎo
小/小 small, little

ADVERBS

yě
也/也 also, too

bù
不/不 no, not

PARTICLES

de
的/的

ne
呢/呢

ma
吗/嗎

EXPRESSIONS

qǐngwèn
请问/請問 may I ask, please tell me

qǐng
请/請 to invite, please

wèn
问/問 to ask, to inquire

四、语法 Grammar

1. 形容词做谓语 Adjectives Used as Predicates

The English structure "to be + adjective" (for example: He is busy.) is expressed in Chinese by dropping the verb "to be." Instead, the adjective plays the role of the predicate.

他好吗?
Is he good (or well)?

老师忙 (máng: busy)。
The teacher is busy.

好!

她小。

一老一小,真好!
(zhēn hǎo: wonderful)

练习一

请在每句话后面用一个形容词(好、小、忙、老)。
Please choose one adjective for each sentence.

(1) 我的爸爸 (bàba: dad) _____。
(2) 我的妈妈 (māma: mom) _____。
(3) 她的娃娃 (wáwa: baby) _____。
(4) 我们的老师 _____。
(5) 我的同学们 _____。
(6) 李同文 _____。

2. 你 and 您 Difference between 你 and 您

Both "你" and "您" correspond to the singular form of "you" in English. But "你" is used among friends and when talking to children, so it is known as the familiar form. "您" is used when addressing an older person and people that you do not know well, as it is often considered the formal (or polite) form. The following are some examples:

第一课 我是你们的老师
I Am Your Teacher

您	
老师	
老板 (lǎobǎn) boss	
爸爸、妈妈 (bàba, māma) dad, mom	
客人 (kèrén) guest	

你	
同学	
朋友 (péngyou) friend	
兄弟姐妹 (xiōngdì jiěmèi) siblings	
小孩子 (xiǎo háizi) kid	

练习二

按照你对"你"和"您"字的理解，为每张照片写一个句子。

Make a sentence for each of the following pictures according to your understanding of the words "你" and "您."

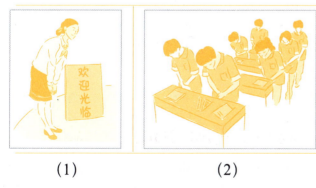 

(1)　　　　　　(2)　　　　　　(3)

(1) _____

(2) _____

(3) _____

3. 动词"是" The Verb "To Be"

Unlike in English and many other western languages, verbs in Chinese remain the same regardless of the singularity or plurality of the subject.

李同文是老师。
Li Tongwen is a teacher.

李同文和 (hé: and) 刘学明是老师。
Li Tongwen and Liu Xueming are teachers.

练习三

请用动词"是"为下面的每张照片写一个句子。
Using the verb "是," make one sentence for each of the following pictures.

(1)　　　　　　(2)　　　　　　(3)

(1) _____

(2) _____

(3) _____ 爸爸 (bàba: dad)

4. 否定词"不" The Negation Word "Not"

"不" is one of the negation words in the modern Chinese language. A verb (except 有: to have) can be changed to the negative when preceded by "不."

他是老师。
He is a teacher.

他不是老师。
He is not a teacher.

第一课 我是你们的老师
I Am Your Teacher

她是我妈妈 (māma)。
She is my mom.

她不是我妈妈。
She is not my mom.

练习四

用下面的句子采访一个同学，请把同学的每一个回答写下来。
Interview one of your classmates, and write down his / her answers to each question.

(1) 你姓王吗？ ＿＿＿＿＿＿＿＿＿。

(2) 你是小学生 (primary school pupil) 吗？ ＿＿＿＿＿＿＿＿＿。

(3) 你是老师吗？ ＿＿＿＿＿＿＿＿＿。

(4) 你爸爸 (bàba: dad) 是老师吗？ ＿＿＿＿＿＿＿＿＿。

(5) 我们的老师老吗？ ＿＿＿＿＿＿＿＿＿。

(6) 我是你的同学吗？ ＿＿＿＿＿＿＿＿＿。

5. "好" 加动词 好 + verb

This structure is equivalent to "easy (or nice) to + verb" in English.

中文好学吗？
Is Chinese easy to learn?

中文不好学。
Chinese is not easy to learn.

练习五

用中文回答下面的问题。
Answer the following questions using Chinese.

(1) 中文好学吗？

(2) 中文字好写 (xiě: to write) 吗？

(3) 王小同的名字好叫吗？

(4) 李小明的名字好听 (hǎo tīng: pleasant to hear) 吗？

6. 如何问问题　How to Ask Questions

There are several ways to form a question using Chinese.

　　A. by using the interrogative particle "吗:"

　　他是李同文。
　　He is Li Tongwen.

　　他是李同文吗？
　　Is he Li Tongwen?

　　B. by using the affirmative and negative form:

　　你是李同文。
　　You are Li Tongwen.

　　你是不是李同文？
　　Are you Li Tongwen?

　　C. by using the rising intonation:

　　他是李同文。
　　He is Li Tongwen.

　　他是李同文？
　　He is Li Tongwen?

练习六

三个人一组做这个练习：将下面的句子变成问句。每个同学做练习时另外两个同学要认真听，因为你不能用你前面的同学用过的疑问方法。
Work in groups of three: transform the following statements into questions. Listen carefully when other group members perform' as you are not allowed to use the same way that the previous student used to form your question.

(1) 我们的老师姓李。

第一课 我是你们的老师
I Am Your Teacher

(2) 我的同学好。

(3) 刘小明是好学生。

(4) 他叫王文生。

(5) 我的爸爸妈妈是老师。

(6) 你们是中学生 (middle school student)。

7. 单数和复数　Singular and Plural Forms

她是老师，我们是学生。

In Chinese the plural is formed by adding the character "们" to the corresponding singular form. For example, "你" means "you" singular, and "你们" means "you" plural.

singular	plural
你	你们
我	我们
他 (tā: he, him)	他们
她 (tā: she, her)	她们
学生	学生们
老师	老师们

Note that if the subject and the object both refer to the same group of people, the plural form marker "们" can be used **only** with the subject.

- ✓ 他们是学生。   They are students.
- ✗ 他是学生们。
- ✗ 他们是学生们。

As in English, the masculine plural form, "他们," is used when both males and females are part of the subject.

李明和 (hé: and)王莉莉(lìli: Lili)，他们都是学生。
Li Ming and Wang Lili, they are both students.

他们是学生。

我们也是学生！

练习七

三个人一组：第一，每个人用单数和复数的主语写三个句子；第二，每个人轮流读自己的三个句子，一个人读的时候另外两个人在下面的图表里做笔记，尤其要注意句子的主语是单数还是复数；三个人都读完后，每个人说出在九个句子中有几个主语是单数，几个主语是复数。

Work in groups of three: first, each one makes three sentences using different subjects (singular and plural); then, take turns to read his/her sentences. While one does the reading, the other two should use the following table to take notes and pay special attention to the form of the subject; finally, when everyone has finished reading, each person should report to the group. Among all nine sentences, how many subjects are singular and how many are plural?

同学1 姓名	同学2 姓名	同学3 姓名
(1)	(1)	(1)
(2)	(2)	(2)
(3)	(3)	(3)
单S.　　复P.	单S.　　复P.	单S.　　复P.

结果：
Result:

单数句 Singular sentences：_____　　复数句 Plural sentences：_____

我们不是老师；我们是 _____ 。

五、练习 Exercises

模式练习 Model exercises

1. 请你离开课桌，在教室里用中文问候同学们并按照例句A、B、C、D和同学们互相问问题。
   Get up from your desk, walk around the classroom to greet each other, and ask each other questions following models A, B, C and D.

您好！

Model A:

A. 你好吗？
B. 我很 (hěn: very) 好，谢谢 (xièxie: thank you)! 你呢？
A. 我也 (yě: also) 好。谢谢你！

(1) 李明，你好吗？
(2) 王莉莉 (lìli)，你好吗？
(3) 李小明、王文生，你们好吗？
(4) 刘小莉，你好吗？
(5) 你们好吗？
(6) 刘文中，你好吗？

第一课 我是你们的老师
I Am Your Teacher

Model B:

A. 你是李明?
B. 我不是李明。

(1) 李明是老师?
(2) 王莉莉是老师?
(3) 你是李明?
(4) 你是王莉莉?
(5) 你们是学生?
(6) 刘文中是学生?

Model C:

A. 你是不是李明?
B. 我是李明。你是谁 (shuí: who)?

(1) 你是不是王莉莉?
(2) 你是不是李明?
(3) 王莉莉是不是学生?
(4) 李明是不是老师?
(5) 您是不是老师?
(6) 你们是不是学生?

Model D:

A. 你好不好?
B. 我很 (hěn: very) 好。

(1) 学生们好不好?
(2) 你好不好?
(3) 李明好不好?
(4) 王莉莉好不好?
(5) 老师好不好?
(6) 你们好不好?

Different gestures when saying "您好"

Han Dynasty 206 BC-220

Qing Dynasty 1644-1911

Today

2. 两个学生一组做这个练习并轮换演 A 和 B 的角色。
   Work in pairs on this exercise and take turns to play the roles of A and B.

用"你"还是用"您"？
Should you use "你" or "您"

Model:

A. 老师好！
B. 老师，您好！

A. 王莉莉 (lìli) 好！
B. 王莉莉，你好！

(1) 王老师好！
(2) 李同文好！
(3) 爸爸 (bàba: dad) 好！
(4) 李老师好！
(5) 妈妈 (māma: mom) 好！
(6) 李明、王莉莉好！

How many "您" characters can you find in this article?

"您" ——金洪远

"您好！我能为您做些什么吗？""请您走好！"这一声声发自志愿者心底的问候和询问是如此的亲切和温暖。在赛场、在地铁站、在候车亭，我总能看见年轻志愿者真诚的面容，听见他们真诚的声音。

一个"您"字，是大家耳熟能详的"你"字下面加个"心"因为有"心"，那问候和询问竟是亲人般的贴近，像春风吹拂的微笑。

一个"您"字，是一条和谐的通道，把人与人的距离拉得更近。

选自：新民晚报 日期：2008年11月1日

第一课 我是你们的老师
I Am Your Teacher

3. 两个学生一组做这个练习，并轮换演 A 和 B 的角色。
Work in pairs on this exercise, and take turns to play the roles of A and B.

单数 (singular) —— 复数 (plural)

Model:

> A. 你是老师吗？
> B. 你们是老师吗？

谁 (shuí: who) 是老师？ 谁是学生？

(1) 你是学生吗？
(2) 你好！
(3) 我不是老师。
(4) 我不是学生。
(5) 你是老师吗？
(6) 你也是老师吗？

4. 两个学生一组做这个练习，并轮换演 A 和 B 的角色。
Work in pairs on this exercise, and take turns to play the role of A and B.

Model:

> A. 李同文是老师，王莉莉呢？
> B. 李同文是老师，王莉莉也是老师。

(1) 我们是学生，你们呢？
(2) 王莉莉很好，刘学明呢？

(3) 我学中文，你们呢？
(4) 王小明姓王，你呢？
(5) 学生们好，老师们呢？
(6) 李明是老师，我们呢？

5. 两个学生一组做这个练习，并轮换演 A 和 B 的角色。
   Work in pairs on this exercise, and take turns to play the roles of A and B.

Model:

A. 我姓王，你呢？　（刘）
B. 我不姓王，我姓刘。

我不姓王，你呢？
我也_____。

(1) 我们的老师姓李，你们的老师呢？　　　（王）
(2) 莉莉姓王，同文呢？　　　（李）
(3) 我学中文，你呢？　　　（中文）
(4) 王莉莉是好学生，李小明呢？　　　（好学生）
(5) 我姓刘，你呢？　　　（王）
(6) 我是老师，你们呢？　　　（学生）

七、文化点滴 Culture Notes

The Word "Teacher" in Chinese

There are two ways to say "teacher" in Chinese: "先生 xiānsheng" and "老师 lǎoshī," and as you can see, both of which represent a combination of two characters. The formation of these words allows for a better understanding of a Chinese tradition: the respect of teachers.

孔子 Confucius

The word "xiānsheng" is composed of "先 xiān (first)" and "生 shēng (to be born)." One can interpret that the original concept for creating the word "teacher" in Chinese is that a teacher is someone who is older and more experienced. The characters that form the word "lǎoshī" are "老 lǎo (old in the sense of experienced)," and "师 shī (model);" therefore, "teacher" in Chinese is also considered as an "experienced role model."

Confucius is respected in China not only because he was a thinker and philosopher but most importantly because he was an educator. He is respected as "师圣 shīshèng" meaning "Saint of Education" or "The Ancestor for Educators." He spent his life and energy educating disciples. Today, Confucius' birthday, September 28, is celebrated as "Teacher's Day" in Hong Kong and Taiwan.

In order to pay respect to someone who has gained fame in an area such as art, music or martial arts, etc., Chinese people tend to address that person as "teacher" although he or she may not practice teaching.

The Chinese saying "一日之师，终身为父 yī rì zhī shī, zhōng shēn wéi fù" (A teacher for a day is a father for life) indicates clearly that Chinese people consider the respect for teachers as an example of moral excellence.

八、自我测试 Self Assessment

1. 请写出下列各音节组的中文词。
Write out the word for each group of syllables.

(1) zhōngwén _____   (6) Liú lǎoshī _____

(2) míngzi _____   (7) shénme _____

(3) xuésheng _____   (8) tāmen _____

(4) wǒmen _____   (9) nǐ xìng Lǐ _____

(5) tóngxué _____   (10) nín hǎo _____

2. 用中文回答下列问题。
Answer the following questions using Chinese.

(1) 你姓什么?
_____

(2) 你叫什么名字?
_____

(3) 你的好朋友 (friend) 姓什么?
_____

(4) 你的中文老师姓什么?
_____

(5) 刘小明是你的同学吗?
_____

第一课 我是你们的老师
I Am Your Teacher

3. 你怎么样向这些人问好?
How would you greet the following people?

(1)

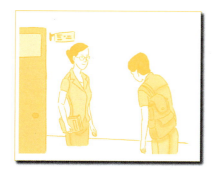

(2)

(3)

4. 对不对?

Read the question (A) and the answer (B). Check "对" if you think the answer is logical with respect to the question, or check "不对" otherwise.

(1) A. 你是学生吗?
    B. 我是学生。　　　　　　　　　　　对＿＿＿　不对＿＿＿

(2) A. 你是李同文吗?
    B. 我是中文老师。　　　　　　　　　对＿＿＿　不对＿＿＿

(3) A. 刘小明,你忙 (máng: busy) 吗?
    B. 我也忙。　　　　　　　　　　　　对＿＿＿　不对＿＿＿

(4) A. 我姓刘,你呢?
    B. 我叫王文生。　　　　　　　　　　对＿＿＿　不对＿＿＿

(5) A. 你们是老师吗?
    B. 我们不是老师,我们是学生。　　　对＿＿＿　不对＿＿＿

(6) A. 你的同学叫什么名字?
    B. 我的同学叫李学明。　　　　　　　对＿＿＿　不对＿＿＿

(7) A. 同学们,你们好!
    B. 老师好!　　　　　　　　　　　　对＿＿＿　不对＿＿＿

(8) A. 你们的中文老师姓什么?
    B. 你不是我们的中文老师。　　　　　对＿＿＿　不对＿＿＿

(9) A. 中文好学吗?
    B. 中文不好学。　　　　　　　　　　对＿＿＿　不对＿＿＿

(10) A. 他是学生吗?
     B. 不,他们是老师。　　　　　　　　对＿＿＿　不对＿＿＿

第二课
LESSON TWO

李新，你好！
Hello, Li Xin!

学习目的
Learning Objectives

介绍别人	To introduce other people
如何礼貌地运用命令式	To politely give a command
零——十的数数及中文哑语手势	To count from (and show using Chinese sign language) 0 to 10
用简单的形容词形容人与事	To describe people and things with some easy adjectives
再谈中国人的姓名	More about Chinese names

本课学习内容
Contents of the chapter

一	学习发音 Pronunciation
	■ 声母 consonants：g, k, h
	■ 韵母 vowels：ai, ei, ui, ao, ou

二	课文：李新，你好！ Text: Hello, Li Xin!

三	生词 Vocabulary
	■ 名词 nouns：人、谢朋、文小英、现在、课、今天、语法、书、页、朋友、中学、介绍、张大卫、中国、美国、北京大学、汉语、文化、高英明
	■ 代词 pronouns：他、她、他们、她们、那、谁、这
	■ 动词 verbs：来、认识、上课、学习、请、打开、介绍、谢、在
	■ 形容词 adjectives：新、大
	■ 副词 adverbs：最
	■ 量词 measure words：个
	■ 虚词 particles：第、吧
	■ 介词 prepositions：在
	■ 连词 conjunctions：和
	■ 词句 expressions：一下(儿)、谢谢

四	数字学习 Study of Numbers: 0 to 10

五	语法 Grammar
	● 量词 "个"　　　　　　　Measure word "个"
	■ "一下(儿)"的用法　　　Usage of the expression "一下(儿)"
	■ "吧"的用法　　　　　　Usage of "吧"
	■ "在"字的作用　　　　　Functions of the character "在"
	■ "第"的用法　　　　　　Usage of "第"
	■ 用"最"字表示最高级　　Use of "最" to indicate the superlative

六	练习 Exercises
七	读报 Newspaper Reading
八	文化点滴 Culture Notes
九	自我测试 Self Assessment

第二课 李新，你好！
Hello, Li Xin!

一、学习发音 Pronunciation 1

g | k | h + ai ei ui ao ou

Drill 1

gē (哥)	gé (格)	gě (葛)	gè (个)
kē (科)	ké (壳)	kě (渴)	kè (克)
hū (乎)	hú (湖)	hǔ (虎)	hù (户)

Drill 2

b		bāi (掰)
d		dāi (呆)
g		gāi (该)
k	+ āi	kāi (开)
p		pāi (拍)
t		tāi (胎)
w		wāi (歪)

b		bái (白)
p		pái (排)
m		mái (埋)
h	+ ái	hái (孩)
t		tái (台)
l		lái (来)

Drill 3

d		dǎi (逮)
g	+ ǎi	gǎi (改)
k		kǎi (凯)

b		bài (败)
d	+ ài	dài (代)
g		gài (丐)

h		hài (害)
l		lài (赖)
m		mài (卖)
p	+ ài	pài (派)
t		tài (太)
w		wài (外)

Drill 4

b		bēi (杯)
p		pēi (胚)
f	+ ēi →	fēi (非)
l		lēi (勒)
h		hēi (黑)
w		wēi (威)

l		léi (雷)
m	+ éi →	méi (梅)
p		péi (陪)
w		wéi (为)

Drill 5

m		měi (美)
n	+ ěi →	něi (馁)
g		gěi (给)

b		bèi (备)
f		fèi (费)
l	+ èi →	lèi (累)
m		mèi (妹)
p		pèi (佩)
w		wèi (卫)

Drill 6

d		duī (堆)
t	+ uī →	tuī (推)
g		guī (规)

| h | + uí → | huí (回) |
| k | | kuí (葵) |

Drill 7

| g | + uǐ → | guǐ (鬼) |
| t | | tuǐ (腿) |

d		duì (对)
t	+ uì →	tuì (退)
g		guì (贵)

Drill 8

b	+ āo →	bāo (包)	+ áo →	báo (薄)	+ ǎo →	bǎo (饱)	+ ào →	bào (报)
p		pāo (抛)		páo (刨)		pǎo (跑)		pào (泡)
m		māo (猫)		máo (毛)		mǎo (卯)		mào (冒)
d		dāo (刀)				dǎo (倒)		dào (到)

第二课 李新，你好！
Hello, Li Xin!

t	tāo (涛)	táo (逃)	tǎo (讨)	tào (套)
n	nāo (孬)	náo (挠)	nǎo (脑)	nào (闹)
l	lāo (捞)	láo (劳)	lǎo (老)	lào (涝)
g + āo	gāo (高) + áo		gǎo (稿) + ào	gào (告)
k	kāo (尻)		kǎo (考)	kào (靠)
h	hāo (蒿)	háo (毫)	hǎo (好)	hào (号)

Drill 9

d		dōu (都)		l		lóu (楼)
t		tōu (偷)				
l	+ ōu	lōu (搂钱)		t	+ óu	tóu (头)
g		gōu (沟)				
k		kōu (抠)		y		yóu (油)
h		hōu (齁咸)				

Drill 10

				d		dòu (斗)
				g		gòu (够)
g		gǒu (狗)		h		hòu (后)
k	+ ǒu	kǒu (口)		k	+ òu	kòu (扣)
y		yǒu (有)		l		lòu (漏)
				t		tòu (透)
				y		yòu (又)

Drill 11

bài (败)	fèi (费)	lǒu (搂)	pǎo (跑)	guì (贵)
kǒu (口)	nǎi (奶)	gāo (高)	tuǐ (腿)	lèi (累)
duì (对)	gěi (给)	lái (来)	hòu (后)	lāo (捞)
gǒu (狗)	gǎi (改)	tōu (偷)	pāi (拍)	nèi (内)
lòu (漏)	kuī (亏)	hēi (黑)	tào (套)	huí (回)

二、课文 Text

李新，你好！

李大友：老师，那两个人是谁？

老　师：来，你们认识一下儿。他们是你们的新同学。这个同学姓谢，叫谢朋；那个同学姓文，她叫文小英。

李大友：谢朋、文小英，你们好！我是你们的同学。我姓李，叫李大友。

谢朋、文小英：李大友，你好！

老　师：好，现在我们上课吧！今天我们学习第二课的语法。请你们打开书，第十页。

我最好的朋友

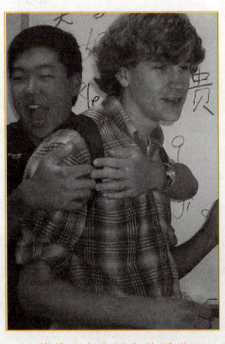 

他是我中文课上的同学　　她是我法语课上的同学

第二课 李新，你好！
Hello, Li Xin!

高英明：我介绍一下，这是我朋友。她姓李，叫李新。她是我的中学同学，也是我最好的朋友。

刘同文：英明，谢谢你的介绍。李新，你好！我叫刘同文。我也介绍一下我的朋友：<u>张大卫</u> (David Johnson)。他是美国人；现在他在北京大学学习汉语和中国文化。

李新、高英明：大卫，你好！

課文

李新，你好！

李大友：老師，那兩個人是誰？

老　師：來，你們認識一下兒。他們是你們的新同學。這個同學姓謝，叫謝朋；那個同學姓文，她叫文小英。

李大友：謝朋、文小英，你們好！我是你們的同學。我姓李，叫李大友。

謝朋、文小英：李大友，你好！

老　師：好，現在我們上課吧！今天我們學習第二課的語法。請你們打開書，第十頁。

我最好的朋友

他是我中文課上的同學

她是我法語課上的同學

高英明：我介紹一下，這是我朋友。她姓李，叫李新。她是我的中學同學，也是我最好的朋友。

劉同文：英明，謝謝你的介紹。李新，你好！我叫劉同文。我也介紹一下我的朋友：張大衛 (David Johnson)。他是美國人；現在他在北京大學學習漢語和中國文化。

李新、高英明：大衛，你好！

LESSON 2

第二课 李新，你好！
Hello, Li Xin!

三、生词 Vocabulary

NOUNS

rén 人 (人) people, person	Xiè Péng 谢朋 (謝朋) a person's name
Wén Xiǎoyīng 文小英 (文小英) a person's name	xiànzài 现在 (現在) now
kè 课 (課) course, lesson, class	

jīntiān 今天 (今天) today	jīn 今：modern, present-day
	tiān 天：sky, day

yǔfǎ 语法 (語法) grammar	yǔ 语 (語)：language
	fǎ 法：law, method, way

shū 书 (書) book	yè 页 (頁) page	péngyou 朋友 (朋友) friend

zhōngxué 中学 (中學) middle school	jièshào 介绍 (介紹) introduction
Zhāng Dàwèi 张大卫 (張大衛) David Johnson	Zhōngguó 中国 (中國) China

Měiguó 美国 (美國) America	měi 美：beautiful, pretty
	guó 国 (國)：country, nation

Běijīng Dàxué 北京大学 (北京大學) Peking University	běi 北：north
	jīng 京：capital

Hànyǔ 汉语 (漢語) Chinese	
wénhuà 文化 (文化) culture	huà 化：change, transform
Gāo Yīngmíng 高英明 (高英明) a person's name	gāo 高：tall, high, a surname
	yīng 英：flower (written language)
	yīngmíng 英明：wise

PRONOUNS

tā
他/他 he, him

tā
她/她 she, her

tāmen
他们/他們 they, them (masculine)

tāmen
她们/她們 they, them (feminine)

nà
那/那 that

shéi (or shuí)
谁/誰 who, whom

zhè
这/這 this

VERBS

lái
来/來 to come

rènshi
认识/認識 to know

shàngkè
上课/上課 to attend a class, to teach a class

xuéxí
学习/學習 to study

qǐng
请/請 to invite, please

dǎkāi
打开/打開 to open

jièshào
介绍/介紹 to introduce

第二课 李新，你好！
Hello, Li Xin!

xiè
谢/謝 to thank

zài
在/在 to be in

ADJECTIVES

xīn
新/新 new

dà
大/大 big, large, great

ADVERBS

zuì
最/最 the most (indicating the superlative)

MEASURE WORDS

gè
个/個 this is the most common measure word used for nouns, denoting people, thing, idea, etc., that don't have a specific measure word.

PARTICLES

dì
第/第 ordinal number marker

ba
吧/吧

PREPOSITIONS

zài
在/在 at, in, on

CONJUNCTIONS

zài
和/和 and, with

EXPRESSIONS

yī xià(r)
一下(儿)/一下(兒) quickly, for a short while (to indicate short duration)

xièxie
谢谢/謝謝 thanks, thank you

四、数字学习 Study of Numbers: 0-10

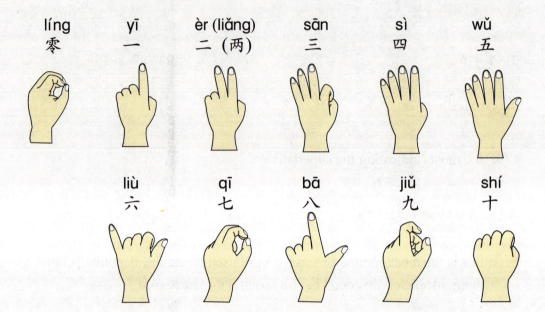

✦ Notes

1. The cardinal number "一" is pronounced "yāo" instead of "yī" in a phone, room or street number.

2. The cardinal number "二" is pronounced "liǎng: 两" in the following cases:
   A. if the single digit number is followed by a measure word.

   两个学生　liǎng gè xuésheng
   two students

   两本书　liǎng běn shū
   two books

   B. when it precedes the words "千 qiān: thousand," "万 wàn: ten thousand," and "亿 yì: one hundred million," the characters "二" and "两" are interchangeable although the pronunciation always remains "liǎng."

   二 (or: 两) 千年 (nián: year)　　　liǎng qiān nián
   two thousand years

   二 (or: 两) 亿美元 (měiyuán: dollar)　liǎng yì měi yuán
   two hundred million dollars

第二课 李新，你好！
Hello, Li Xin!

3. The pronunciation is optional when the word "百 bǎi: hundred" follows "二."

二百五十个老师　liǎngbǎi wǔshí gè lǎoshī/èrbǎi wǔshí gè lǎoshī
two hundred fifty teachers

4. In all other cases it remains the pronunciation "èr."

十二个学生　　　shí èr gè xuésheng
twelve students

二十本书　　　　èr shí běn shū
twenty books

第二个学生　　　dì èr gè xuésheng
the second student

练习

1. 两个人一组：轮流一个人说出下面的数字，另一个人用手势表示听到的数字。
   Work in pairs: take turns to pronounce the number and show it using Chinese sign language.

   五　九　二　八　六　三　一　七　四　十

2. 两个人一组：轮流一个人大声读下面的数字，另一个人用中文把听到的数字写出来。请把"一"字读作"yāo"。
   Work in pairs: take turns to read aloud each of the following numbers and write out the numbers you hear in Chinese. Please pronounce number one "yāo."

   1. 三三六一
   2. 四七九二
   3. 二零一一
   4. 八三七七
   5. 九零二四
   6. 一六一五
   7. 二一一三
   8. 七四七八
   9. 五八二一
   10. 六零九九

五、语法 Grammar

1. 量词 "个" Measure Words "个"

In Chinese, a number is almost never directly connected to a noun ("一 + measure word" is sometimes an exception). A measure word is always needed to link the number and the noun except for some idioms or proverbs. The most commonly used measure word "个" is introduced in this chapter. This measure word can be used for people, some things and institutions.

一个老师	one teacher
十个学生	ten students
这个系 (xì)	this department (as division of a university)
那个电影 (diànyǐng)	that movie

练习一

1. 请按照例句做对话。
   Make conversation following the model.

    这个人是谁？   他/她是我的同学。

   (1) 我的朋友
   (2) 你们的新同学
   (3) 我们的中文老师
   (4) 他们的英语老师
   (5) 我的化学 (chemistry) 课同学
   (6) 张学友，我们的好朋友
   (7) 我的中学老师
   (8) 谢文新，我的老同学

2. 请你离开课桌，按照下面的例子和五个同学进行对话，然后用中文将对话的结果写下来。
   Get up from your desk, walk around the classroom, carry out the dialogue of the following model, and then write down the results of the dialogues.

    我有 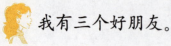 两个好朋友。你呢？

   我有三个好朋友。

Bob 有两个好朋友。　　　　Laura 有三个朋友。

(1) _____

(2) _____

(3) _____

(4) _____

(5) _____

2. "一下(儿)" 的用法　Usage of Expression "一下(儿)"

"一下(儿)" is an adverbial expression indicating the short duration of the action expressed by the related verb. For example:

我介绍一下(儿)我的朋友。
Let me quickly introduce my friend.

请你来一下(儿)。
Please come (for a short time.)

Note that in the second example, English speakers would say "Do you have a minute?"

练习二

这样说更礼貌：请在每个句子前面加"请"字。
It is more polite to say it this way: add the word "请" in front of each sentence.

(1) 你介绍一下你的朋友。
_____

(2) 你们来一下。
_____

(3) 你问一下他姓什么。
_____

(4) 你介绍一下你的同学。
_____

(5) 你问一下她叫什么名字。
_____

(6) 你开一下门 (mén: door)。

(7) 你们认识一下。

(8) 你介绍一下你的文学课。

3. "吧" 的用法 Usage of the Character "吧"

Used in an imperative sentence, the particle "吧" softens the command.

你来吧!
Please come.

我们说 (shuō: to speak) 汉语吧!
Let's speak Chinese.

我来介绍一下我的学生们吧!
Let me introduce my students.

练习三

将下面的问句变成命令式句子。
Transform the following interrogative sentences into imperative sentences.

 你们打开书, 好吗?   (请) 你们打开书吧!

(1) 你来一下, 好吗?
(2) 你们打开语法书, 好吗?
(3) 我们学汉语, 好吗?
(4) 你们介绍一下这个同学, 好吗?
(5) 我们学习化学, 好吗?
(6) 你们认识一下, 好吗?
(7) 我们上课, 好吗?
(8) 你打开门 (mén: door), 好吗?

4. "在" 的用法 Fuctions of the Character "在"

The character "在" has three major functions. As a verb, "在" equals "to be in" in English.

第二课　李新，你好！
Hello, Li Xin!

老师在吗？
Is the teacher in?

现在大卫在中国。
David is in China now.

李明在北京大学。
Li Ming is at Peking University.

If "在" is followed by a noun which denotes a place and another verb exists in the same sentence, "在" then serves as a preposition.

大卫在中国学习中文。
David studies Chinese in China.

李明在北京大学教书 (jiāoshū: teach).
Li Ming teaches at Peking University.

When directly followed by a verb, "在" plays the role of a helping verb to indicate that the action of the verb is in progress.

老师在上课。
The teacher is teaching now.

学生们在学习语法。
Students are learning the grammar.

练习四

请指出在下面的句子里"在"是动词、助动词还是介词。
Please indicate the function of the word "在" in the following sentences.

	动词 verb	助动词 helping verb	介词 preposition
(1) 刘大卫在学法语 (French)。			
(2) 刘大卫在法国 (France)。			
(3) 刘大卫在法国学习法语。			
(4) 他们在上化学 (chemistry) 课。			
(5) 谁在北京？			
(6) 我朋友在北京大学学习汉语。			
(7) 你们在上课吗？			
(8) 你在哪儿学习中国文化？			

5. "第" 的用法 Usage of "第"

In Chinese, the ordinal numbers are formed by adding the character "第" to the corresponding cardinal number, and they are normally used as adjectives.

这是我的第一个中文老师。
This is my first Chinese teacher.

今天是我们来北京大学的第二天。
Today is our second day at Peking University.

Note that, as an ordinal number, "二" is always pronounced /èr/ even when it precedes a measure word.

练习五

1. 请按照例句做对话。
   Make conversation following the model.

    现在你在上什么课？ 现在我在上汉语课。

   (1) 汉语课
   (2) 英文 (English) 课
   (3) 中国文化课
   (4) 英国文学课
   (5) 法语 (French) 语法课
   (6) 化学课
   (7) 汉语语法课
   (8) 数学 (shùxué: mathematics) 课

2. 请按照例句做对话。
   Make conversation following the model.

    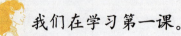今天在中文课上，你们学习第几课？

    我们在学习第一课。

    明天呢？

   明天我们学习第二课。

第二课　李新，你好！
Hello, Li Xin!

(1) 在<u>英文</u> (English) 课上
(2) 在<u>化学</u> (chemistry) 课上
(3) 在<u>法语</u> (French) 课上
(4) <u>法国文学</u> (French literature) 课上
(5) <u>英美文学</u> (English American literature) 课上
(6) 在汉语课上
(7) 在中国文化课上
(8) 中文语法课上

6. 用"最"字表示最高的 Usage of "最" to Indicate the Superlative

In Chinese, the superlative is formed by adding the character "最" immediately before an adjective, an adverb or a verbal phrase.

他个子最高。
He is the tallest.

她是最美的人。
She is the most beautiful.

汉语最不好学吗?
Is Chinese the hardest (language) to learn?

谁最英明?
Who is the wisest person?

那<u>本</u> (běn: measure word)书最新。
That book is the newest.

练习六

请按照例句做对话。
Make conversation following the model.

 你们的英文书好吗?　 我们的英文书最好。

(1) 北京大学 / 老
(2) 这<u>本</u> (běn: measure word) 书 / 新
(3) 那个人 / <u>英明</u> (wise)
(4) 谢文来<u>个子</u> (height, size) / 高
(5) 这个学生 / <u>聪明</u> (cōngming: intelligent)
(6) 高小英 / 美
(7) 你的朋友 / 好
(8) 英语 / 好学

57

六、练习 Exercises

样式练习 Model exercises

1. 两个人一组，用下列中国人姓名做练习。
Work in pairs to do exercises with the following Chinese names.

两个人轮换：一个人高声读下列中国人名并注意每个字的声调，另一个人用中文写出你听到的名字。
Take turns to read aloud the following Chinese names (be careful with the tone of each character) and write out the names that you hear using Chinese.

Names likely for men

刘汉文	文京生	张大明	谢书朋	王小卫
李明生	张学友	师文友	卫一明	高中国
刘卫国	李法生	英明	谢文来	马(Mǎ)大友

Names likely for women

王文美	文英	那美英	谢文新	张英英	李娜(nà)
国新英	刘文文	谢一娜	王新新	高小英	刘来娣(dì)
安娜	师小妹	卫莉莉(lìlì: jasmine)			

2. 请按照例句做对话。
Make conversation following the model.

我介绍一下，这是我的同学；她叫师小妹。

谢谢你的介绍。师小妹，你好！

(1) 刘汉文
(2) 王文美
(3) 李京生
(4) 李娜

(5) 张大明
(6) 那美英
(7) 谢书朋
(8) 文英

3. 请按照例句做对话。
Make conversation following the model.

 谁是你最好的朋友?

 师小妹是我最好的朋友。你最好的朋友是谁?

 我最好的朋友叫李京生。

(1) 谢文新
(2) 王小卫
(3) 张英英
(4) 文国明
(5) 刘文文
(6) 张学友
(7) 谢一娜
(8) 卫一明

4. 请按照例句做对话。
Make conversation following the model.

 谁是北京大学的学生?

 师小妹是北京大学的学生。

(1) 刘大友
(2) 王新新
(3) 高中国
(4) 刘来娣
(5) 刘卫国
(6) 安娜

(7) 李法生
(8) 高小英

5. 请按照例句做对话。
Make conversation following the model.

我们是朋友,也是汉语课的同学。

 师小妹是谁?

 她是我的中学同学,也是我的好朋友。

(1) 张大明 / 小学同学、好朋友
(2) 国新英 / 汉语老师、英语老师
(3) 刘卫国 / 中学同学、小学同学
(4) 那美英 / 大学同学、老朋友
(5) 李娜 / 新同学、新朋友
(6) 刘汉文 / 我的朋友、他的朋友
(7) 谢文新 / 我的好朋友、她的好朋友
(8) 马友友 / 我们的老师、他们的老师

6. 请按照例句做对话。
Make conversation following the model.

 你认识她吗? 认识,她叫师小妹。

(1) 英明
(2) 师小妹
(3) 谢文来
(4) 卫莉莉
(5) 师文友

(6) 张小明

(7) 王英

(8) 高朋

7. 请用中文回答问题。
Answer the questions using Chinese.

(1) 你在哪学习汉语?

(2) 谁是你的中文老师?

(3) 在中文课上，你们学习语法吗?

(4) 中文语法好学吗?

(5) 在汉语课上，你们也学习中国文化吗?

(6) 在中文课上，谁是你最好的朋友?

(7) 在中文课上，现在你们学习第五课吗?

(8) 你认识一个姓李的同学吗?

8. 请按照例句做对话。
Make conversation following the model.

 这是中文书吗? 不是，这是英文书。

 这是谁的书？是你的吗? 不是，这是老师的书。

(1) 中文书 / 法文书
(2) 英文书 / 德文 (Déwén: German)
(3) 文学书 / 化学书
(4) 语法书 / 数学 (shùxué: math) 书

9. 请按照下面的例子采访三个同学。
   Interview three classmates following the model questions.

   英文 (English)　　　　法文 (French)　　　　文学 (literature)
   化学 (chemistry)　　　汉语和中国文化　　　英语和英国文化
   中国文学　　　　　　法国文学　　　　　　美国文学

   (1) 你学习英语吗?
   (2) 你的英语课老师姓什么?
   (3) 这是你的英文书吗?
   (4) 现在你们学习第二课吗?
   (5) 英语好学吗?

10. 请按照例句做对话。
    Make conversation following the model.

    你想 (xiǎng: to want) 有 (yǒu: to have) 一个中文名字吗?
    Do you want to have a Chinese name?

     你想有一个中文名字吗?

     我想有一个中文名字。

     你的英文名字是什么?

     我的英文名字是 Brianna Daughton。

     好,你的中国姓是"刁 diāo,"你的中文名字是"碧娜 bìnà"。

     "刁碧娜,"这个名字好!

    (1) Andrew Lee / 李安竹 ānzhú
    (2) Danielle Shiver / 师丹妮 dānnī
    (3) Kevin Gordon / 高开文

第二课　李新，你好！
Hello, Li Xin!

(4) Camille Weiss / 卫佳敏 jiāmǐn
(5) Anna Goodson / 国安娜
(6) Rob Johnson / 张浩伯 hàobó
(7) Ashley Malave / 马诗莉 shīlì
(8) David Lively / 刘大卫
(9) Bob Schneider / 谢宝伯 bǎobó
(10) Marc Vance / 王马克 mǎkè

11. 小故事

Mini-story

两个人一组：首先，在下面的空格里填上适当的字，把整段连成一个小故事。然后把你的两个小故事讲给对方听。
Work in pairs: first, fill in the blanks to complete each of the following stories. Afterwards, tell each other your mini-stories.

(1) 这是我的好朋友。_____ 姓 _____，叫 _____。我的朋友不是中国人，也不是 _____，他/她是英国人。现在他/她在法国学习_____。他/她也学习 _____。

(2) 我的好朋友姓 _____，叫 _____。他/她是我的 _____同学。他/她个子高，人很聪明 (rén hěn cōngming: to be a smart person)。现在他/她在北京大学学习汉语。

实况演练 Real situation exercises

1. 两个人一组：轮流一个人说，另一个人写，完成下列任务。
Work in pairs: take turns to speak and write in order to complete the following tasks.

(1) 请你介绍一下你的好朋友。

(2) 请你们介绍一下你们的汉语老师。

(3) 谁是你最好的朋友？请介绍一下。

(4) 你认识一个中国学生吗？请你介绍一下这个学生。

(5) 你们的英语老师姓什么？叫什么？他/她是美国人吗？

(6) 你认识他吗？他叫什么名字？
他是你的同学吗？

第二课 李新，你好！
Hello, Li Xin!

LESSON 2

七、读报　Newspaper Reading 7

How Many Characters Do You Know?

1. Read the following article.
2. While reading, underline the characters you know.

结缘微软，回国创业

上大学前的张亚勤

　　1998年10月的一天，一个越洋电话来找他。电话那端是在业内名气颇响的李开复博士。那年，比尔·盖茨决定在中国建立一个"全世界最高水准的研究机构"，李开复接受邀请，到中国筹建微软中国研究院。李开复希望张亚勤能回来一起创业。

　　1998年11月，张亚勤回到阔别已久的祖国，感受到了改革开放20年后的中国巨大的发展潜力。从此，张亚勤正式加盟微软。不久，微软中国研究院成立，李开复任院长，张亚勤担任副院长兼首席科学家。

　　2000年的8月2日，张亚勤正式成为微软中国研究院院长兼首席科学家，当时研究院的规模接近50人。次年11月，微软中国研究院发展为微软亚洲研究院。

　　2002年夏，美国前国务卿基辛格率团访华，纪念30年前尼克松总统的"破冰之旅"。他的好友、微软全球CTO克瑞格·蒙迪和他同行。张亚勤陪同基辛格和克瑞格·蒙迪吃饭时，谈了很多事。

　　张亚勤说："当时他跟我们讲了很多故事，讲完之后，他兴勃勃地与我们一起去北京饭店吃饭。到了北京饭店的顶层，他回忆说1972年时，周总理在这儿指着北京的烟囱对他介绍当时北京的情况。"

　　这时基辛格问站在身边的张亚勤："微软在中国做得怎么样？"张亚勤向他介绍了研究院的基本情况，基辛格十分感兴趣，并决定第二天前往微软中国研究院参观。

　　次日，在张亚勤开始介绍前，基辛格说，我想问一下，你们都有什么背景？大致介绍一下。每个人都回答了是在哪里读的书，结果很有意思，"我们一圈十几个人都是在国内出生，在美国读完博士，然后又回来。"

　　张亚勤说："听完大家的介绍，我看到他有一种特别自豪的感觉。我们这一群人都是中美建交的受益者，我们都在为中美科技的交流做贡献，我能看到基辛格老人脸上的那份满足感、那份自豪感。"

选自：新民晚报
日期：2009年3月31日

3. Pronounce the characters you have recognized.
4. Tell the meaning of each character to your class (or study group).

65

八、文化点滴 Culture Notes

Chinese First Names

Chinese given names carry a very special culture. There is no resource of names comparable to the Bible and mythology for Westerners. Chinese parents create names for their children by choosing one character or by combining two characters.

Some parents name their children to commemorate the time or place where their child was born: 沪生 hùshēng (born in Shanghai), 鲁平 Lǔpíng (born or coming from Shan Dong), 小川 Xiǎochuān (born in the province of Sichuan), 京汉 Jīnghàn (a man born in Beijing); 晓明 Xiǎomíng (born at dawn), 冬冬 Dōngdong (born in winter).

Some parents place hope or wish on their children when naming them. They hope their boys are: strong and powerful like 钢 Gāng (steel), 石 Shí (stone), 山 Shān (mountain); frank and openhearted like 海 Hǎi (sea) or 洋 Yáng (ocean), 天 Tiān (sky); smart, diligent, and capable, etc. like 明 Míng (bright), 飞 Fēi (to flight), 超 Chāo (super), 学 Xué (like to study), 勤 Qín (hard-working); 康 Kāng (healthy), 福 Fú (have good fortune and happiness), 富 Fù (wealthy), and 贵 Guì (noble). They wish their girls are: beautiful like 莉莉 Lìli (jasmine), 莲 Lián (lotus), 兰 Lán (orchid), 春月 Chūnyuè (Spring Moon), and 白雪 Báixuě (white snow); kind, gentle, virtuous, and skillful like 淑 Shū, 贤 Xián, 巧 Qiǎo, etc.

In many families, one of the two characters is used in names of several members to indicate that they are from the same generation. For example, three children from one family may be named "周天明 Zhou Tianming," "周路明 Zhou Luming" and "周海明 Zhou Haiming."

第二课 李新，你好！
Hello, Li Xin!

九、自我测试 Self Assessment

1. 读出下面的音节并用中文写出每个名字。
Read the following syllables and write out the Chinese characters for each name.

(1) Zhāng Dàmíng ☐　　(2) Liú Láidì ☐

(3) Xiè Wénxīn ☐　　(4) Shī Wényǒu ☐

(5) Lǐ Jīngshēng ☐　　(6) Gāo Xiǎoyīng ☐

(7) Mǎ Shūpéng ☐　　(8) Nà Měilì ☐

2. 用中文回答问题
Answer the questions using Chinese

(1) 这是谁的书？
_____

(2) 你们的新同学叫什么名字？
_____

(3) 在中国，北京大学是最老的大学吗？
_____

(4) 你学中文，也学英文吗？
_____

(5) 你们在上什么课？
_____

3. 对不对？

Read the question (A) and the answer ((B). Check "对" if you think the answer is logical with respect to the question or check "不对" otherwise.

(1) A. 这是语法书吗？
　　B. 这是我的书。　　　　　　　　　　对_____ 不对_____

(2) A. 他是你们的新老师吗？
　　B. 是，这个新老师是我们的中文老师。对_____ 不对_____

(3) A. 你的朋友是美国人吗？
    B. 不是，他是法国人。　　　　　　　对_____ 不对_____

(4) A. 在汉语课上，你们学习中国文化吗？
    B. 我们上化学课。　　　　　　　　　对_____ 不对_____

(5) A. 你们认识那个学生吗？
    B. 认识。他姓谢，叫谢小明。　　　　对_____ 不对_____

(6) A. 请介绍一下你的同学，好吗？
    B. 好，我姓刘，叫刘文生。　　　　　对_____ 不对_____

(7) A. 王文莉在哪儿学习法语？
    B. 她在法国学习法语。　　　　　　　对_____ 不对_____

(8) A. 你们在学习第八课吗？
    B. 不，我们在学习第六课。　　　　　对_____ 不对_____

4. 阅读下列短文，并用中文回答问题。
Read the following paragraph and answer the questions using Chinese.

我叫师开文，是美国人。现在我在中国人文大学学习汉语。高安娜和 (hé: and) 刘大卫是我的两个最好的朋友。高安娜是英国人；刘大卫是法国人。他们也在这个大学学习中文。今天我们上中国文化课，也上汉语语法课。

(1) 师开文是哪国人？

(2) 师开文在北京大学学习汉语吗？

(3) 师开文和谁是好朋友？

(4) 刘大卫是哪国人？

(5) 今天这三个学生上什么课？

第三课
LESSON THREE

我的家人
My Family

学习目的
Learning Objectives

介绍家人	To introduce family members
询问别人与介绍自己的工作	To ask and tell professions
询问别人与介绍自己的年龄	To ask and tell age
什么是"全家福"	The meaning of "全家福"

本课学习内容
Contents of the chapter

一	学习发音 Pronunciation	
	■ 声母 consonants：j, q, x	
	■ 韵母 vowels：ia, iao, ie, iu, ue, er	
二	课文：我的家人 Text: My Family	
三	生词 Vocabulary	
	■ 名词 nouns：家、安娜、爸爸、妈妈、哥哥、姐姐、弟弟、妹妹、孩子、工作、医生、医院、银行、律师所、岁、年、生日、照片、全家福、爷爷、奶奶、姥姥、姥爷	
	■ 动词 verbs：给、有、做、工作、上学、住、看	
	■ 代词 pronouns：几(个)、哪(儿)	
	■ 形容词 adjectives：男、女、多	
	■ 副词 adverbs：没、只、还在、一起	
	■ 量词 measure words：家、口、所、张	
	■ 连词 conjunctions：还是	
	■ 介词 prepositions：给	
	■ 词句 expressions：你多大，您多大岁数，和……一起	
四	数字学习 Study of Numbers: 11-50	
五	语法 Grammar	
	■ 动词"有"的肯定及否定式	The verb "有" in the affirmative and negative forms
	■ "给"字用作动词和介词	The word "给" used as a verb and a preposition
	■ 副词"只"的用法	Usage of the adverb "只"
	■ 连词"还是"	The conjunction word "还是"
	■ 连词"和"	The conjunction word "和"
六	练习 Exercises	
七	读报 Newspaper Reading	
八	文化点滴 Culture Notes	
九	自我测试 Self Assessment	

一、学习发音 Pronunciation

Drill 1

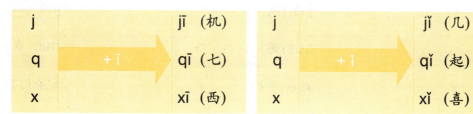

Drill 2

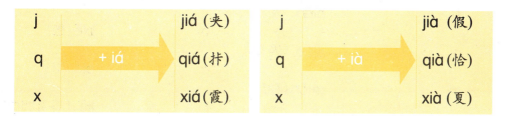

Drill 3

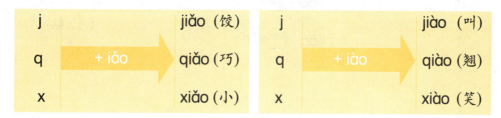

Drill 4

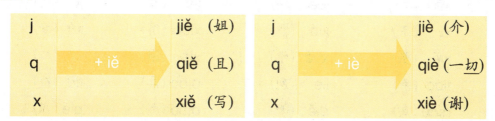

Drill 5

Drill 6

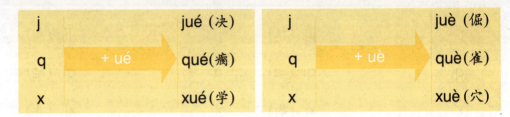

Drill 7 **Drill 8**

Drill 9

qù (去)	qiǎo (巧)	quē (缺)	qí (其)
jiāo (交)	jué (决)	jiě (姐)	jí (及)
xì (系)	xiá (霞)	xiāo (消)	xú (徐)
xiē (些)	xué (学)	xiè (谢)	èr (二)
tiáo (条)	liè (列)	piào (票)	tiě (铁)
niǎo (鸟)	diē (爹)	biāo (彪)	piē (撇)

第三课 我的家人 My Family

二、课文 Text 2

我的家人

安　娜：小英，你给我介绍一下你的家人，好吗？你家有几口人？

高小英：我家有六口人：我爸爸、妈妈、哥哥、姐姐、弟弟和我。

安　娜：你没有妹妹？

高小英：没有，我爸爸妈妈有两个男孩子，两个女孩子。

安　娜：你爸爸妈妈做什么工作？

高小英：我爸爸是医生，在一家医院工作；妈妈在一家银行工作。

安　娜：你哥哥姐姐呢？他们在哪儿工作？

这家有几个孩子？
_____

高小英：我哥哥在一个 (or: 一家) 律师所工作，他是律师。我姐姐只有十九岁，她还在上大学。

安　娜：你弟弟今年多大？(or: 你弟弟今年几岁？)

高小英：他十五岁。明天是他的生日。你看，这张照片是我们家的全家福。

安　娜："全家福"是什么意思？

高小英：全家人在一起照的照片是"全家福"。

安　娜：这两个人是你的爷爷奶奶，还是你的姥姥姥爷？

高小英：是我的爷爷奶奶。他们和我们住在一起。(or: 他们和我们一起住。)

这家有几口人？爷爷和奶奶在哪儿？

第三课 我的家人 / My Family

课文

我的家人

安　娜：小英，你給我介紹一下你的家人，好嗎？你家有幾口人？

高小英：我家有六口人：我爸爸、媽媽、哥哥、姐姐、弟弟和我。

安　娜：你沒有妹妹？

高小英：沒有，我爸爸媽媽有兩個男孩子，兩個女孩子。

安　娜：你爸爸媽媽做什麼工作？

高小英：我爸爸是醫生，在一家醫院工作；媽媽在一家銀行工作。

安　娜：你哥哥姐姐呢？他們在哪兒工作？

這家有幾個孩子？

高小英：我哥哥在一個 (or: 一家) 律師所工作，他是律師。我姐姐祇有十九歲，她還在上大學。

安　娜：你弟弟今年多大？(or: 你弟弟今年幾歲？)

高小英：他十五歲。明天是他的生日。你看，這張照片是我們家的全家福。

安　娜："全家福"是什麼意思？

高小英：全家人在一起照的照片是"全家福"。

安　娜：這兩個人是你的爺爺奶奶，還是你的姥姥姥爺？

高小英：是我的爺爺奶奶。他們和我們住在一起。(or: 他們和我們一起住。)

這家有幾口人？爺爺和奶奶在哪兒？

第三课 我的家人
My Family

三、生词 Vocabulary

NOUNS

jiā 家(家) home, family		
Ānnà 安娜 (安娜)	ān 安：	
	nà 娜： elegant, graceful (often used in girls' names)	
bàba 爸爸(爸爸)		māma 妈妈(媽媽) mom
gēge 哥哥(哥哥)		jiějie 姐姐(姐姐) elder sister
dìdi 弟弟(弟弟) younger brother		mèimei 妹妹(妹妹) younger sister
háizi 孩子(孩子) child		gōngzuò 工作(工作) work, job
yīshēng 医生(醫生) doctor		
yīyuàn 医院(醫院) hospital	yī 医(醫)：	
	yuàn 院： yard, public places	
yínháng 银行(銀行)	yín 银(銀)： silver	
	háng 行：	
lǜshīsuǒ 律师所(律師所) law firm	lǜ 律：	
	lǜshī 律师(律師)： lawyer	
	suǒ 所：	

suì 岁 (歲) year, age	nián 年 (年) year, annual
shēngrì 生日 (生日) birthday	rì 日：sun, day
zhàopiàn 照片 (照片) picture, photograph	
quánjiāfú 全家福 (全家福) family picture	quán 全：complete, entire
	fú 福 (福)：good fortune, happiness
yéye 爷爷 (爺爺) grandfather (paternal)	nǎinai 奶奶 (奶奶) grandmother (paternal)
lǎolao 姥姥 (姥姥) grandmother (maternal)	lǎoye 姥爷 (姥爺) grandfather (maternal)

VERBS

gěi
给/給 to give

yǒu
有/有 to have

zuò
做/做 to do, to make

gōngzuò
工作/工作 to work

shàng xué
上学/上學 to attend school, to go to school

zhù
住/住 to live

kàn
看/看 to look at, to watch

PRONOUNS

jǐgè
几(个)/幾(個) how many

nǎr
哪(儿)/哪(兒) where

ADJECTIVES

nán
男/男 male

nǚ
女/女 female

duō
多/多 many

第三课 我的家人
My Family

LESSON 3

ADVERBS

méi
没/沒 not

háizài
还/還 still, also

zhǐ
只/祇 only

yīqǐ
一起/一起 together

MEASURE WORDS

jiā
家/家 for families, enterprises, restaurants, movie theaters, banks, hotels, etc.

suǒ
所/所 for schools, houses, hospitals, etc.

kǒu
口/口 for number of people in a family or village

zhāng
张/張 for flat things such as paper, pictures, maps, tables, beds, sheets, etc.

CONJUNCTIONS

háishì
还是/還是 or

PREPOSITIONS

gěi
给/給 to, for

EXPRESSIONS

nǐ duōdà
你多大？/你多大？ How old are you? (used for young people)

nín duōdà suìshu
您多大岁数？/您多大歲數？ How old are you? (used for elder people)

hé…… yīqǐ
和……一起/和……一起 Together with...

79

四、数字学习 Study of Numbers: 11-50

shíyī	shí'èr	shísān	shísì	shíwǔ
十一	十二	十三	十四	十五
shíliù	shíqī	shíbā	shíjiǔ	èrshí
十六	十七	十八	十九	二十
èrshí yī	èrshí èr	èrshí sān	èrshí sì	èrshí wǔ
二十一	二十二	二十三	二十四	二十五

练习

1. 下面的数字怎么数？
   How would you say the following numbers using Chinese?

   21 24 26 27 28 29 30 31 32 34 36
   37 39 40 41 43 44 45 47 48 49 50

2. 两个人一组做这个练习：从前到后，从左到右每个人读一个运动员的号码。
   Work in pairs: take turns to read the numbers of the players from the front to the back row, from left to right.

3. 两个人一组按照例句做这个练习。
   Work in pairs: do this exercise following the model.

   Model:

   一号 (hào: number) 叫什么名字?
   我不知道 (zhīdào: to know) 一号叫什么名字。你知道吗?
   我知道。他叫 _____。

4. 比赛：先三个人一组练习读下面的绕口令 (ràokǒulìng)；然后选出最好的一个代表你们组参加全班范围的比赛。
   Competition: First, work in groups of three to practice the following tongue twister; afterwards, select the best one to represent your group in the class competition.

   绕口令

   十是十，四是四，
   十四是十四，四十是四十。
   十四不是四十，四十也不是十四。

五、语法 Grammar

1. 动词"有"的肯定及否定式 The Verb "有" in the Affirmative and Negative Forms

The verb "有" is different from most other verbs in the way that it is negated by adding "没" in front of the verb instead of "不."

李明没有弟弟。
Li Ming does not have any younger brothers.

他没有姐姐吗?
He doesn't have elder sister?

练习一

请按照你自己的情况回答下面的问题。
Please give your own answers.

(1) 你有哥哥/姐姐吗? 有几个哥哥/姐姐?

(2) 你哥哥有没有女朋友? 他的女朋友叫什么名字?

(3) 你姐姐有男朋友吗? 她的男朋友是她的同学吗?

(4) 你有没有弟弟/妹妹? 有几个弟弟/妹妹?

(5) 你有没有好朋友? 有几个好朋友?

(6) 你有你好朋友的照片吗?

(7) 今天你有汉语课吗?

(8) 你有中文书吗?

(9) 你有没有你们家的全家福?

2. "给" 字用做动词和介词 The Word "给" Used as a Verb and a Preposition

The word "给" is used as both a verb and a preposition. "给" is always a verb when there are no other verbs present in the sentence. In other cases, it should be a preposition.

A. As a verb:

老师给赵文生一张照片。
The teacher gave a picture to Zhao Wensheng.

我们给他一个工作。
We gave him a job.

B. As a preposition:

老师给我们介绍新同学。
The teacher introduces new schoolmates to us.

他给我们照全家福。
He is taking a family picture for us.

练习二

请指出在下面的句子里"给"是动词还是介词。

Please indicate the function of the word "给."

	动词 verb	介词 preposition
(1) 我朋友给我两张照片。		
(2) 刘小明给他的朋友们照一张照片。		
(3) 老师给我们上课。		
(4) 老师给我们功课 (gōngkè: homework)。		
(5) 王律师给他一个工作。		
(6) 爸爸给我一枝笔 (yì zhī bǐ: a pen)		
(7) 你给爷爷买 (mǎi:to buy) 生日礼物 (lǐwù: gift)。		
(8) 你给奶奶什么?		
(9) 我给他打开书。		
(10) 妈妈给安娜一个礼物。		

3. 副词"只"的用法 Usage of the Adverb "只"

While most adverbs in Chinese are used to modify verbs, adjectives and other adverbs, the adverb "只" can be used to describe not only a verb but also a noun, a pronoun and even a prepositional phrase.

他在中国只学习汉语。
He only studies Chinese in China. (verb)

他只(是)在中国学习汉语。
It is only in China that he studies Chinese. (prepositional phrase)

When the adverb "只" precedes a subject noun or pronoun, "只有" replaces "只."

只有李明是我的好朋友。
Li Ming is my only good friend. (noun)

只有他在中国学习汉语。
Only he studies Chinese in China. (pronoun)

Conclusion:

只　　　+ verb
只(是)　+ prepositional phrase
只有　　+ subject noun or pronoun

练习三

1.请按照例句做对话。
Make conversation following the model.

你学习英语和法语,是吗?

不是,我只学习英语,不学习法语。

(1) 你爸爸妈妈有男孩子也有女孩子,是吗?
(2) 今天是你姥姥的生日也是你姥爷的生日,是吗?
(3) 你给我们介绍新朋友也介绍老朋友,是吗?
(4) 李新是小明的朋友也是安娜的朋友,是吗?
(5) 王大明是我们的同学也是你们的同学,是吗?
(6) 今天你有英语课也有汉语课,是吗?
(7) 你给我们照全家福也给他们照全家福,是吗?
(8) 你有中文书也有法语书,是吗?

2. 请用中文回答下面的问题。
Answer the following questions using Chinese.

(1) 在你们家，只有你哥哥 / 姐姐是大学生吗？

(2) 在中文课上，只有你们的老师是中国人吗？

(3) 在你的朋友中，只有你学习中文吗？

(4) 只有他/她是你的好朋友吗？

(5) 只有你认识这个新同学吗？

(6) 在中文课上，只有他姓李，是吗？

4. 连词"还是"的用法 The Conjuction Word "还是"

Although the conjunction word "还是" is equivalent to the word "or" in English, its function is not quite the same in Chinese because "还是" can be used only in a question.

你们今天来，还是明天来？
Are you coming today or tomorrow?

这是英文书还是法文书？
Is this an English or a French book?

谁是英语老师，是你还是他？
Who is the English teacher, you or him?

If it is not a question, another conjunction word will be used instead of "还是."

你可以叫他Bill 或者 (huòzhě: or) Willam.
You can call him Bill or Willam.

练习四

1. 请按照例句做对话。
   Make conversation following the model.

    你朋友是中国人还是美国人？

    他不是中国人，也不是美国人，他是法国人。

   (1) 王文国是学生还是老师？
   (2) 他是你哥哥还是你弟弟？
   (3) 你们的汉语老师是中国人还是美国人？
   (4) 这是中文书还是英文书？
   (5) 他爸爸是医生还是律师？
   (6) 你们今天还是明天有化学课？

2. 请按照你自己的情况回答下面的问题。
   Please give your own personal answers to the following questions.

   Model:
   A. 你哥哥大，还是你姐姐大？
   B. 我哥哥大。他今年二十岁；我姐姐十八岁。

   (1) 你弟弟大，还是你妹妹大？

   (2) 你大，还是你朋友大？

   (3) 李英大，还是李娜大？

   (4) 这个男孩子大，还是那个女孩子大？

   (5) 你爸爸岁数大，还是你妈妈岁数大？

   (6) 你爷爷老，还是你奶奶老？

5. 连词 "和" The Conjuction Word "和"

Although translated as "and," the conjunction word "和" does not always function as its English equivalent. It can be used between nouns in a list.

李新、谢大明、张朋和赵文生是学生。
Li Xin, Xie Daming, Zhang Peng and Zhao Wensheng are students.

他有弟弟和妹妹，没有哥哥和姐姐。
He has younger brothers and sisters but no elder brother and sisters.

今天、明天和后天 (hòutiān: the day after tomorrow) 我们没有化学课。
We don't have chemistry class today, tomorrow, and the day after tomorrow.

It cannot, however, be used to express logical modification, consequence or supplementary explanation (while the English word "and" can: He was late, and missed the quiz.). In other words, "和" links nouns but not sentences.

练习五

请按照例句做对话。
Make conversation following the model.

你和谁一起住？

我和姥姥、姥爷一起住。

(1) 你和谁一起学习？
(2) 你妈妈和谁一起工作？
(3) 你和谁一起上中文课？
(4) 你和谁一起做功课 (gōngkè: homework)？
(5) 大卫和谁一起在中国学习汉语？
(6) 他和中国学生一起住吗？

六、练习 Exercises

模式练习 Model exercises

1. 三个人一组按照范例做练习1, 2, 3 和 4。A 向 B 提问，B 再向 C 提问。提问时要把对方的回答记下来。然后每个人再用第三人称 (他 / 她) 讲述组员的家庭情况。

   In groups of three, take turns to ask the following questions in exercises 1, 2, 3, and 4. A asks B, who will then ask C. Take note of the answers and afterwards use a third person subject (他 / 她) to report the results of the interview.

   (1) 你家有几口人？
   　　A. 你家有几口人？
   　　B. 我家有＿＿＿口人：我爸爸、妈妈、姐姐……
   　　A. 请你介绍一下你的家人，好不好？
   　　B. 好，现在我介绍一下我的家人。我爸爸是医生……

   (2) 老大、老二、老三、老四……
   　　A. 你爸爸妈妈有几个孩子？谁是<u>老大</u> (eldest child)？
   　　B. 我爸爸妈妈有三个孩子；我哥哥是老大。
   　　A. 你是老几？
   　　B. 我是老三。
   　　A. 谁是老二？
   　　B. 我姐姐是老二。

你们三个，谁是老大？

(3) 大哥、二哥、三哥……，哥哥、姐姐、弟弟、妹妹、儿子、女儿 (nǚér: daughter)

A. 你有几个哥哥？
B. 三个。我大哥今年二十四岁，是律师；我二哥十九岁，是大学生。
A. 你三哥呢？
B. 我三哥今年十七岁，明年上大学。
A. 你爸爸妈妈有三个儿子；有几个女儿？
B. 只有我一个。我没有姐姐，也没有妹妹。

(4) 男孩子、女孩子

A. 你们家老大是男孩子还是女孩子？
B. 男孩子。
A. 老三呢？
B. 我们家没有老三。我爸爸妈妈只有两个孩子：一男一女。

2. 按照下面照片的内容回答问题。
Answer the questions according to what you see in the following pictures.

谁是大姐？谁是小妹？

(1) 这家有几个孩子？

(2) 这家有男孩子吗？

(3) 谁是二姐？

(4) 谁是小妹？

(5) 大姐有几个妹妹？

文娣　　　大卫　　　莉莉

他是哥哥还是弟弟？

(6) 这家有几个孩子？

(7) 这家有几个男孩子？几个女孩子？

(8) 你看大姐有几岁？

(9) 你看小弟弟有几岁？

(10) 谁有妹妹？

(11) 谁有弟弟和妹妹？

3. 请两个人一起做下面的练习：一个人读，另一个人把家谱画出来。

Work in pairs: one person reads the paragraph, and the other completes the family tree.

我的家谱 (jiāpǔ: family tree)

这是我的爷爷和奶奶。他们有一个儿子、一个女儿。我爸爸是他们的老大。我爸爸的妹妹是我的姑姑 (gūgu)。我爸爸妈妈有三个孩子：一个男孩子，两个女孩子。我姐姐是老大，我妹妹是老三，我呢？我是老几？我姑姑和姑父 (gūfu: 姑姑's husband) 只有一个男孩子。

4. 请你找两个同学，按照例句 A 和 B 做对话。要注意用不同的方法问不同年龄的人。

Make conversation following models A and B. Make sure that you use the appropriate ways of asking people their age.

Model A:

你哥哥今年多大 (used when asking young people's age)

A. 你哥哥今年多大？
B. 他今年十八岁。
A. 你弟弟呢？
B. 我弟弟今年十二岁。

| 哥哥 | 姐姐 | 弟弟 | 妹妹 |
| 你朋友 | 你同学 | 学生 | 你 |

Model B:

你爸爸今年多大岁数 (used for asking elder people's age)

A. 你爸爸今年多大岁数？
B. 我爸爸今年四十五岁。
A. 你妈妈今年也四十五岁吗？
B. 不是，我妈妈四十岁。

| 爸爸 | 妈妈 | 爷爷 | 奶奶 | 姥爷 |
| 姥姥 | 这个医生 | 那个老师 | 你们的律师 | |

5. 阅读下列短文，并用中文回答问题。
   Read the following paragraphs and answer the questions using Chinese.

A. 你们认识我吗？

你们认识我吗？对，我姓魏(Wèi)，叫魏敏芝(Wèi Mǐnzhī)。我十三岁，是一个老师。我不是大学老师，也不是中学老师；我是一个小学老师。我有二十多个学生。

(1) 你认识这个女孩子吗？

(2) 她姓什么？叫什么名字？

(3) 她有工作吗？

(4) 她做什么工作？

(5) 魏老师有多少个学生？

B. 大家 (everyone) 好！
　　大家好！我叫李文中，三十二岁。我是一个医生，在北京 (Běijīng) 第二医院工作。这所医院很大，有三百 (bǎi: hundred) 八十八个医生。我家有三口人：我，我太太 (tàitai: wife) 和一个女儿。我太太是中学英文老师，女儿今年七岁，是小学生。

(6) 李医生在哪儿工作？

(7) 他工作的医院有多少个医生？

(8) 李医生家有几口人？

(9) 李医生的太太也是医生吗？

(10) 他的女儿几岁？

6. 请按照例句做对话。
Make conversation following the model.

 现在你在做什么？　　 现在我在上中文课。

(1) 现在张学友在做什么？（看书: to read）
(2) 现在那美英在做什么？（学中文）
(3) 现在刘卫国在做什么？ 做功课 (gōngkè: homework)
(4) 现在刘来娣在做什么？（看照片）
(5) 现在你们在做什么？（上中文课）

7. 请按照例句做对话。
Make conversation following the model.

 你在哪儿住？　　 我在上海(Shànghǎi)住。

(1) 谢家朋在哪儿学习英语？(美国)
(2) 李卫明在哪儿工作？(一家银行)
(3) 高小英的爷爷奶奶在哪儿住？(北京)
(4) 安娜在哪儿学汉语？(中国)
(5) 你在哪儿看书？(家)
(6) 你们在哪儿学习中文？(英国)

8. 学习下面的对话，然后用"几个"或"多少个"填空。
Study the following dialogues and then fill in the blanks with "几个" or "多少个."

 那所大学有多少个汉语老师？　　 有二十五个。

 你爸爸妈妈有几个孩子？　　 有三个。

几个 (when the speaker expects the answer is less than ten) vs 多少 shǎo 个

(1) 你有 ☐ 姐姐？
(2) 你有 ☐ 同学？
(3) 你们学校 (xuéxiào: school) 有 ☐ 英语老师？
(4) 你们学校有 ☐ 学生？
(5) 你有 ☐ 新朋友？
(6) 你们有 ☐ 中文老师？

9. 和一个同学一起先决定"工作"一词在对话中的词性，然后按照例句做对话。请注意工作单位的量词用法。
Work in pairs: first decide the nature of the word "工作" in the dialogue, then make conversation following the model. Please pay attention to the measure words you use for each of the workplaces.

这是一家银行　　一所大学　　这是一家(所)医院

第三课 我的家人 My Family

Model:
A. 王同卫有工作吗？
B. 有，他在一家银行工作。
A. 他做什么工作？
B. 他是 行长 (hángzhǎng: president of a bank)。

名词	动词

(1) 刘汉生 / 一家银行 / 行长 (hángzhǎng: president of a bank)。
(2) 张英明 / 一所中学 / 校长 (xiàozhǎng: principal)
(3) 文美英 / 一家医院 / 医生
(4) 李新来 / 一所大学 / 老师
(5) 谢一娜 / 一家律师所 / 律师
(6) 王文英 / 一所小学 / 老师

实况演练 Real situation exercises

1. 请用中文完成下列任务。
   Complete the following tasks using Chinese.

   (1) 请你介绍一下你的家人。

   (2) 你有你们家的全家福吗？请给你的同学们看看。

   (3) 你认识一个大家庭 (jiātíng: family) 吗？请你介绍一下这个家庭，好吗？

(4) 你爸爸有几个兄(xiōng: 哥哥)弟姐妹(siblings)？你妈妈呢？

(5) 你的好朋友家有几口人？有什么人？请你介绍一下。

(6)

A. 这个人是中国人还是美国人？

B. 他多大岁数？

C. 他是大学老师吗？

D. 他的中国名字叫什么？(比尔·盖茨：Bǐ'ěr Gàicí)

(7)

A. 你认识这两个人吗？

B. 他们是律师吗?

C. 他们有几个孩子？有儿子还是有女儿?

D. 他们的孩子叫什么名字?

(8)

A. 他是医生吗?

B. 他家有几口人?

C. 他的生日是几月几号?

D. 他有几个孩子？男孩子还是女孩子?

七、读报 Newspaper Reading

How Many Characters Do You Know?

1. Read the following article.
2. While reading, underline the characters you know.

妈妈的生日

李凯玲　年龄：11岁　七年级二班　辅导教师：黄晓冬

　　那一年是2004年，我十岁。我和妈妈从美国回中国度假。那天是七月二十一日，你也许会觉得这一天很普通，但是对我来说，那是一个特别的日子，七月二十一日是我妈妈的生日。

　　那天实在是太热了，中午妈妈睡午觉。我也想睡觉，可是我连给妈妈的生日礼物都没有准备，我怎么祝贺她的生日呢？我正在想要给妈妈一份什么样的礼物时，我的表姐羽栖来了，我让她帮我拿主意。她想了想，突然说："哎，要不我们送她几朵花吧？我们现在就去办。""这个……"我脑子飞快转了起来。

　　是是是，这个主意是不错，可是如果我们现在出门，妈妈突然起来问我和羽栖去哪儿了，我们怎么解释？肯定会说我们的。我正在犹豫，想到底去不去呢？可是我也不能没有礼物吧。"好，我们去跟我的外婆说了一声"，羽栖说着就去问了外婆。还好她答应了，"早点回家！"外婆嘱咐道。我们便悄悄地走了。

　　当我的脚踏上了上海的马路时，我一点也不知道我们要去哪儿。我只是跟着羽栖走。一边走着一边聊着，我们来到了一个卖花的地方。我们挑了又挑，买了一束各种鲜花的花束。我以为我们买了花就回去，但是羽栖说我们要去买一张卡。我们又来到了一个小商店。我们挑了一张，羽栖还是没让我走。她说："你还想要什么东西？"她问我这个问题我觉得很奇怪，我不想要什么东西，就说："我不知道。"她说，"你的生日是在八月份，到那时你就要回去了，我也不能给你礼物了。"她说得有道理，我就挑了一些折纸用的长条纸。

　　回家的时候，妈妈还没睡醒呢。我放心多了。外婆把花藏起来，我赶快地把卡做好。正好我们买了那些长条，我和羽栖就把那些长条做成一颗颗的小星星，贴在卡上。我们等了一会儿，妈妈才醒过来。她把门一打开，我们就喊了起来，"生日快乐！"妈妈很惊讶，也很高兴，捧着鲜花和我们一起唱"祝你生日快乐"的歌。

　　到了晚上，妈妈也给了我一个小惊喜。她的朋友请她吃饭，可是她婉言推辞了。她要待在家里和我一起看电视呢！

选自：中美导报　日期：2008年3月14日

一起过生日

段玉梅

　　今天是女儿16岁的生日。

　　昨天，我问她："冉冉，你过生日时，想吃些什么？"女儿说："我什么都不要，但我有个要求，你得答应我。"我说："那好，你说吧，只要是合理的要求，妈妈都会答应的。"女儿说："妈，我请同学来家和我一起过生日，你看可以吗？"我说："好呀。你准备请几个同学？我给你买一个大点儿的生日蛋糕吧？"

　　女儿很高兴，连连拍手说："好，好。谢谢妈妈！上次，我同桌穗穗过生日时，是一个人过的。她父母在南方打工，她住在学校寝室里，只有到了周末，才能到她姑妈家。我看她父母不在身边，缺少家庭温暖，我想在过生日那天邀请穗穗到我们家来一起吃生日蛋糕。"

　　女儿生日这天上午，我都在厨房忙，菜饭做好了，摆满了一桌子。我为她订的奶油水果蛋糕，也放在了餐桌上。

　　过12点了，这小寿星还没回来。我一会儿跑到窗前望望，一会儿朝着大门听听。同住一幢楼的学生都陆陆续续回来了，还不见女儿，我有点心急了。披上衣服走出家门，在小卖部的门口，我远远看见女儿跟穗穗、婷婷两个女孩，正往这边走来，边走边兴致勃勃地聊着。

　　进了家门，女儿赶紧请同学"上座"，热情地请她们吃菜。女儿还点起蜡烛，大家一起唱了《生日歌》，然后切蛋糕，分蛋糕。孩子们吃得很开心。

　　看着这一切，我想：女儿这一代90后，虽说是独生子女，在蜜罐里长大的，但待人接物、互助友爱的精神却真令人欣慰。她们的未来，一定很美好。

选自：新民晚报　日期：2008年11月5日

3. Pronounce the characters you have recognized.
4. Tell the meaning of each character to your class (or study group).

八、文化点滴 Culture Notes

Chinese Surnames

According to recent surveys, there are currently over one thousand Chinese surnames in use throughout the world. The top ten account for 44% of the Chinese population.

There are two different kinds of Chinese surnames: single-character surnames and double-character ones. Most Chinese surnames belong to the single-character type, but some popular double-character surnames are 司马 Sīmǎ, 上官 Shàngguān, 欧阳 Ōuyáng and 诸葛 Zhūgě.

The top ten popular Chinese surnames are: 李 Lǐ, 王 Wáng, 张 Zhāng, 刘 Liú, 陈 Chén, 杨 Yáng, 赵 Zhào, 黄 Huáng, 周 Zhōu, 吴 Wú.

Unlike in the western tradition, the Chinese surname comes before the given name. For example, in the name of 孙中山, Sūn Zhōngshān (Sun Yat-sen), 孙 (Sūn) is the surname while 中山 (Zhōngshān or 逸先 Yat-sen) is the given name.

In mainland China, women do not change their surnames after marriage; however, in Hong Kong and Taiwan, very often the husband's surname is added to the woman's full name in order to form her conjugal name. 王淑珍 Wáng Shūzhēn would become 赵王淑珍 Zhào Wáng Shūzhēn if her husband's surname were Zhào.

孙中山 (Sūn Zhōngshān) 1866-1925

诸葛亮 (Zhūgě Liàng) 181-234

九、自我测试 Self Assessment

1. 用中文回答问题。
   Answer the following questions using Chinese.

(1) 你家有几口人?

(2) 你爸爸、妈妈多大岁数?

(3) 我们能看看你的全家福吗?

(4) 你爸爸是做什么工作的?

(5) 你妈妈工作吗?

(6) 你有几个兄 (xiōng: 哥哥) 弟姐妹 (siblings)?

2. 请你说说每张照片上的家庭。
   Talk about the families in each picture using Chinese.

(1)

3. 对不对？

Read the question (A) and the answer (B). Check "对" if you think the answer is logical with respect to the question or check "不对" otherwise.

(1) A. 你认识我哥哥吗？
    B. 不认识。我认识你弟弟。　　　　对 _____ 不对 _____

(2) A. 你妈妈是大学老师？
    B. 我妈妈在大学工作，可 (kě: but)
       她不是大学老师。　　　　　　　　对 _____ 不对 _____

(3) A. 谁是你的好朋友？
    B. 你有两个好朋友。　　　　　　　　对 _____ 不对 _____

(4) A. 同学们，请你们打开书，好吗？
    B. 请问，老师，第几页？　　　　　　对 _____ 不对 _____

(5) A. 今天是你的生日还是你朋友的生日？
    B. 今天是我们两个人的生日。　　　　对 _____ 不对 _____

(6) A. 这是你家人的照片吗？
    B. 是，这是我们的全家福。　　　　　对 _____ 不对 _____

(7) A. 你是你们家的老大吗？
    B. 是，我是我爸爸妈妈的第二个孩子。
                                              对 _____ 不对 _____

(8) A. 李明和谁住在一起？
    B. 他和他的姥姥、姥爷住在一起。　　对 _____ 不对 _____

(9) A. 谁是医生？
    B. 刘小明的爷爷是一个老医生。　　　对 _____ 不对 _____

(10) A. 谁在律师所工作？
     B. 这个律师所有五个律师。　　　　　对 _____ 不对 _____

4. 阅读下列短文，并用中文回答问题。
Read the following paragraph and answer the questions using Chinese.

我们家是老北京人。我爷爷的爸爸 (或者说 or 我爸爸的爷爷) 出生 (chūshēng: to be born) 在北京；我爷爷出生在北京；我爸爸也出生在北京。我出生在美国。

我爷爷今年八十六岁，他还在北京住，他是一个老中医 (doctor of traditional Chinese medicine)。我爸爸妈妈也是医生，可是 (kěshì: but) 他们不是中医。

(1) "我们家"是哪里人？ Where does "my family" come from?

(2) "我"的爷爷今年多大岁数？

(3) "我"出生在哪儿？

(4) "我"的爸爸妈妈是做什么的？

(5) "我们家"谁是中医？

在我的家庭，我有四口人和一个狗。有我的爸爸,妈妈,妹妹和我。我的狗叫"Buddy." 我的爸爸是一个律师, 我妈妈是一个医生。我妹妹和我是高中学生。

戴开文
Kevin Davis

我的家庭有四口人。我的爸爸妈妈，妹妹和我。我的家庭也有一只狗。我的爸爸是一个律师,他花很多的时间工作。我的妈妈是一个很好的医生。我的妹妹是一个小学四年级的学生。

苏南欧
Neel Swami

我的家庭有五口人和一只狗。我有爸爸,妈妈,两个弟弟和我。除了我的大弟弟以外,我们都有咖啡颜色的头发。我的爸爸是一个售货员,我妈是一个医生。我们都上学,我的狗真长。我喜欢我的家庭。

卢侯骏
Jose Luna

第四课
LESSON FOUR

生日快乐!
Happy Birthday!

学习目的
Learning Objectives

生日祝贺	To wish people happy birthday
表达正在做的事	To tell what you or others are doing
表达打算要做的事	To tell what you or others plan to do
年、月、日、星期表达法	To express dates, days of the week, months and year
"最"的用法	To use "最" to express superlative
用"了"和"过"叙述过去的事情与经验	To use "了" and "过" to talk about past events and experiences

本课学习内容 Contents of the chapter

一	学习发音 Pronunciation
	■ 声母 consonants：z, c, s ■ 韵母 vowels：an, ian, en, in, un, uan
二	课文：生日快乐！ Text: Happy Birthday!
三	生词 Vocabulary
	■ 名词 nouns：赵、长江、周、号、月、下、星期、瓶、花、蛋糕、卡、长寿、面条、明天、男朋友、饭、餐馆、日本、意大利、长城、公园 ■ 代词 pronouns：那里、那儿 ■ 动词 verbs：到、打算、过、要、买、喜欢、祝贺、想、吃、知道、去、听说、觉得、试 ■ 形容词 adjectives：漂亮、长、快乐、错 ■ 副词 adverbs：快、怎么、很 ■ 介词 prepositions：里 ■ 连词 conjunctions：那么、可是 ■ 量词 measure word：次 ■ 虚词 particle：了 ■ 词句 expressions：再见、明天见
四	数字学习 Study of Numbers: 51-99
五	语法 Grammar
	■ "认识"与"知道"的区别　　"认识" versus "知道" ■ "要"的用法　　Usage of "要" ■ 虚词"了"　　The modal particle "了" ■ "过"和"了"字的区别　　Difference between "过" and "了" in indicating the past ■ "打算"用作名词和动词　　"打算" used as a noun and a verb ■ 动词"想"的作用　　Functions of the verb "想"
六	练习 Exercises
七	读报 News paper Reading
八	文化点滴 Culture Notes
九	自我测试 Self Assessment

第四课 生日快乐！
Happy Birthday!

LESSON 4

一、学习发音 Pronunciation 1

z　c　s　+　an　ian　en　in　un　uan

Drill 1

z +

āi （栽）	é （则）	ǎi （宰）	è （仄）
			ài （在）
	éi （贼）		
āo （遭）	áo （凿）	ǎo （早）	ào （造）
ōu （邹）		ǒu （走）	òu （揍）
		uǐ （嘴）	uì （最）

Drill 2

c +

ā （擦）		ǎ （礤）	
ū （粗）			ù （促）
āi （猜）	ái （才）	ǎi （采）	ài （菜）
uī （催）		uǐ （璀）	uì （萃）
āo （操）	áo （曹）	ǎo （草）	
			è （策）
			òu （凑）

Drill 3

s +

ā （仨）		ǎ （洒）	à （萨）
			è （色）
ū （苏）	ú （俗）		ù （素）
āi （腮）			ài （赛）
ōu （搜）		ǒu （擞）	òu （嗽）
uī （虽）	uí （随）	uǐ （髓）	uì （岁）
āo （搔）		ǎo （嫂）	ào （臊）

107

Drill 4

b		bān (班)
p		pān (潘)
d	+ ān →	dān (丹)
t		tān (滩)
z		zān (糌)
w		wān (弯)

f		fán (烦)
l		lán (兰)
m	+ án →	mán (蛮)
p		pán (盘)
t		tán (谈)
z		zán (咱)

b		bǎn (板)
d		dǎn (胆)
f		fǎn (反)
l	+ ǎn →	lǎn (揽)
m		mǎn (满)
s		sǎn (伞)
w		wǎn (晚)
z		zǎn (攒)

b		bàn (办)
d		dàn (蛋)
f		fàn (饭)
l	+ àn →	làn (烂)
m		màn (慢)
s		sàn (散发)
w		wàn (万)
z		zàn (赞)

Drill 5

b		biān (边)
p	+ iān →	piān (篇)
d		diān (颠)
t		tiān (天)

l		lián (连)
m	+ ián →	mián (棉)
n		nián (年)
t		tián (田)

b		biǎn (贬)
d	+ iǎn →	diǎn (点)
l		liǎn (脸)
m		miǎn (免)

b		biàn (变)
d		diàn (电)
l	+ iàn →	liàn (恋)
m		miàn (面)
n		niàn (念)
p		piàn (片)

Drill 6

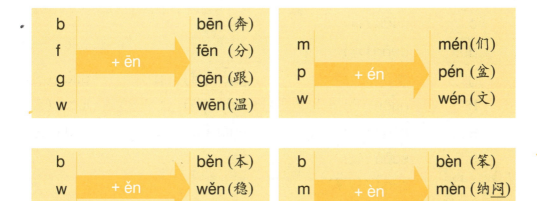

Drill 7

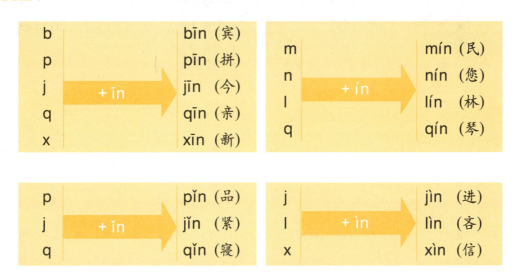

Drill 8

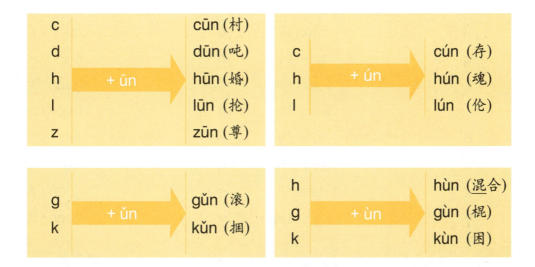

Drill 9

c		cuān (撺)					
d		duān (端)					
g		guān (官)	g		guǎn (馆)	g	guàn (贯)
h	+ uān →	huān (欢)	l	+ uǎn →	luǎn (卵)	l	+ uàn → luàn (乱)
k		kuān (宽)	n		nuǎn (暖)	s	suàn (算)
s		suān (酸)					
z		zuān (钻探)					

Drill 10

j		jūn (军)	q		qún (群)	j	jùn (俊)
x	+ ūn →	xūn (勋)	x	+ ún →	xún (询)	x	+ ùn → xùn (迅)
y		yūn (晕)	y		yún (云)	y	yùn (运)

Drill 11

j		juān (娟)			
q		quān (圈套)	q		quán (全)
s	+ uān →	suān (酸)	x	+ uán →	xuán (旋)
x		xuān (宣)	y		yuán (园)
y		yuān (鸳)			

Drill 12

d		duǎn (短)	c		cuàn (篡)
g		guǎn (管)	d		duàn (段)
k		kuǎn (款)	g		guàn (贯)
l	+ uǎn →	luǎn (卵)	h	+ uàn →	huàn (换)
n		nuǎn (暖)	l		luàn (乱)
q		quǎn (犬)	q		quàn (劝)
x		xuǎn (选)	s		suàn (算)
y		yuǎn (远)	y		yuàn (院)

第四课　生日快乐！
Happy Birthday!

Drill 13

zán (咱)	zài (在)	zěn (怎)	zāi (栽)
zuì (最)	zǒu (走)	zì (自)	sēn (森)
sān (三)	sūn (孙)	sài (赛)	sǎo (嫂)
sú (俗)	sì (四)	cún (存)	cān (参)
cǎo (草)	cài (菜)	cū (粗)	cì (次)
cè (策)	tiān (天)	luàn (乱)	xún (询)
juǎn (卷)	biàn (变)	yuán (园)	duǎn (短)

二、课文 Text

祝妈妈生日快乐！

赵长江：大利，今天几号？
周大利：今天是五月二十一号。
赵长江：我妈妈的生日快到了。
周大利：是吗？你妈妈的生日是几月几号？
赵长江：五月二十七号。
周大利：那就是下个星期。下个星期三是二十七号。你打算怎么给你妈妈过生日？
赵长江：我要给她买一瓶花，我妈妈很喜欢花，一个漂亮的大蛋糕和一张生日卡。我还要给她做长寿面(条)，祝贺她的生日。
周大利：我也祝你妈妈生日快乐！
赵长江：谢谢你！

明天是我男朋友的生日

江小妹：明天是我男朋友的生日，我想请他吃饭，可是不知道去哪家餐馆好。

祝文英：你男朋友喜欢吃什么饭？中国饭、法国饭、日本饭，还是意大利饭？

江小妹：他最喜欢吃意大利饭。

贺　亮：我听说长城公园里有一家意大利餐馆，可是我没在那儿吃过。

祝文英：我和我家人在那里吃过一次。我们觉得不错。

江小妹：那我们去试试。

祝文英：祝你男朋友生日快乐！

江小妹：谢谢你们。

贺亮、祝文英：不谢。再见！

江小妹：明天见！

課文

祝媽媽生日快樂！

趙長江：大利,今天幾號?
周大利：今天是五月二十一號。
趙長江：我媽媽的生日快到了。
周大利：是嗎? 你媽媽的生日是幾月幾號?
趙長江：五月二十七號。
周大利：那就是下個星期。下個星期三是二十七號。你打算怎麼給你媽媽過生日?
趙長江：我要給她買一瓶花,我媽媽很喜歡花,一個漂亮的大蛋糕和一張生日卡。我還要給她做長壽面(條),祝賀她的生日。
周大利：我也祝你媽媽生日快樂!
趙長江：謝謝你!

明天是我男朋友的生日

江小妹：明天是我男朋友的生日，我想請他吃飯，可是不知道去哪家餐館好。

祝文英：你男朋友喜歡吃什麼飯？中國飯、法國飯、日本飯，還是義大利飯？

江小妹：他最喜歡吃義大利飯。

賀　亮：我聽說長城公園裏有一家義大利餐館，可是我沒在那兒吃過。

祝文英：我和我家人在那裏吃過一次。我們覺得不錯。

江小妹：那我們去試試。

祝文英：祝你男朋友生日快樂！

江小妹：謝謝你們。

賀亮、祝文英：不謝。再見！

江小妹：明天見！

三、生词 Vocabulary

NOUNS

Zhào 赵(趙) a surname	Chángjiāng 长江(長江) the Yangtze River	
Zhōu 周(周) week, cycle, a surname		
hào 号(號) date of the month, number	yuè 月(月) month, moon	xià 下/下 lower, inferior, next
xīngqī 星期(星期) week	xīng 星: star	
	qī 期: a period of time, term	
píng 瓶(瓶) bottle, vase, jar	huā 花(花) flower	
dàngāo 蛋糕(蛋糕) cake	dàn 蛋: egg	
	gāo 糕: cake	
kǎ 卡(卡) card	chángshòu 长寿(長壽) longevity	miàntiáo 面条(面條) noodles
míngtiān 明天(明天) tomorrow	fàn 饭(飯) meal, food	nán péngyou 男朋友(男朋友) boyfriend
cānguǎn 餐馆(餐館) restaurant	Rìběn 日本(日本) Japan	Yìdàlì 意大利(義大利) Italy
Chángchéng 长城(長城) the Great Wall		
gōngyuán 公园(公園) park	gōng 公: public	
	yuán 园(園) garden, public recreation area	

第四课　生日快乐！
Happy Birthday!

PRONOUNS

nàli
那里/那裏 there

nàr
那儿/那兒 (informal) there

VERBS

dào
到/到 to arrive

dǎsuan
打算/打算 to plan, to intend

guò
过/過 to spend, to pass, to go through

yào
要/要 to ask, to want

mǎi
买/買 to buy

xǐhuan
喜欢/喜歡 to like, to be fond of

zhùhè
祝贺/祝賀 to congratulate ⟶

zhù
祝/祝 to wish (express good wishes)

xiǎng
想/想 to think, to plan, to miss, to want

chī
吃/吃 to eat

zhīdào
知道/知道 to know, to be aware of

qù
去/去 to go

tīng
听/聽 to listen

tīngshuō
听说/聽說 to be told, to hear that

shuō
说/說 to speak, to say

juéde
觉得/覺得 to feel, to think

shì
试/試 to try, to test

ADJECTIVES

piàoliang
漂亮/漂亮 pretty

cháng
长/長 long

kuàilè
快乐/快樂 happy, joyful

cuò
错/錯 wrong

117

ADVERBS

kuài
快/快 fast, quickly, soon

zěnme
怎么/怎麼 how

hěn
很/很 very, quite, awfully

PREPOSITIONS

lǐ
里/裏 inside, in

CONJUNCTIONS

nà
那/那 so, then, in that case

kěshì
可是/可是 but, yet, however

MEASURE WORD

cì
次(次) time (recurring instances)

PARTICLES

le
了/了

EXPRESSIONS

zàijiàn
再见/再見 goodbye

míngtiān jiàn
明天见/明天見 see you tomorrow

第四课 生日快乐！
Happy Birthday!

LESSON 4

四、学习数字 Study of Numbers 51-99

wǔshí yī	wǔshí èr	wǔshí sān	wǔshí sì	wǔshí wǔ
五十一	五十二	五十三	五十四	五十五
wǔshí liù	wǔshí qī	wǔshí bā	wǔshí jiǔ	liùshí
五十六	五十七	五十八	五十九	六十

★ 练 习

1. 三个人一组：从六十一开始，每个人数一个数，一直数到九十九。
   Work in groups of three: starting from number 61, each person counts one number until you reach 99.

2. 请朗读下面的口诀，并想一想"得 dé"字是什么意思。
   Read aloud the following table, and try to figure out the meaning of the word "得."

乘法口诀 (chéngfǎ kǒujué)
Multiplication Table

一一得一
一二得二，二二得四
一三得三，二三得六，三三得九
一四得四，二四得八，三四十二，四四十六
一五得五，二五一十，三五十五，四五二十，五五二十五
一六得六，二六十二，三六十八，四六二十四，五六三十，六六三十六
一七得七，二七十四，三七二十一，四七二十八，五七三十五，六七四十二，七七四十九
一八得八，二八十六，三八二十四，四八三十二，五八四十，六八四十八，七八五十六，八八六十四
一九得九，二九十八，三九二十七，四九三十六，五九四十五，六九五十四，七九六十三，八九七十二，九九八十一

五、语法 Grammar

1. "认识"与"知道"的区别 "认识" versus "知道"

Both verbs "认识" and "知道" can be translated as "to know" in English. However, they are not used in the same situation in Chinese. While "认识" is more or less the equivalent of "to be familiar with" somebody or something,

你认识赵长江吗?
Do you know Zhao Changjiang?

他认识(去)北京大学(的路)吗?
Does he know (how to get to) Peking university?

你们认识这个字吗?
Do you know this word?

"知道" is used in the sense of "to find out something" or "to know thoroughly" through study, memorization, investigation, and inquiry, that is, more than just being familiar or acquainted with something. This verb is very often used to introduce a sentence which denotes what is happening and what is going on and why, when, and how to do something.

我知道这个男孩子的名字。
I know this boy's name.

我知道你的意思。
I know what you mean.

他知道你们是好朋友。
He knows that you are good friends.

学生们知道中文不好学。
Students know that Chinese is not easy to learn.

Note that "知道" can also be followed by a noun that refers to a person. In this case the meaning is different from "认识 + person." For example:

我知道他。
I have heard of him. or: I know who he is.

我认识他。
I know him.

第四课　生日快乐！
Happy Birthday!

练习一

1. 请按照例句做对话。
   Make conversation following the model.

    你知道你爸爸的生日是哪天吗？

    我知道，是六月十七号。你呢？你知道你妈妈的生日是几月几号吗？

    我也知道，我妈妈的生日是一月二十二号。

   (1) 你爸爸 / 妈妈
   (2) 你哥哥 / 姐姐
   (3) 你弟弟 / 妹妹
   (4) 你爷爷 / 奶奶
   (5) 你姥姥 / 姥爷
   (6) 你女朋友 / 男朋友
   (7) 大明 / 二明
   (8) 安娜 / 开文

2. 请按照例句做对话。
   Make conversation following the model.

    你认识张天月吗？

    认识，她是张天星的姐姐。

    你认识张天星的哥哥吗？

    不认识。可(是)我知道他叫张天明。

   (1) 周学文 / 周学美 / 周学亮
   (2) 谢小明 / 谢小朋 / 谢小英
   (3) 贺长江 / 贺长城 / 贺长安
   (4) 祝文英 / 祝明英 / 祝新英
   (5) 高新卫 / 高新莉 / 高新国

2. "要" 的用法 Usage of "要"

The word "要" can be used simultaneously as a verb and a helping verb. As a verb, "要" is equivalent to the expression "to want something."

你要什么?
What do you want?

我要一个蛋糕。
I want a cake.

But as a helping verb, "要" is followed by another verb to express the idea of "to want to do something" or the future tense.

你要吃什么?
What do you want to eat?

我弟弟要来北京。
My brother wants to come to Beijing. / My brother will come to Beijing.

这个星期天我们要去李老师家。
This Sunday, we are going to Professor Li's home.

他要来北京上学。
He will come to Beijing for school. / He wants to come to Beijing for school.

练习二

在下面的句子里,"要"是动词还是助动词?
Is the character "要" a verb or a helping verb in the following sentences?

	动词 verb	助动词 helping verb
(1) 你要买什么?		
(2) 他们要吃意大利饭。		
(3) 我要一张他的照片。		
(4) 你要不要看我们的照片?		
(5) 明天你们要做什么?		
(6) 她想要花。		
(7) 你要哪本书?		
(8) 他要见谁?		

3. 虚词 "了" The Modal Particle "了"

As a modal particle, the word "了" has several functions in Chinese. The most popular one is that "了" indicates that the action of the verb has been completed. When this particle appears after a verb or an adjective (not necessarily immediately after), it indicates that the action of the verb or a change of the state took place.

今天我吃了很多蛋糕。
I ate a lot of cake today.

今天我们学了六个中文字。
Today we have learned six Chinese characters.

他是大学生了!
He became a college student! / He is already a college student!

In the dialogue of this chapter, however, "了" is used to indicate the future change that is pre-determined in the speaker's mind. 我妈妈的生日快到了 (My mother's birthday is coming soon). Here are some more examples:

天快冷 (lěng: cold) 了。
The weather is becoming cold.

大卫要去北京学汉语了。
David will study Chinese in Beijing.

他不想来上海 (Shànghǎi) 了。
He (has made his mind that he) will not come to Shanghai.

In the above sentences, "了" is used to announce the change that will soon take place. The first example should be understood as "It has become evident that the weather will soon be cold," and in the last two, "了" indicates "a decision has been made that ...."

练习三

请用中文回答下列问题。
Answer the following questions using Chinese.

(1) 你给爷爷买生日卡了吗?

(2) 你给大家介绍你的朋友了吗?

(3) 今天你们学了几个汉字?

(4) 在长城, 你们照了几张照片?

(5) 谁去银行了?

(6) 昨天 (zuótiān: yesterday) 他们上化学课了吗?

(7) 学生们打开书了吗?

(8) 这个孩子几岁了? 他上学了吗?

4. "过" 和 "了" 字的区别 Difference between "过" and "了" in Indiating the Past

In the dialogue for this chapter, the two basic functions of the character "过" are introduced. As a verb, it means to spend.

他们在日本过了两个星期。
They spent two weeks in Japan.

她请了很多朋友给她儿子过生日。
She invited a lot of friends to celebrate (spend) her son's birthday.

As a helping verb, "过" appears after a verb. In this case, just like the character "了," it indicates the completion of the action of the verb. For example:

你买那本书了吗?
Did you buy that book?

你们学过这个字吗?
Have you learned this character?

However, there is a subtle difference, and one should comprehend the nuance

between the two characters so as to understand both and use them accurately. See the following examples:

他去中国了。
He went to China.

他去过中国(了)。
He has been to China.

昨天我们吃了意大利饭。
Yesterday we ate Italian food.

你们吃过意大利饭吗?
Have you ever had Italian food?

As one can see, when a verb is followed by "过," it emphasizes a past experience, a message that a verb followed by "了" does not deliver. Note that when "过" and "了" are negated by 没 (有), the character "了" is dropped while "过" remains with the negation.

他去中国了吗?
Did he go to China?

他没去中国。
He didn't go to China.

他去过中国吗?
Has he been to China?

他没去过中国。
He hasn't been to China.

When both characters "过" and "了" appear in one sentence (过 + object + 了), it plays the role of the adverb "already." For example:

我们吃过中饭了。
We already had lunch.

你们看过这张照片了吗?
Have you (already) seen this picture?

练习四

先在空格里填上"过"或"了"字,然后读每一个小对话。如果有读不懂的地方,请你们问老师。
First, fill in the blanks with the word "过" or "了," then read each of the following dialogues, and ask your instructor questions if there is anything you do not understand.

(1) A. 昨天你们去哪儿吃饭 _____？
    B. 去来利餐厅。你在那里吃 _____ 饭吗?
    A. 没有。那个餐厅的饭好吃吗?
    B. 不错 (bú cuò: not bad)。

(2) A. 你上 _____ 王老师的语法课吗?
    B. 没有。这是第一次 (dì yī cì: the first time)。

(3) A. 上个 (last) 周末 (zhōumò: weekend) 你做什么 _____？
    B. 我去朋友家 _____ 。

(4) A. 大卫在上海 (Shànghǎi) 住 _____ 吗?
    B. 住过。去年，他在那里住 _____ 两个月。

(5) A. 你买这本书 _____ 吗?
    B. 没买，我看 _____ 这本书了。

(6) A. 今天你们学 _____ 几个汉字?
    B. 八个。

(7) A. 你们学 _____ "家"字了吗?
    B. 学过了。

5. "打算"用作名词和动词 "打算" Used as a Noun and Verb

As a helping verb, "打算" must be immediately followed by a verb.

学生们打算去中国。
The students are planning to go to China.

谁打算学中文?
Who is planning to learn Chinese?

今天他们不打算买书。
They are not planning to buy books today.

"打算" can also be used as a noun.

这是你的打算吗?
Is this your plan?

这个打算很好。
This is a nice plan.

你们有什么打算?
What kind of plan do you have?

练习五

请按照例句做对话。
Make conversation following the model.

 我爷爷的生日快到了。

 你打算怎么给你爷爷过生日？

 我打算给爷爷做长寿面，给他祝寿。

 我也祝你爷爷生日快乐！祝他长寿！

 谢谢你！

(1) 爷爷的生日/做长寿面、祝寿/祝生日快乐、长寿
(2) 哥哥的生日/去意大利餐馆吃饭、买生日卡/祝生日快乐
(3) 妈妈的生日/去法国餐馆吃饭、买花、吃生日蛋糕/祝生日快乐
(4) 新年/买贺年卡、请爷爷奶奶来我们家过年/新年好 (or: 过年好)
(5) 周末 (zhōumò: weekend) /请朋友来我家、做好吃的/周末好

6. 动词"想"的作用 Functions of the Verb "想"

This verb has several commonly used functions:

A. When followed by another verb, "想" means to **WANT** to do something.

你想做什么？
What do you want to do?

我想学英语。
I want to learn English.

我不想看书。
I do not want to read.

B. When followed by a noun (normally a person) or a pronoun, "想" means to **MISS**.

你想谁？
Whom do you miss?

我想我爸爸、妈妈。
I miss my father and mother.

你想她吗？
Do you miss her?

C. When followed by a noun (thing), "想" means to **THINK ABOUT**.

你在想什么？
What are you thinking about?

我在想(我的)工作。
I'm thinking about my work.

他在想(他的)<u>前途</u> (qiántú: future)。
He is thinking about his future.

D. When followed by a sentence, "想" is used to give one's opinion. It is the equivalent of the verbs to **BELIEVE** or to **THINK**.

我想他是一个好学生。
I believe that he is a good student.

我想他们在学习第三课。
I think they are learning Lesson Three.

练习六

1. 请按照例句做对话。
   Make conversation following the model.

 你想谁？   我想爸爸、妈妈。

 你在想什么？   我在想怎么给爸爸过生日。

谁	什么
(1) 爸爸、妈妈	爸爸的生日怎么过
(2) 爷爷、奶奶	今天做什么饭
(3) 哥哥和姐姐	怎么学习中文
(4) 弟弟和妹妹	买几张贺年卡
(5) 朋友	去哪里买生日蛋糕

2. 请用中文回答下列问题。
   Answer the following questions using Chinese.

   (1) 你们想吃什么？

(2) 学生们想学什么？

(3) 孩子们想去哪个餐馆吃饭？

(4) 谁想介绍一下长城？

(5) 你们想谢谁？

(6) 他想说什么？

(7) 你想和谁一起学习？

(8) 谁想看我们的全家福？

(9) 谁想打开生日卡？

(10) 生日那天，你想请几个朋友来你家？

3. 请按照例句做对话。

   Make up conversation following the model.

    他是一个好老师吗？   我想他是一个好老师。

   (1) 现在学生们在上课吗？
   (2) 他来过中国吗？
   (3) 她和她的同学们在一起吗？
   (4) 这是妈妈最喜欢的照片吗？
   (5) 他们在看书吗？
   (6) 刘欢认识你的数学老师吗？
   (7) 赵长江有女朋友吗？

六、练习 Exercises

模式练习 Model exercises

1. 请用中文回答下列问题。
Answer the following questions in Chinese.

(1) 今天几月几号？

(2) 你的生日是几月几号？

(3) 谁的生日快到了？

(4) 今天是星期几？明天呢？

(5) 你星期几有数学课？

(6) 你星期几最忙 (máng: busy)？

(7) 一个星期有几天？

(8) 你们一个星期上几天课？

2. 请按照例句做对话。
Make up conversation following the model.

 上个星期你们学了多少个汉字？ 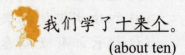 我们学了十来个。
(about ten)

第四课 生日快乐！
Happy Birthday!

 这个星期呢？ 这个星期我们也要学十来个。

 下个星期呢？ 下个星期我们打算学二十来个。

(1) 十来个 (about ten)
(2) 十多个 (more than ten)
(3) 十五六个
(4) 十七八个
(5) 二十来个 (about twenty)
(6) 二十一二个
(7) 二十四五个
(8) 二十多个

3. 请按照例句用提供的词汇做对话。
Use the provided vocabulary to make up conversations following the model.

 我哥哥去年是大学二<u>年级</u> (niánjí: grade) 的学生，今年呢？

 今年他是大学三年级的学生。

 明年呢？

 明年他是大学四年级的学生。

(1) 大哥
(2) 二哥
(3) 弟弟
(4) 妹妹
(5) 姐姐
(6) 朋友

4. 两个人一组：轮流用中文问问题及回答问题。
Work in pairs: take turns to ask and answer the following questions in Chinese.

(1) 今年一月有多少天？

(2) 今年的哪个月有三十天？

(3) 今年的哪个月有二十八天？

(4) 一年有几个月有三十一天？

(5) 上个月的二十六号是星期几？

(6) 这个月的十号是星期几？

(7) 下个月有几个星期？

(8) 上个星期四是几号？

(9) 人们 (one, people) 一个星期工作几天？

(10) 今年的新年是星期几？

5. 请按照例句做对话。
  Make up conversation following the model.

 你听说什么了？ 我听说大卫明年要去中国学习汉语。

 你听谁说的？ 我听大卫本人 (himself) 说的。

(1) 今天高老师不在学校，我们没有英语课 / 周老师
(2) 这家律师所有五十多个律师 / 我的律师
(3) 那个学校 (xuéxiào: school) 有很多学生学汉语 / 李明
(4) 祝小英的妈妈是法语和意大利语老师 / 祝小英本人
(5) 刘江北的爷爷是一个有名的 (famous) 律师 / 刘江北的朋友
(6) 贺安生家有十二口人 / 贺安生本人
(7) 他的爸爸是英国人，妈妈是意大利人 / 同学们
(8) 中国人过生日吃长寿面 / 我的中国朋友们

6. 请按照例句做对话。
Make up conversation following the model.

 这是你们第一次上王老师的课吗？

 不是。

 你们上过几次王老师的课了？

 上过两次了，这是第三次。

(1) 你们照全家福
(2) 你爸爸妈妈去法国
(3) 你做日本饭
(4) 她给姥姥做长寿面
(5) 你给他介绍朋友
(6) 你哥哥来美国
(7) 他看朋友的照片
(8) 他们和你说中文

7. 请按照例句做对话。
Make up conversation following the model.

 我听说周大利还没有女朋友。

 是吗？那我们给他介绍一个吧。

 好，我们试试吧！

(1) 赵长江不喜欢吃日本饭 / 去一个法国餐馆
(2) 下个星期是大卫的生日 / 请同学们来一起给他过生日
(3) 他们家还没有全家福 / 我们给他们照一张
(4) 开文也在学习中文 / 我们和他一起学
(5) 朋友们明天来我家 / 你给他们做中国饭
(6) 安娜还没去过长城公园 / 这个周末我们和她一起去
(7) 江文新在这家医院住院 / 我们去看看她
(8) 贺天明和我是同一天生日 / 你们一起过生日

实况演练 Real situation exercises

1. 三个人一组做下面的练习：首先每个人把自己每天的课程名字填在图表(1)里，然后三个人轮流把每一天的课程告诉其他组员。每个人在听的同时要把大家每天的课程数量用中文填写在图表(2)里。最后，三个人一起为图表(2)中的问题(谁的课最多？)找出答案。

Work in groups of three with the following exercise: first, each group member fills out Table (1) with the name of courses you are taking, then the three of you take turns to tell the courses you have for each day of the week. While listening, you need to write down in Chinese the number of courses that each member has on each day in Table (2). Finally, together you will answer the question in Table (2).

图表 Table (1)　　　　课程表 Course Schedule

星期	一	二	三	四	五
有什么课？					
一共 Total					

第四课　生日快乐！
Happy Birthday!

图表 Table (2)　　　　谁的课最多？

姓　名	星期一	星期二	星期三	星期四	星期五
谁的课最多？					

2. 两个人一组：每个人问四个问题，答四个问题，并把对方的回答用中文写下来。

   Work in pairs: each one asks and answers 4 questions, and writes down the partner's answers in Chinese.

(1) 你觉得汉语好学吗？

(2) 你觉得法国饭好吃，还是日本饭好吃？

(3) 你觉得买的蛋糕好吃，还是做的蛋糕好吃？

(4) 你觉得这个课文 (text) 长吗？

(5) 你觉得那个女孩子／男孩子漂亮吗？

(6) 你觉得她的名字好听吗？

(7) 你觉得赵先明是一个好律师吗？

(8) 你觉得这张生日卡好看吗？

3. 四个人一组：每个人轮流问自己右边的组员他/她喜欢、不喜欢或最喜欢吃什么饭 (美国饭、中国饭、法国饭、德国饭、意大利饭、日本饭)。一个人回答问题时其他人用图表(1)做记录。

Work in groups of four: take turns to ask the group member to your right what kinds of foods (American, Chinese, French, Germany, Italian, or Japanese) he /she likes, doesn't like and likes the most to eat. Use Table (1) to take notes when other group members talk.

图表 Table (1)

姓名	喜欢	最喜欢	不喜欢

然后，把调查的结果写在图表(2)中，准备向全班汇报。

Afterwards, work on an outcome of the results of your interviews in Table (2) so that you can report to the class.

几个人喜欢？几个人最喜欢？几个人不喜欢？

图表 Table (2)

A. 中 国 饭： ☐ 喜欢 ☐ 最喜欢 ☐ 不喜欢

B. 德 国 饭： ☐ 喜欢 ☐ 最喜欢 ☐ 不喜欢

C. 法 国 饭： ☐ 喜欢 ☐ 最喜欢 ☐ 不喜欢

D. 美 国 饭： ☐ 喜欢 ☐ 最喜欢 ☐ 不喜欢

E. 日 本 饭： ☐ 喜欢 ☐ 最喜欢 ☐ 不喜欢

F. 意大利饭： ☐ 喜欢 ☐ 最喜欢 ☐ 不喜欢

第四课 生日快乐!
Happy Birthday!

现在每个组汇报图表(2)上的结果。在听汇报的同时每个人都做记录,然后再和本组的人一起比较记录,汇集数字,以便按照例句回答问题,并写进图表(3)。

Each group presents the results of Table (2). Take notes while listening to the reports, then work again with your group to compare notes and sum up the information from each group in order to be able to answer questions following the model, and write down the answers in Table (3).

A. 我们班 (bān: class) 有几个人喜欢吃中国饭?
B. 我们班有几个人最喜欢吃中国饭?
C. 我们班有几个人不喜欢吃中国饭?

图表 Table (3)

饭	喜欢	最喜欢	不喜欢
中国饭			
德国饭			
法国饭			
美国饭			
日本饭			
英国饭			
意大利饭			

这是哪国饭?　　　　　这是法国饭吗?　　　　　这是不是意大利饭?
_____。　　　_____。　　　_____。

七、读报　Newspaper Reading

How Many Characters Do You Know?

1. Read the following article.
2. While reading, underline the characters you know.

钱包"丢"了

马溯　长宁区实验小学四(4)班

那是一个平常的星期四，但对我来说却有着特殊的含义，因为那天是妈妈生日。过去我从来没有想过要在妈妈生日那天做点什么，这一次我却早有打算——拿自己的钱给妈妈买束鲜花。

一放学，我就揣着钱包迫不及待地冲向了花店。那时的心情既兴奋还伴有点紧张，这不仅是我第一次为妈妈买生日礼物，而且还是我第一次自己花钱购物。

这家花店很小，但很干净，各种我叫不出名字的鲜花簇拥在一起，姹紫嫣红，争奇斗艳。迎接我的是一位和蔼可亲的老先生。等我说明来意后，他的脸变得更加笑容可掬了。他向我耐心地介绍各种花卉的名称和寓意，最后向我推荐"康乃馨"，说这是最适合送给妈妈的花了，祝愿妈妈身体健康、生活温馨。我一听正合我意，于是请老先生赶紧扎起来，付了50元钱后抱起"康乃馨"就往回赶。

一路上我在想象着妈妈看到我送的鲜花后那种惊喜的表情，很为今天的自作主张而自鸣得意，就像歌中唱的那样：懂事的我长大啦！

事情果然像我预料的那样，妈妈看到鲜花很开心，找了个花瓶插上去，摆在了家里最醒目的位置。爸爸回来后，我再一次得到了表扬。一家三口出去吃了个生日晚餐，我的心情就像放飞的鸽子，轻松而快乐。

然而这份好心情并没有持续多久。回到家整理书包的时候，妈妈问我："你的钱包呢？"我一下子懵了，猛然想起放在花店柜台上忘拿了，钱包里还有80元钱。爸爸安慰我说，"没关系，老爷爷会帮你保管的，明天放学后去拿，老人不会欺骗小朋友的。"妈妈反驳说，"想得美，这年头哪有这样的好人？人家肯定说没看到什么钱包嘛！"听着爸爸妈妈的争辩，我的心情变得十分沮丧。我在回想花店老先生那张慈祥的脸，他会像爸爸说的那样把钱包还给我？还是会像妈妈说的那样推说没见过呢？带着满肚子的问号，我进入了梦乡。

第二天，我在忐忑不安中等到了放学时间。我应该怎样向那位老爷爷开口要钱包？他会不会把钱包还给我？这世上究竟好人多还是坏人多？走到花店门口，我还在被这些问题困扰着。

但当我再一次看到老爷爷时，刚才的那些疑问全都有了答案。老爷爷一看见走进花店，就从抽屉里拿出我的那个钱包，笑着问我："是不是来找钱包的？"

离开花店时，我的心情似乎比前一天还要好。这世上当然是好人多，我得赶紧回去告诉爸爸妈妈……

选自：新民晚报　日期：2007年11月4日

3. Pronounce the characters you have recognized.
4. Tell the meaning of each character to your class (or study group).

八、文化点滴 Culture Notes

算盘 (pán) Abacus

According to *Supplementary Notes on the Art of Figures* (术数记遗), a book written in 190 A.D. by Xú Yuè (徐岳), the abacus was already in use in China by that time. It remained very popular in Chinese society until electronic calculator arrived.

A typical Chinese abacus is composed of a rectangular frame with 9, 11, 13, 15 or even more columns inside. From right to left, each column represents a place value. There are 7 beads on each column divided into two sections by a crossbar: the lower set of five beads (called earth beads) represents ones and the upper set of two beads (called haven beads) represents fives. One can use an abacus to perform all arithmetic functions: addition, subtraction, multiplication and division.

The long history of abacus in China is seen in proverbs, sayings and expressions derived from this tool. For example, these idioms are formed based on abacus:

"精打细算 jīng dǎ xì suàn (careful calculation and strict budgeting)" is used to describe a person who knows how to use his/her time, money, and things in an economical way. "如意算盘 rúyì suànpán" means wishful thinking. "打小算盘 dǎ xiǎosuànpán" means selfish calculations, and "打错算盘 dǎcuò suànpán (miscalculate)" is used to signify misjudge and be injudicious.

The following fixed expressions are taken directly from pithy formulas of the Chinese abacus:

"三下五除二 sān xià wǔ chú èr" meaning the quickness and preciseness of doing something, and "二一添作五 èr yī tiān zuò wǔ" means to split something evenly into two parts.

Finally, the word "打算 dǎsuàn (to plan)" that you are learning in this chapter is taken directly from the action of using this tool.

While new technology may have made this instrument outdated, the abacus will exist forever as part of Chinese culture and language.

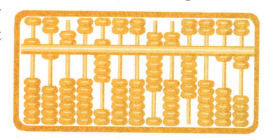

九、自我测试 Self Assessment

1. 用中文回答问题。
   Answer questions in Chinese.

   (1) 你在这家意大利餐馆吃过饭吗？

   (2) 你想试试做法国饭吗？

   (3) 你的生日快到了吗？

   (4) 你觉得这个律师好吗？

   (5) 一个月有几个星期？

   (6) 今年是二〇一二年，明年呢？

2. 用中文回答问题。
   Answer questions in Chinese.

   (1) 中国人怎么过生日？英国人怎么过生日？

   (2) 去年你做了什么？今年你在做什么？明年你打算做什么？

第四课 生日快乐! Happy Birthday!

(3) 你的英语课上有多少个学生？数学课上有多少个学生？
中文课上有多少个学生？哪门课上的学生人数最多？

(4) 在中文课上你们上个星期学了几个汉字？这个星期呢？
这两个星期你们一共学了多少个汉字？

(5) 我听说大卫去中国学汉语了。这是他第一次去中国吗？
你呢？你去过哪个<u>国家</u> (country) ？你打算去哪个国家？

3. 对不对？
   Read the question (A) and the answer (B). Check "对" if you think the answer is logical with respect to the question or check "不对" otherwise.

   (1) A. 长江在哪里？
       B. 长江在中国。   对_____ 不对_____

   (2) A. 今天是你的生日？
       B. 不，明天是。   对_____ 不对_____

   (3) A. 今天是星期几？
       B. 一个星期有七天。   对_____ 不对_____

   (4) A. 你做过长寿面吗？
       B. 我想做长寿面。   对_____ 不对_____

   (5) A. 这瓶花好看吗？
       B. 我觉得好看。   对_____ 不对_____

   (6) A. 那个公园好吗？
       B. 那个公园不大，可是很漂亮。   对_____ 不对_____

   (7) A. 你朋友哪天来北京？
       B. 我朋友很喜欢北京。   对_____ 不对_____

(8) A. 这个学生是第一次去美国吗？
　　B. 不是，他去过两次了，这是第三次。　　对____　不对____

(9) A. 这是新年卡吗？
　　B. 不是，这是生日卡。　　　　　　　　对____　不对____

(10) A. 你买了几瓶花？
　　 B. 这瓶花最漂亮。　　　　　　　　　　对____　不对____

4. 阅读下列短文，并用中文回答问题。
Read the following paragraph, and answer questions in Chinese.

　　今天是一月二十五号，我妈妈的生日快到了。去年妈妈生日那天，我和爸爸给她买了生日卡和蛋糕。今年我们怎么给妈妈过生日呢？……<u>有了</u>！(I got an idea!)

　　今年我们再给她买一张漂亮的生日卡，可是不买蛋糕了<u>因为</u> (yīnwèi: because) 妈妈<u>不太</u> (tài: very) 喜欢吃蛋糕。我们给她买一瓶花。我要给妈妈做长寿面。我们请妈妈的朋友们来，和我们一起给妈妈过生日。

(1) 你知道妈妈的生日是几月几号吗？
_____
_____

(2) 去年"我和爸爸"给妈妈买什么了？
_____
_____

(3) 今年"我"<u>为什么</u> (wèishénme: why) 不想买蛋糕了？
_____
_____

(4) "我"打算给妈妈做什么？
_____
_____

(5) "我们"打算请谁来给妈妈过生日？
_____
_____

第一单元 结尾活动
First Unit End Activities

说说唱唱学中文
Learning Chinese in singing and speaking

 学唱歌曲：《找朋友》
Learning the song: Making Friends

词汇源
Vocabulary Support

gēcí 歌词/歌詞 lyrics	zuòqǔ 作曲/作曲 composer	zuòcí 作词/作詞 to write lyrics
gēqǔ 歌曲/歌曲 song	zhǎo 找/找 to look for	yā (or: ya) 呀/呀 ah, oh
zhǎodào 找到/找到 to find	xiào 笑/笑 to smile	diǎntóu 点头/點頭 to nod one's head
jìnglǐ 敬礼/敬禮 to salute	wòshǒu 握手/握手 to shake hands	dàjiā 大家/大家 everybody

Note: Very often, the word "的" is pronounced "dì" in a song.

找朋友

找呀找呀找朋友，
找到一个好朋友。
笑一笑，点点头，
我是你的好朋友。

找呀找呀找朋友，
找到一个好朋友。
你姓王，我姓刘，
你是我的好朋友。

找呀找呀找朋友，
找到一个好朋友。
敬个礼，握握手，
大家都是好朋友。
再见！

你看，在这张照片里学生们在干什么？
他们在_____。

听歌曲，练中文。
Learn Chinese while listening to music.

词汇源
Vocabulary Support

xún
寻/尋 to look for, search, seek

xīn
心/心 heart

chūn (tiān)
春(天)/春(天) in Table (2) spring

jiéshí
结识/結識 to become acquainted with

yuàn
愿/願 to hope, to wish, to desire

nán
难/難 difficult, hard

rúguǒ
如果/如果 if

lù
路/路 road, way, journey, route

jīn
金/金 metals, gold

yǒngyuǎn
永远/永遠 always, forever

biànchéng
变成/變成 to change into, to turn into

dàochù
到处/到處 everywhere

cóngcǐ
从此/從此 from now on

* 难 + verb = hard to do something; 好 + verb = easy to do something
Note: Very often, the word "了" is pronounced "liǎo" in a song.

Unit 1 第一单元 结尾活动
First Unit End Activities

⭐ 练习

1. 三个人一组：轮流读下面的句子，并把不明白的句子记下来，然后全班讨论。
   Work in groups of three: take turns to read the sentences, and mark down the ones you do not understand to bring them to class discussion.

   (1) "寻"和"找"这两个字有一样的意思。有的时候一起用，也有的时候分开 (separate) 用。比如：寻人、找路、寻找机会 (opportunity, chance)。
   (2) 我知道他的心思 (thought, idea, state of mind)；他一心想当医生。
   (3) 大卫一心一意想去长城，可就是找不到时间。
   (4) 我姐姐在大学学习心理学，因为她的理想是当心理医生。
   (5) 今天我们上中文课的时候学唱歌，汉语课变成了音乐课。
   (6) 大家都在复习考试，所以图书馆里到处是学生。
   (7) 他到处都找了，还是没找到他的手机 (shǒujī: cell phone)。
   (8) 我最喜欢春天，因为春天到处是花，很漂亮。
   (9) 高路明是我新结识的朋友，不过我认识他的弟弟高天明两年多了。
   (10) 没有人永远年轻 (niánqīng: young)，你说是不是？

2. 请听歌曲《永远是朋友》，并用中文填空。
   Listen to the song "永远是朋友," and fill in the blanks using Chinese.

永远是朋友
任卫新　作词
刘　青　作曲

千里难寻_____朋友，朋友_____了路_____走。
以诚相见心诚则灵，让_____从此是_____。
千金难_____是朋友，朋友_____了春常留。
以心相许心灵相通，让我们永远_____朋友。
结识_____朋友，_____忘_____朋友。
_____少新朋友，变成_____朋友。
_____高地_____厚，山_____水长流。
愿_____到处都_____好朋友。
千_____难寻是朋友，朋友多_____路好走。
以诚相_____心诚则灵，让我们从此是朋友。

千金难＿＿＿＿是朋友，朋友＿＿＿＿春常留。
以心相许心灵相通，让我们永远＿＿＿＿＿＿。
结＿＿＿＿新朋友，不忘＿＿＿＿＿＿，
多少＿＿＿＿＿＿，变成老朋友。
＿＿＿＿＿＿地也厚，山＿＿＿＿水＿＿＿＿流，
愿我们＿＿＿＿处都＿＿＿＿＿＿好朋友。
结识＿＿＿＿朋友，＿＿＿＿忘老朋友，
多少＿＿＿＿朋友，变成老＿＿＿＿＿＿。
天高地＿＿＿＿厚，山＿＿＿＿水长流，
愿＿＿＿＿＿＿处都＿＿＿＿好朋友。
愿我们到处都＿＿＿＿＿＿＿＿。

3. 请用中文回答下列问题。

Answer the following questions using Chinese.

(1) 这<u>首</u> (shǒu: measure word for song and poem) 歌的歌名是什么？

(2) 这<u>首</u> (shǒu) 歌的<u>作词人</u> (lyric writer) 是谁？他/她姓什么？叫什么？

(3) 这<u>首</u> (shǒu) 歌的<u>作曲人</u> (composer) 是谁？他/她姓什么？叫什么？

(4) "千里难<u>寻</u> (xún) 是朋友"
请你看看<u>上下文</u> (context)，想一想"寻"字是什么意思。

(5) 我们<u>可以</u> (kěyǐ: can, may) 买书，也可以买花；可以买朋友吗？

(6) 你觉得朋友多了好不好？你想有很多朋友吗？

(7) 谁是你的新朋友？谁是你的老朋友？

Unit 1 第一单元 结尾活动
First Unit End Activities

(8) 你的新朋友多，还是老朋友多？

(9) 你怎么样结识 (jiéshí: to get acquainted with) 新朋友？

(10) 你和你的爸爸妈妈是好朋友吗？

(11) 你有了新朋友会忘 (wàng: to forget) 了老朋友吗？

(12) 你的新朋友和老朋友也是朋友吗？

(13) 如果 (rúguǒ: if) 一个中文字是一个朋友，在这首 (shǒu) 歌里你认识多少个老朋友？结识 (jiéshí) 了多少个新朋友？

(14) 你喜欢这首 (shǒu) 歌的词，还是喜欢这首歌的曲子 (melody)？

(15) 在英文里，有没有一首 (shǒu) 歌和"永远是朋友"一样 (same, similar)？如果 (rúguǒ: if) 有，这首歌的名字叫什么？

4. 角色扮演：我介绍一下……

Role-play: Let me introduce ...

In groups of three, create a role-playing dialogue in which you each adopt a specific role (one as I, one as my old friend, and one as my new friend). "I" introduce the Old Friend and the New Friend to each other, and the two friends should also ask each other questions.

Try to use a variety of words and expressions you have learned from the first unit to make your dialogue as interesting as possible. After you finish the dialogue, practice it several times to the degree that you would feel comfortable to present it in front of class.

Model:

I: 王小亮，你好！我介绍一下，这是大卫，我新认识的朋友。
Old Friend (王小亮): 你好，大卫！
New friend (大卫): 你好！你是……？
I: 噢 Oh! 这是我的小学同学，也是我的老朋友，他叫王小亮。
……

看电影学中文
Learning Chinese while watching movie

看电影：《变脸王》
Movie screening: The King of Masks

看电影之前
Before watching the movie

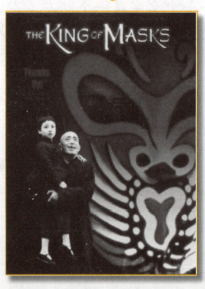

词汇源
Vocabulary Support

sìchuān xì
四川戏/四川戲 Sichuan opera

sìchuān jù
四川剧/四川劇 Sichuan opera

yǎnyuán
演员/演員 actor, actress

dǎoyǎn
导演/尊演 director (of a film or play)

diànyǐng
电影/電影 movie

bāngzhù
帮助/幫助 to help

biàn
变/變 to change

liǎn
脸/臉 face

Unit 1 第一单元 结尾活动
First Unit End Activities

wáng
王/王 king

hóu
猴/猴 monkey

wá (wa)
娃(娃)/娃(娃) baby, newborn animal

sūnzi
孙子/孫子 grandson

tiāncì
天赐/天賜 God-send, God's Gift

zhǔtí
主题/主題 theme

chuán
船/船 boat, ship

gǒu
狗/狗 dog

lǎobǎn
老板/老板 boss

sūnnǚ
孙女/孫女 granddaughter

zhǔyào
主要/主要 main, chief, major

dìfāng
地方/地方 place

练 习

1. 用下面的问题采访一个同学，并用中文将同学的回答写下来。
Interview a classmate using the following questions and write down his/her answers using Chinese.

(1) 当演员是你的理想吗？

(2) 你最喜欢的演员是谁？

(3) 你每个星期都看电影吗？

(4) 你喜欢和谁一起看电影？

(5) 你认识一家餐馆的老板吗？

(6) 你爷爷奶奶有几个儿子？几个孙子和孙女？

(7) 你觉得多大的孩子是娃娃？三个月大？十个月大？五岁大？

(8) 你们家有狗吗？有几只 (zhī: measure word)？你们的狗叫什么名字？

(9) Tom Hanks 是演员还是导演？

(10) 你喜欢猴子吗？

看电影之后
After watching the movie

2. 请在网上查找有关回答下列问题的信息。你可以先用英语回答问题，但最终要给出中文的回答。

Search online for the information you need to answer the following questions. You may first answer the questions using English, but ultimately, you should write out the answers using Chinese.

网上调查研究题目：
Online research topics:

(1) 《变脸王》这个电影的导演是谁？他的中文名字是什么？
Who is the director of the movie *King of Masks*? What is the director's name in Chinese?

(2) 《变脸王》这个电影里的故事发生在什么时候？什么地方？
When and where did the story in the movie happen?

(3) 什么是四川剧？川剧有什么特点？你能在中国地图上找到四川吗？
What is Sichuan Opera? What are the characteristics of this kind of opera? Can you find Sichuan Province on the map of China?

(4) 这个电影里有几个主要人物 (rénwù)？这几个人物是谁？
How many major characters are there in this movie? Who are they?

(5) 你觉得这个电影的主题是什么？说说为什么。
What are the themes of this movie? Explain why.

3. 请用中文回答下列问题。
Answer the following questions using Chinese.

(1) 王先生住在哪儿？

(2) 王先生家有几口人？

(3) 王先生买的孩子几岁？这个孩子叫什么名字？

(4) 谁姓杨 (Yáng)？

(5) 王先生家有狗吗？

(6) 王先生为什么不喜欢狗娃？

(7) 这个电影里有几个孩子？几个男孩子？几个女孩子？男孩子叫什么名字？女孩子叫什么名字？

(8) 这个电影里有没有爷爷、奶奶、姥爷和姥姥?

(9) 谁有爷爷,没有奶奶? 谁有姥爷和姥姥?

(10) 狗娃喜欢爷爷吗?

(11) 谁给王先生和狗娃照了一张"全家福"?

(12) 你喜欢电影里的猴子吗? 为什么?

(13) 谁给了爷爷一个孙子?

(14) 谁帮助了狗娃?

(15) 电影结束 (jiéshù: end) 的时候,王先生是老板还是爷爷?

4. 按照剧情需要,两个人或三个人一组做这个练习:先从下面的三个题目中选择一个,编写一个小剧本。然后排练,准备给全班人演出。
Work in pairs or groups according to the need of your mini-play: first, choose one from the following three topics and write the scripts of your play. Afterwards, practice in order to perform in front of the class.

(1) 王先生买孩子 (王先生、人贩子 fànzi: dealer、孩子)
(2) 小弟弟,别哭 bié kū: don't cry (狗娃、天赐)
(3) 你是谁家的孩子 (or: 你是哪家的孩子)? (王先生、天赐)

第二单元
Unit Two

学校生活
School Life

第五课
LESSON FIVE

今天你有几节课？
How Many Classes Do You Have Today?

学习目的
Learning Objectives

表达时间	To tell time
表达在某一时间做某事	To express doing a certain thing at a certain time
介绍各种学科	To talk about different course subjects
制订和介绍课程表	To make and express daily school schedules
评论各种课程	To comment on school courses
"再见"的不同说法	To say "goodbye" in different ways

本课学习内容
Contents of the chapter

一	学习发音 Pronunciation
	■ 声母 consonants：zh, ch, sh, r
	■ 韵母 vowels：ang, iang, eng, ing, ong, iong
二	课文：今天你有几节课？ Text: How Many Classes Do You Have Today?
三	生词 Vocabulary
	■ 名词 nouns：莉、点、钟、刻、地理、历史、生物学、音乐、政治、经济、物理、美术、体育、数学、书包、几何、题、意思、零、半、中午、百、分钟、千
	■ 动词 verbs：解题、得
	■ 形容词 adjectives：差、忙、每、满、难、容易、对
	■ 副词 adverbs：都、怎么样、为什么
	■ 连词 conjunctions：因为、所以、不过
	■ 量词 measure words：节、门、本
	■ 词句 expressions：看来、一会(儿)见、回头见、有意思、对不起
四	数字学习 Study of Numbers: hundred and thousand
五	语法 Grammar
	■ "一门课"和"一节课"的区别　"一门课" versus "一节课"
	■ 时间表达法　Telling time
	■ "几"字的不同意思　Different meanings of the character "几"
	■ "怎么"与"怎么样"的区别　Difference between "怎么" and "怎么样"
	■ "都"字的基本用法　Basic functions of the adverb "都"
六	练习 Exercises
七	读报 Newspaper Reading
八	文化点滴 Culture Notes
九	自我测试 Self Assessment

LESSON 5

第五课 今天你有几节课?
How Many Classes Do You Have Today?

一、学习发音 Pronunciation 1

Drill 1

zh ch sh	+ ā	zhā (扎) chā (插) shā (沙)

zh ch sh	+ á	zhá (闸) chá (茶) shá (啥)

zh ch sh	+ ǎ	zhǎ (眨) chǎ (衩) shǎ (傻)

zh ch sh	+ à	zhà (炸) chà (岔) shà (厦)

Drill 2

zh ch sh r	+ ē	zhē (遮) chē (车) shē (奢)

zh ch sh r	+ é	zhé (哲) shé (蛇)

zh ch sh r	+ ě	zhě (褶) chě (扯) shě (舍) rě (惹)

zh ch sh r	+ è	zhè (这) chè (彻) shè (社) rè (热)

157

Drill 3

zh		zhū (猪)
ch	+ ū	chū (出)
sh		shū (书)
r		

zh		zhú (竹)
ch	+ ú	chú (除)
sh		shú (熟悉)
r		rú (如)

zh		zhǔ (主)
ch	+ ǔ	chǔ (楚)
sh		shǔ (暑)
r		rǔ (乳)

zh		zhù (住)
ch	+ ù	chù (到处)
sh		shù (树)
r		rù (入)

Drill 4

chāi (拆)	zhài (债)	chuí (垂)	shàn (善)	shén (神)
chūn (春)	zhēn (真)	chén (陈)	rén (人)	chún (纯)
rùn (润)	shǒu (手)	cháo (潮)	zhào (赵)	shǎo (少量)
rào (绕)	rǔ (乳)	chú (除)	zhū (朱)	shān (山)
shí (十)	rì (日)	zhǐ (纸)	ruì (瑞)	rán (然)
zhòu (宙)	chóu (仇)	ròu (肉)	shuǐ (水)	zhàn (站)

Drill 5

	āng (帮)	ǎng (榜)	àng (棒)
b +	ēng (崩)	éng (甬)	èng (蹦)
	īng (兵)	ǐng (饼)	ìng (并)

Drill 6

	áng (狼)		áng (囊)			áng (忙)	
l +	ěng (冷)	n +	éng (能)	m +		ēng (蒙骗)	
	ìng (令)		ǐng (柠)			íng (明)	
	óng (隆)		óng (农)				

第五课 今天你有几节课?
How Many Classes Do You Have Today?

Drill 7

t +
- āng (汤)   áng (糖)   ǎng (躺)   àng (趟)
- éng (疼)
- īng (听)   íng (停)   ǐng (艇)
- ōng (通)   óng (同)   ǒng (桶)   òng (痛)

Drill 8

c +
- āng (苍)
- èng (蹭)
- óng (从)

ch +
- āng (昌)
- èng (称杆)
- óng (虫)

s +
- ǎng (嗓)
- ēng (僧)
- òng (送)

sh +
- āng (伤)
- ēng (生)

Drill 9

zh +
- āng (张)   ǎng (掌)   àng (涨痛)
- ēng (争)   ěng (整)   èng (政)
- ōng (中)   ǒng (肿)   òng (种田)

Drill 10

r +
- àng (让)
- ēng (仍)
- óng (容)

Drill 11

d, t, y, p + īng
- dīng (丁)
- tīng (听)
- yīng (英)
- pīng (乒)

d, t, y, p + àng
- dàng (荡)
- tàng (烫)
- yàng (样)
- pàng (胖)

Drill 12

w + āng (汪)　áng (王)　ǎng (网)　àng (忘)
　　ēng (翁)　　　　ěng (蓊)　èng (甕)

Drill 13

l　　　　　liàng (亮)
n　+ iàng　niàng (酿)
q　　　　　qiàng (呛)
x　　　　　xiàng (向)

j +　iāng (江)
　　iǎng (讲)
　　iàng (降落)

Drill 14

q　+ ióng　qióng (穷)
x　　　　　xióng (雄)

j + iǒng　jiǒng (炯)

Drill 15

nóng (农)	dōng (东)	zāng (脏)	sòng (宋)
xíng (形)	sēng (僧)	gòng (共)	kāng (康)
hóng (红)	hèng (蛮横)	zǒng (总)	lèng (愣)
wàng (望)	sāng (桑)	cèng (蹭)	hēng (亨)
liǎng (两)	xiōng (兄)	zhāng (张)	chōng (充)
tǐng (挺)	dèng (邓)	rǎng (壤)	shèng (胜)

第五课 今天你有几节课?
How Many Classes Do You Have Today?

二、课文 Text 2

今天你有几节课?

史小莉：何天明，现在几点(钟)了？

何天明：现在差一刻九点。今天你有几节课？

史小莉：今天我有四节课：地理、历史、生物和音乐。你呢？今天你忙吗？

何天明：星期一是我最忙的一天。

史小莉：为什么？

何天明：因为我有五节课。

史小莉：你有五节什么课？

何天明：政治、经济、物理、美术和体育。

史小莉：我知道你这个学期有五门课；看来今天每一门课你都要上课。

何天明：对，所以我的书包都满了。每一门课都有一两本书。

史小莉：这几门课你都喜欢吗？

这是什么课？
_____

学生们在上什么课？
_____

何天明：政治、经济、物理和美术我都很喜欢，只有体育课差一点，因为我的体育不好。这个学期你没有数学课吗？

史小莉：有。不过今天我没有数学课。

何天明：在这门课上你们在学什么？

史小莉：我们在学习几何。

何天明：你觉得几何难学吗？

史小莉：不容易。不过我觉得解题很有意思。

何天明：对不起，现在都九点零三分了，我得去上课了。十二点半我们一起吃中午饭，怎么样？

史小莉：好。一会儿见！

何天明：回头见！

地理课下课以后

第五课 今天你有几节课?
How Many Classes Do You Have Today?

課文

史小莉：何天明，現在幾點(鐘)了？
何天明：現在差一刻九點。今天你有節課？
史小莉：今天我有四節課：地理、歷史、生物和音樂。你呢？今天你忙嗎？
何天明：星期一是我最忙的一天。
史小莉：為什麼？
何天明：因為我有五節課。
史小莉：你有五節什麼課？
何天明：政治、經濟、物理、美術和體育。
史小莉：我知道你這個學期有五門課；看來今天每一門課你都要上課。
何天明：對，所以我的書包都滿了。每一門課都有一、兩本書。
史小莉：這幾門課你都喜歡嗎？

這是什麼課？
_____

學生們在上什麼課？
_____

何天明： 政治、經濟、物理和美術我都很喜歡，祇有體育課差一點，因為我的體育不好。這個學期你沒有數學課嗎？

史小莉： 有。不過今天我沒有數學課。

何天明： 在這門課上你們在學什麼？

史小莉： 我們在學習幾何。

何天明： 你覺得幾何難學嗎？

史小莉： 不容易。不過我覺得解題很有意思。

何天明： 對不起，現在都九點零三分了，我得去上課了。十二點半我們一起吃中午飯，怎麼樣？

史小莉： 好。一會兒見！

何天明： 回頭見！

地理課下課以後

LESSON 5

第五课 今天你有几节课?
How Many Classes Do You Have Today?

三、生 词 Vocabulary

NOUNS

lì 莉 *(莉)* jasmine	diǎn 点 *(點)* dot, point	zhōng 钟 *(鐘)* bell, clock

kè
刻 *(刻)* quarter (of an hour)

dìlǐ 地理 *(地理)* geography	dì 地：earth, land, soil
	lǐ 理：texture, reason

lìshǐ 历史 *(歷史)* history	shǐ 史：a surname

shēngwùxué 生物学 *(生物學)* biology	wù 物：thing, substance

yīnyuè 音乐 *(音樂)* music	yīn 音：sound, tone
	yuè 乐 *(樂)*：music, a surname

zhèngzhì 政治 *(政治)* politics	zhèng 政：politics, political affairs
	zhì 治：to rule, to govern, to cure

jīngjì 经济 *(經濟)* economy, economics	jīng 经 *(經)*：to go through, to manage
	jì 济 *(濟)*：to help, to cross a river

wùlǐ
物理 *(物理)* physics

měishù 美术 *(美術)* fine arts, art	shù 术 *(術)*：skill, art, technique

tǐyù 体育 (體育) sports, physical education		shùxué 数学 (數學) mathematics
shūbāo 书包 (書包) book bag	bāo 包: bag, to wrap	
jǐhé 几何 (幾何) geometry	hé 何: a surname	
tí 题 (題) topic, title, problem	yìsi 意思 (意思) meaning	líng 零 (零) zero
bàn 半 (半) half, semi-	zhōngwǔ 中午 (中午) noon	
bǎi 百 (百) hundred	fēnzhōng 分钟 (分鐘) minute	
qiān 千 (千) thousand		

VERBS

jiětí
解题/解題 to solve a problem

děi
得/得 to have to

ADJECTIVES

chà
差/差 short of

máng
忙/忙 busy

měi
每/每 every, each

mǎn
满/滿 full, filled, packed

róngyì
容易/容易 easy

duì
对/對 correct, yes, right

Lesson 5

第五课 今天你有几节课?
How Many Classes Do You Have Today?

ADVERBS

dōu
都/都 both, all, already

zěnmeyàng
怎么样/怎麽樣 how, how about

wèishénme
为什么/爲什麽 why

CONJUNCTIONS

yīnwèi
因为/因爲 because, since, as

suǒyǐ
所以/所以 therefore, thus, as a result

bùguò
不过 but, however

MEASURE WORDS

jié
节/節 for sections of things

mén
门/門 for academic courses

běn
本/本 for things that are bound, such as books and magazines

EXPRESSIONS

kànlái
看来/看來 to seem, to look as if

yīhuì (r) jiàn
一会(儿)见/一會(兒)見 see you soon

huítóu jiàn
回头见/回頭見 see you later, see you soon

yǒu yìsi
有意思/有意思 interesting

duìbuqǐ
对不起/對不起 sorry

四、数字学习 Study of Numbers: Hundred and Thousand

bǎi 百 hundred

yībǎi líng yī 一百零一	yībǎi líng èr 一百零二	yībǎi líng sān 一百零三	yībǎi líng sì 一百零四
yībǎi líng wǔ 一百零五	yībǎi líng liù 一百零六	yībǎi líng qī 一百零七	yībǎi líng bā 一百零八
yībǎi líng jiǔ 一百零九	yībǎi yīshí 一百一十	yībǎi yīshí yī 一百一十一	yībǎi yīshí èr 一百一十二
yībǎi yīshí sān 一百一十三	yībǎi yīshí sì 一百一十四	yībǎi yīshí wǔ 一百一十五	yībǎi yīshí liù 一百一十六
yībǎi yīshí qī 一百一十七	yībǎi yīshí bā 一百一十八	yībǎi yīshí jiǔ 一百一十九	yībǎi èrshí 一百二十

★ 练 习

1. 请用中文朗读下面的数字。
Read aloud the following numbers using Chinese.

159	201	236	240	371
323	382	397	399	400
404	418	463	480	500
515	530	577	586	608
635	669	681	692	700
709	724	752	793	799
800	815	843	861	888
909	926	957	983	999

第五课 今天你有几节课?
How Many Classes Do You Have Today?

qiān 千 thousand

yīqiān yībǎi èrshí yī 一千一百二十一	yīqiān yībǎi èrshí èr 一千一百二十二	yīqiān yībǎi èrshí sān 一千一百二十三
yīqiān yībǎi èrshí sì 一千一百二十四	yīqiān yībǎi èrshí wǔ 一千一百二十五	yīqiān yībǎi èrshí liù 一千一百二十六
yīqiān yībǎi èrshí qī 一千一百二十七	yīqiān yībǎi èrshí bā 一千一百二十八	yīqiān yībǎi èrshí jiǔ 一千一百二十九
yīqiān yībǎi sānshí 一千一百三十	yīqiān yībǎi sānshí yī 一千一百三十一	yīqiān yībǎi sānshí èr 一千一百三十二
yīqiān yībǎi sānshí sān 一千一百三十三	yīqian yībǎi sānshí sì 一千一百三十四	yīqiān yībǎi sānshí wǔ 一千一百三十五

★ 练 习

2. 两个人一组做这个练习：轮流一个人用中文朗读，一个人听并写下面的数字。
   Work in pairs: take turns to read and write the following numbers using Chinese.

   1562 1741 1986 2001 2534 2980 3000 3006 3115 3328
   4059 4802 4100 5005 5173 5804 5019 6012 6102 6112
   6309 6666 6807 6901 7111 7370 7605 7822 8000 8008
   8260 8374 8505 8700 8826 9015 9281 9404 9616 9999

3. 请用中文回答下列问题。
   Answer the following questions using Chinese.

   (1) 一年有多少天？十年呢？
   _____

   (2) 中国有多少年的文字历史？
   _____

   (3) 长城有多少年的历史？
   _____

   (4) 你们学校 (xuéxiào: school) 有多少年历史？现在有多少个学生？
   _____

五、语法 Grammar

1. "一门课"和"一节课"的区别 一门课 versus 一节课

As measure words, both characters "门" and "节" can be used for school classes. However, there is a major difference between them. While "门" is used for academic courses, subjects or disciplines, "节" represents sections of things and class periods at school. Therefore, "一门课" is "a course" meaning a number of lectures or other activities dealing with a subject, and "一节课" is "a class" meaning a time period during which the class meets.

	一	二	三	四	五
数　　学		★		★	
英美文学	★		★		★
汉　　语	★	★	★	★	★
美国历史	★		★		★
化　　学		★		★	
体　　育	★				★
这个学期我有六门课	今天我有四节课	今天我有三节课	今天我有三节课	今天我有三节课	今天我有四节课

这个学期我有六门课，可是今天我只有三节课。
I'm taking six courses this semester, but I have only three classes today.

教 (jiāo: to teach) 这门课的是一个女老师。
The professor who teaches this class is female.

在这节课上我们学了十个新字。
We learned ten new characters during this class period.

练习一

两个人一组：互相提问下列问题，并将对方的回答用中文写下来。
Work in pairs: ask each other the following questions and write down your partner's answers using Chinese.

(1) 这个学期你有几门课？上个学期呢？
_____

(2) 下个学期你打算上几门课？
_____

(3) 在这个学期的课里你最喜欢哪门课?

(4) 今天你有几节课? 明天呢?

(5) 你星期几上课最多? 星期几上课最少?

(6) 今天你的第一节课是什么课?

(7) 第二节呢, 是什么课?

(8) 一节课是多少分钟?

2. 时间表达法 (shíjiān biǎodá fǎ) Telling Time

A. The following questions are often used to ask time:

现在几点钟 (了)?
What time is it now?
十点整 (zhěng: exact)。
It's ten o'clock.

妈, 几点了?
Mom, what time is it now?
十一点 (了)。
Eleven o'clock.

B. The adjective "差" is used to express a certain time to ... o'clock:

现在差十分 (钟) 八点。
It's ten to eight now.

现在差二十(分钟)九点。
It's twenty to nine now.

现在差二十五(分)十点。
It's twenty five to ten now.

Note that, in the first example, since the number "十" has only one syllable, the measure word "分" must be pronounced while in the last two examples it is optional.

C. The word "零" is not required even though some people like to use it to express a certain time after an hour.

现在七点(零)五分。
It is now five after seven.

现在是六点(零)十分吗?
Is it ten after six o'clock now?

D. AM. and PM. are expressed using "早上 (zǎoshang: early morning) or 上午 (shàngwǔ: morning)," "中午 (zhōngwǔ: noon)," "下午 (xiàwǔ: afternoon)," and "晚上 (wǎnshang: evening)."

赵文生上午九点有课。
Zhao Wensheng has class at nine o'clock AM.

我晚上七点半来看你。
I will come and see you at seven thirty in the evening.

Note that in China, the twenty four hour system is used in public places such as radio stations, train stations and airports, etc.

现在是二十二点钟。
It is now ten o'clock PM.

E. In Chinese, an expression of time always precedes the place expression and can be stressed at the beginning of a sentence.

我们十一点钟在一家餐馆吃饭。
We will eat in a restaurant at eleven o'clock.

晚上六点半,我们在餐馆见面。
We will meet in the restaurant at six thirty PM.

练习二

1. 请按照例句做对话。
Make conversation following the model.

第五课 今天你有几节课?
How Many Classes Do You Have Today?

 现在几点钟(了)?   现在差两分钟八点。

(1) 7:58   (4) 3:45
(2) 6:40   (5) 8:47
(3) 4:50   (6) 9:53
(7) 1:55   (8) 2:50

2. 请按照例句做对话。
   Make conversation following the model.

 现在几点钟(了)?   现在两点零一分。

(1) 2:01   (2) 3:05
(3) 5:06   (4) 8:08
(5) 11:02   (6) 9:05
(7) 1:08   (8) 10:04

3. 请按照例句做对话。
   Make conversation following the model.

 现在是七点一刻,还是差一刻七点?

 现在是七点一刻。

(1) 7:15   (2) 1:45
(3) 4:15   (4) 3:15
(5) 10:45   (6) 5:45
(7) 8:15   (8) 6:45

4. 请按照例句做对话。
   Make conversation following the model.

 现在几点钟(了)?   现在上午九点半。

(1) 9:30am   (2) 12:30pm
(3) 4:30pm   (4) 10:30am
(5) 2:30pm   (6) 3:30pm
(7) 1:30pm   (8) 11:30am

3. "几"字的不同意思 Different Meanings of the Character "几"

You have learned that when "几" appears in an interrogative phrase, it means "how many." But, when this word is used in a statement, the meaning is "some" or "several" (if preceded by 好). See the following comparisons:

你们有几天假 (jià: vacation)?
How many days of vacation do you have?

我们有几天假。
We have a few days of vacation.

大卫有几个中国朋友?
How many Chinese friends does David have?

大卫有好几个中国朋友。
David has several Chinese friends.

他们在这里住 (zhù: to live) 了几年?
How many years did they live here?

他们在这里住了好几年。
They have lived here for several years.

练习三

请按照例句做对话。
Make conversation following the model.

 你买了几张贺年卡?

 我买了好几张(贺年卡)。

(1) 买贺年卡
(2) 请朋友
(3) 上课
(4) 认识新同学
(5) 买蛋糕
(6) 照照片
(7) 学新字
(8) 介绍朋友
(9) 来北京 (几次)
(10) 去长城 (几次)

4. "怎么"与"怎么样"的区别 Difference between "怎么" and "怎么样"

The interrogative adverbs "怎么" and "怎么样" should be translated differently into English according to the following situations:

A. When used at the beginning of a question, "怎么" implies a surprise on the part of the speaker.

怎么，你不喜欢这门课？
What, you don't like this course?

怎么，他们没去长城？
What, they did not go to the Great Wall?

B. When followed by a verb in the affirmative, "怎么" is used to ask the manner or the way that the action of the verb will be carried out.

你怎么学英语？
How do you study English?

他怎么来北京？坐火车 (huǒchē:train)还是坐飞机 (fēijī: airplane)？
How will he come to Beijing, by train or by airplane?

C. "怎么样" is used to ask about the situation or quality of a person or thing.

你们的历史课老师怎么样？
How is your history professor?

这个蛋糕怎么样？好吃吗？
How is this cake? Is it delicious?

你爸爸妈妈怎么样？他们好吗？
How are your parents? Are they doing well?

D. When "怎么样" appears after a statement, it can also be used to ask the other party's opinion.

这个周末我们去北海公园，怎么样？
How about we go to Beihai Park this weekend?

我们去上海过年，你看怎么样？
What do you think if we spend the New Year in Shanghai?

练习四

1. 请按照例句做对话。
   Make conversation following the model.

你的音乐课怎么样？ 我的音乐课很有意思。

(1) 数学课/很难
(2) 长城公园/不错
(3) 经济课/不容易
(4) 那个餐馆/最好
(5) 这道几何题/不难
(6) 他的书包/很大
(7) 这张照片/很漂亮
(8) 政治课/没有意思

2. 请按照例句做对话。
   Make conversation following the model.

    我们一起学中文，怎么样？

    好啊 (hǎo a: fine)！我们一起学吧！

   (1) 照一张照片
   (2) 去奶奶家过年
   (3) 学法语
   (4) 周末去长城
   (5) 请朋友吃饭
   (6) 给她买一瓶花
   (7) 做法国饭
   (8) 解数学题

3. 用中文，你怎么回答下面的问题？
   Using Chinese, how would you answer the following questions?
   (1) 你们打算怎么去上海？
   _____

   (2) 怎么，你们没去上海？
   _____

   (3) 下个星期我们去上海，怎么样？
   _____

第五课 今天你有几节课?
How Many Classes Do You Have Today?

(4) 怎么，你也在学习法语?

(5) 你怎么学习法语?

(6) 你和我一起学习法语，怎么样?

(7) 你们怎么给妈妈过生日?

(8) 怎么，你们不打算给妈妈过生日?

(9) 你们都回家来给妈妈过生日，怎么样?

(10) 你怎么做意大利饭?

(11) 今天你做意大利饭，怎么样?

(12) 怎么，你不想做意大利饭!

5. "都"字的基本用法 Basic Functions of the Adverb "都"

The character "都" appears several times in the dialogue of this chapter. In order to have a better understanding of each of the sentences where it appears, one needs to learn the following basic functions of this adverb.

A. When the subject is in plural form and the verb of the sentence is affirmative, "都" can be translated as "both" or "all."

我爸爸妈妈都是医生。
Both my parents are doctors.

他们都是你的老师吗?
Are they all your professors?

B. However, "都" should be translated as "neither" or "none" when the verb of the sentence is in negative form.

我爸爸妈妈都不说英语。
Neither of my parents speaks English.

数学、物理和文学课都不容易。
Math, physics and literature classes, none of them is easy.

Note that the adverb "都" can also be used to stress the object. In this case, the object needs to be placed at the beginning of the sentence. For example:

政治、经济、历史和音乐课我都喜欢。
Political science, economics, history and music classes, I love them all.

中国饭、美国饭和日本饭他都不喜欢。
Chinese, American and Japanese foods, he likes none of them.

C. The meaning of the adverb changes to "already" when the subject of the sentence (which normally ends with "了") appears in singular form.

她都是妈妈了。
She is already a mother.

现在都十点钟了。
It's already ten o'clock now.

练习五

1. 请按照例句做对话。
   Make conversation following the model.

    你的爸爸妈妈都是医生吗?

    不,我的爸爸妈妈都不是医生。

   (1) 物理课和化学课容易
   (2) 他们的两个孩子学习美国文学
   (3) 学生们的书包满了
   (4) 大卫和大牛在中国学汉语
   (5) 这两个人是意大利人
   (6) 两个律师来
   (7) 星期一、二、三我们有体育课
   (8) 你和弟弟说法语

2. 请按照例句做对话。

   Make conversation following the model.

    我知道你做了蛋糕；你也做长寿面了吗？

    对，蛋糕和长寿面我都做了。

   (1) 这个学期他学英语／法语和汉语
   (2) 她买了花／蛋糕和生日卡
   (3) 你们去过中国／日本
   (4) 他们没吃过法国饭／意大利饭
   (5) 你们认识王老师／周老师
   (6) 你们介绍了新同学／老同学
   (7) 他看了这本书／那本书
   (8) 他们去了爷爷奶奶家／姥姥姥爷家

3. 请按照例句做对话。

   Make conversation following the model.

    你知道吗，她是两个孩子的妈妈？

    什么，她都是两个孩子的妈妈了！

   (1) 他去中国
   (2) 今天星期五
   (3) 她是大学生
   (4) 安娜有工作
   (5) 今天二十六号
   (6) 我朋友来美国
   (7) 我看见他
   (8) 现在八点半

六、练习 Exercises

模式练习 Model exercises

1. 首先两个人一组互相问下面的问题，并将对方的回答用中文写下来；
   First, work with one partner: ask each other the following questions and take notes on his / her answers using Chinese;

   (1) 你每天几点钟吃早饭 (zǎofàn: breakfast)?

   (2) 你每天几点钟来学校 (xuéxiào: school)?

   (3) 你几点钟上第一节课?

   (4) 上午你有几节课?

   (5) 你几点钟吃中午饭?

   (6) 你喜欢和谁一起吃中午饭?

   (7) 下午你有几节课?

   (8) 你几点钟上最后 (zuìhòu: the last) 一节课?

   (9) 你每天几点钟回 (huí: to return) 家?

   (10) 你们家每天几点钟吃晚饭 (wǎnfàn: dinner)?

第五课 今天你有几节课？
How Many Classes Do You Have Today?

然后再和另外一个人一组，用第三人称互相讲述他／她的情况。请按照例句做这个练习。

Afterwards, work with another partner: use a third person subject (he or she), to tell each other his / her story based on the information you collected from the answers. Please follow the model.

Model:

> 史小莉每天七点钟吃早饭；她七点四十来学校。

2. 请用"因为……所以"回答下列问题。

Answer the following questions with "因为……所以."

Model: 你为什么不介绍这个学生？

> 因为我不认识这个学生，所以我不介绍他。

(1) 你为什么买书？

(2) 今天你为什么很忙？

(3) 他为什么去中国？

(4) 你为什么不打开书？

(5) 他们为什么买花？

(6) 你为什么喜欢这张生日卡？

(7) 你们为什么要买一个大书包？

(8) 今天你们为什么没有英语课？

(9) 你为什么不和我们一起去长城？

(10) 你为什么不和你的同学们说中文？

3. 比赛。
Competition.

(1) 两个人一组：按照下面的例子，在三分钟之内用"每"字组成词组（越多越好）。然后每个组在全班面前大声朗读两次你们的词组；与此同时，其他人把听到的新词组加到自己的词组里。比赛的结果是看哪个组最终的词组最多。

Work in pairs: follow the model and make as many expressions as possible using the character "每" within three minutes. Afterwards, each pair should read aloud your expressions twice in front of the class while the other pair takes notes in order to add new ones to the list. The result of the competition will be based on the number of expressions that each pair has on the final list.

Model:

每个人、每节课

4. 请按照例句做对话。
Make conversation following the model.

 你们得解几何题吗？   我们不用解几何题。

(1) 你们得解几何题
(2) 他得去北京大学上课
(3) 大家都得工作
(4) 学生们每个学期都得买新书
(5) 我们得请律师
(6) 今天我们得学习语法
(7) 我得告诉老师他为什么不来

(8) 爸爸得给我们一家人做饭
(9) 我得给大家介绍我的朋友
(10) 今天老师得上四节课

5. 请按照例句做对话。
Make conversation following the model.

 你知道不知道"生日"是什么意思?

 我知道,生日的意思是"<u>出生</u> (chūshēng: to be born) 的日子"。

(1) 贺年卡 = 祝贺新年的卡
(2) 姥爷 = 妈妈的爸爸
(3) 长寿面 = 过生日吃的面条
(4) 大家 = 每个人
(5) 同学 = 在同一个<u>学校</u> (xuéxiào: school) 上学的人
(6) 上学 = 去学校学习
(7) 看书 = 学习
(8) 容易 = 不难

6. 请按照例句做对话。
Make conversation following the model.

 地理课有意思吗?
那你觉得哪门课有意思?

 没有意思,我不喜欢。
我觉得历史课有意思。

地理课	历史课	生物课	政治课	经济课
物理课	文学课	语法课	音乐课	中文课
英文课	体育课	美术课	数学课	化学课
英国历史课	美国经济课	法国音乐课	中国地理课

7. 请按照例句做对话。
Make conversation following the model.

 这个学期你上几门课?

五门。

 哪门课最难？哪门课最容易？

 我觉得地理课最难；历史课最容易。

 你的同学们都觉得地理课最难吗？

 不是，只有几个同学觉得这门课最难。

地理课	历史课	生物课	政治课	经济课
物理课	文学课	语法课	音乐课	中文课
英文课	体育课	美术课	数学课	化学课
英国历史课	美国经济课	法国音乐课	中国地理课	

实况演练 Real situation exercises

1. 两个人一组：按照例句互相问问题，并把对方的课程表填好。
   Work in pairs: following the model sentence below, ask each other questions and fill out the school schedule for each other.

   Model:

   八点钟到九点钟 (from 8:00 to 9:00)
   你有课吗？有什么课？

课程表 kèchéngbiǎo

星期	一	二	三	四	五
8:00 - 9:00					
9:00 - 10:00					
10:00-11:00					
11:00-12:00					
12:00-1:00					
1:00 - 2:00					
2:00 - 3:00					
3:00 - 4:00					

第五课 今天你有几节课?
How Many Classes Do You Have Today?

然后，轮流读下面的问题，并一起用中文写出你们的回答。
Afterwards, take turns to read the questions and together write out your answers using Chinese based on the information written on both of your schedules.

1) 几点钟你们两个人都有课？

2) 几点钟你们两个人都没有课？

2) 星期几的几点钟你们两个人有同一节课 (the same class)？

4) 星期几你最忙，可是他/她不忙？

5) 星期几你们两个人都忙？

6) 这个学期你上几门课？他/她上几门课？

7) 星期几你上午没有课？他/她呢？

8) 你觉得哪门课最难？他/她呢？

9) 你觉得哪门课最容易？他/她呢？

10) 你最喜欢哪门课？他/她最喜欢哪门课？

2. 两个人一组。一个人是A，一个人是B：读下面的对话，并用适当的英语词填空。
Work in pairs to play the roles of A and B: read the dialogue and fill in the blanks using appropriate English words.

A. 你知道"音乐"是什么意思，对不对？
B. 我知道。"音乐"的意思是"music"。

A. 好。现在我们学习一个新词 (cí: word)。

B. 什么新词?

A. 你认识这三个字吗：音乐家?

B. 认识，可是我不知道"音乐家"是什么意思。

A. "音乐家"的意思是"musician"。

B. 有意思。我们再学一个新词 (cí: word)，怎么样?

A. 好。现在请你想一想"美术家"、"政治家"、"文学家"和"数学家"是什么意思。

B. 我知道了，"美术家"是 ⬚ ，"政治家"是 ⬚ ，"文学家"是 ⬚ ，"数学家"是 ⬚ 。

A. 看，你学了几个新词 (cí)?

B. 我学了好几个新词 (cí)。

A. 容易不容易?

B. 太容易了!

A. 还想学吗?

B. 想学!

A. 好。请你听我说。你认识"历史"两个字，对不对?

B. 认识。

A. "历史学家"的意思是"historian"。现在请你想想"生物学家"、"经济学家"、和"物理学家"是什么意思。

B. 我想这不难。"生物学家"的意思是 ⬚ ，"经济学家"的意思是 ⬚ ，"物理学家"的意思是 ⬚ 。

A. <u>今天我们到这里吧</u> (Let's stop here today)，下次再学。

B. 好，谢谢你。再见!

---

3. 比赛。
Competition.

(1) 三个人一组用十分钟的时间把你们知道的信息填在下面的表格里，如果你们不知道这些人的中文名字可以写他们的英文或法文名字。

Work in groups of three: you have ten minutes to fill out the following table with the information you know. You may write their English or French names if you do not know them in Chinese.

	法国	美国	英国	中国
美术家				
音乐家				
文学家				
政治家				
历史学家				
经济学家				
物理学家				
体育明星				

然后，按照例句用中文 (除了名字以外) 向全班汇报你们做这个练习的结果。比赛的结果取决于每个组能说出的名人数量多少。

Afterwards, following the model below, present the information you collected in front of the class using Chinese (except the names if you do know them). The result of the competition will be based on the total number of famous people you can name.

例句：我们知道两个法国美术家，他们的名字是……

(1) _____
(2) _____
(3) _____
(4) _____
(5) _____
(6) _____
(7) _____
(8) _____

七、读报 Newspaper Reading

How Many Characters Do You Know?

1. Read the following article.
2. While reading, underline the characters you know.

[文忠老弟是真天才]

季羡林：他是我50年教学生涯中所见最具备语言天才的人

季羡林

钱文忠是幸运的，在他人生的几个关时期遇到了两位好师。

"优秀教师可以传授给学生知识和做人的道理，伟大的教师却可以影响、改变乃至决定一个人的生命轨迹。"这是钱文忠在为启蒙恩师郝陵生先生所著的《茶余琐话》一书题"跋"中的一段话。

对郝老师，钱文忠一直满怀感恩之情。

对郝陵生是二十多年前钱文忠读华东师范大学第一附属中学时的高中历史老师。在那个"重理轻文"的年代，郝先生教授的历史课却让年少的钱文忠听得如痴如醉。郝先生将历史美学和"图式教学法"带入课堂，最大限度地激发了学生学习历史的兴趣。

"郝老师确实让我感受到了学术的魅力，尤其是历史学诱人的美妙。这种美妙必将诱惑我的一生。"

高二时，郝老师在一次历史课上提到季羡林先生研究的梵文、巴利文已是后继无人，17岁的钱文忠听之入心，遂给时任北大副校长的季羡林写信，表达了自己想学习这两种语言的意愿。

如果说郝陵生先生开启了钱文忠年少时懵懂的心智，那么，另一位恩师季羡林先生，则引领他把历史研究作为了自己毕生的"志业"。

1984年，钱文忠以上海市外语类第二名的高考成绩，考入北京大学东方语言文学系，就读梵文、巴利文专业，师从季羡林先生学习印度学。这个专业，北大仅在1960年招收过本科班。时隔24年后，季羡林先生能重开此班，不能不说与钱文忠当年给他的那封信有关。

钱文忠的天资聪颖和勤奋好学让季羡林大为赞赏。"这个孩子，是我50年教学生涯中所见过的最具备语言天才的人，所以我把那古怪的语言教给他了。"季羡林曾经这样说。

在给钱文忠学士学位论文的评语中，季羡林先生毫不惜墨："这篇论文其学术水平，实际上早已超过一篇学士论文。即使对一个成熟的梵文学者来说，也是一篇极有价值的、有独立新见解的论文，应该给他满分。"

季先生对于钱文忠，不仅是老师，更是朋友，甚至是亲人。

2007年1月，钱文忠著书《季门立雪》诠释了季先生在学术史上的贡献、地位；抒发了对恩师的崇敬之情。《季门立雪》的书名，也自然让人联想起古时"程门立雪"的典故。

"这是北大的一个传统。每到下雪的时候，一些北大的学生就会在季先生门前雪地上写下祝福的话，季先生家住一楼，推开窗子就能看到。我也写过呢。"钱文忠告诉记者。

在这本书的前言中，钱文忠写下了这样一段话："恩师是我这艘飘零小舟的缆绳。恩师系着我，使我心里永远有岸。"

今年，季羡林先生96岁寿辰，钱文忠特赴北京为老师祝寿，恭恭敬敬地向恩师行叩拜大礼。季先生送给钱文忠一本《季羡林说自己》，并在书的扉页上写下："文忠老弟，是真才子，但不要有才子气；有傲骨，但不要有傲气。"

"这是季先生教训我的话！他会在人生最合适的阶段，用最直接的语言来点拨你，这就是好老师。"钱文忠说。

如今，钱文忠自己也已为人师。他秉承恩师的教诲，努力将教学变成一项"志业"，而不仅仅是一种职业。他也希望能影响自己的学生，去和他共同完成这项"志业"。

刚从复旦旅游管理系毕业的林姓同学，曾经选修过钱文忠开设的梵文课。"我是慕名去听钱老师课的，他知识渊博，讲课很风趣。虽然梵文真的很难懂，但是我还是很喜欢他讲课的风格。"

选自：新民晚报　日期：2007年11月15日

3. Pronounce the characters you have recognized.
4. Tell the meaning of each character to your class (or study group).

八、文化点滴 Culture Notes

Chinese Ethnic Groups

China has 56 ethnic groups in total. The largest one is the Han (汉) which represents 92% of the country's population. All other 55 ethnic groups are considered minorities (少数民族), and the five largest are Zhuang, Man, Hui, Miao and Uyghur.

Zhuang (壮) (population of approximately 16.2 million). Most of the Zhuang live in southwestern China's Guangxi Zhuang Autonomous Region, which is about the size of New Zealand. The rest have settled in Yunnan, Guangdong, Guizhou and Hunan provinces.

Man (满) (population of approximately 10.7 million). The Man are an ethnic group that originally lived in the forests and mountains of northeastern China. Beginning in the 1640s, large numbers of Man moved south of the Shanhaiguan Pass (east end of the Great Wall). The Man have their own script and language, which belongs to the Tungusic group of the Altaic language family, but gradually adopted Mandarin Chinese as their spoken language after they conquered China during the Qing Dynasty (1644-1911).

Hui (回) (population of approximately 9.8 million). People of Hui ethnicity live in most counties and cities throughout China, but especially in the Ningxia Hui Autonomous Region and Gansu, Qinghai, Henan, Hebei, Shandong and Yunnan provinces and the Xinjiang Uygur Autonomous Region.

Miao (苗) (population of approximately 8.9 million). The Miao people are one of the largest ethnic minorities of southwestern China. They live mainly across Guizhou, Yunnan, Hunan and Sichuan provinces and Guangxi Zhuang Autonomous Region, with a small number living in Hainan, Guangdong and in southwest Hubei Provinces.

Uygur (维吾尔) (population of approximately 8.4 million). Almost all Uygurs are found in Xinjiang Uygur Autonomous Region. As the largest ethnic group, the Uygurs live along with several other ethnic groups such as Han, Kazak, Hui, Mongolian, Kirgiz, Tajik, Xibe, Ozbek, Manchu, Daur, Tatar and Russian in Xinjiang.

九、自我测试 Self Assessment

1. 用中文回答问题。
Answer the questions using Chinese.

(1) 你每天吃早饭吗？几点钟吃？

(2) 今天你有几节课？第一节是什么课？

(3) 你的英文课怎么样？有意思吗？

(4) 你们在哪门课上学几何？

(5) 你们几点钟上汉语课？

(6) 你的书包满吗？你的书包里有几本书？

2. 请在下面的图片中选择五个名人，并尽量用这一课和以前学过的中文词汇对他们加以介绍。
Choose five famous people from the following pictures and introduce them using Chinese vocabulary that you have learned from this and previous chapters.

Claude Monet

Ernest Hemingway

Richard Nixon

第五课 今天你有几节课?
How Many Classes Do You Have Today?

Mao Zedong

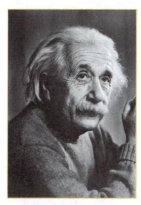
Albert Einstein

Sun Yat-sen

Jacques Chirac

Michael Jordan

Jackie Chan

Amy Tang

Alan Greenspan

Marie Curie

Yao Ming

Barack Obama

Elvis Presley

(1)

(2)

(3)

(4)

(5)

第五课 今天你有几节课？
How Many Classes Do You Have Today?

3. 对不对？

Read the question (A) and the answer (B). Check "对" if you think the answer is logical with respect to the question or check "不对" otherwise.

(1) A. 我星期一有三节课；星期三有四节课；星期五有三节课。我哪天最忙？
　　B. 你星期三最忙。　　　　　　对 _____　不对 _____

(2) A. 怎么，今天你们没有数学课？
　　B. 数学课很有意思。　　　　　对 _____　不对 _____

(3) A. 你为什么不解题？
　　B. 所以我看书。　　　　　　　对 _____　不对 _____

(4) A. 老师给了你们几道几何题？
　　B. 老师给了我们好几道几何题。对 _____　不对 _____

(5) A. 你们学习哪国地理？
　　B. 美国地理不难学。　　　　　对 _____　不对 _____

(6) A. 政治课难吗？
　　B. 不容易，不过很有意思。　　对 _____　不对 _____

(7) A. 你体育好吗？
　　B. 我很喜欢体育。　　　　　　对 _____　不对 _____

(8) A. 你们老师哪天忙？
　　B. 我们老师天天都忙。　　　　对 _____　不对 _____

(9) A. 现在几点钟？
　　B. 我十点钟有化学课。　　　　对 _____　不对 _____

(10) A. 她是美术家？
　　 B. 对，她很美。　　　　　　　对 _____　不对 _____

4. 阅读下列短文，并用中文回答问题。
Read the following paragraph and answer the questions using Chinese.

今年开学 (to start school) 的时候妈妈给我买了一个新书包。这个书包很大，是绿色 (lǜsè: green color) 的；我喜欢我的新书包。因为有很多同学有这样的 (this kind) 书包，所以我在书包上写 (xiě: to write) 了我的名字。我的书包每天都很满，因为这个学期我有五门课，每门课都有一、两本书。

(1) 谁给"我"买了一个新书包？

(2) "我"的新书包是什么颜色的？

(3) "我"为什么在新书包上写我的名字？

(4) "我"的书包里大概 (dàgài: approximitely) 有几本书？

(5) 在你的同学中，谁有绿色的书包？

第六课
LESSON SIX

你们在中文课上做什么?
What Do You Do in Chinese Class?

学习目的
Learning Objectives

表达语言课课堂活动	To express language class activities
表达在校班级	To express seniority in school
出题和解算术题	To give and solve arithmetic problems
成段表达自己	To express oneself in paragraphs

本课学习内容 Contents of the chapter

一	学习发音 Pronunciation
	• 韵母 vowels：ua, uai, uang, uo, üan, ün
二	课文：你们在中文课上做什么？ Text: What Do You Do in Chinese Class?
三	生词 Vocabulary
	• 名词 nouns：黄安竹、年级、初级、班、活动、时间、语音、发音、声、生词、语言、时候、用法、课文、对话、练习、作业、考试、测验、花 • 动词 verbs：干、告诉、开始、花、卖、会、书写、写、读、教、唱歌、练习、起名字、留、完、考试 • 形容词 adjectives：一样 • 介词 prepositions：至 • 副词 adverbs：刚刚、差不多、尽量、几乎、就、平时、常常 • 量词 measure words：堂、次 • 词语 expressions：也就是说、截然不同、除了……以外，也、除……以外，都、有时(候)
四	数字复习 Study of Numbers: Addition
五	语法 Grammar
	• 刚(刚)＋动词　　　　　　　刚(刚)＋verb • "除了……以外，也 (or: 　"除了……以外，也 (or: 还)" 　还)"和"除了……以外，　 versus "除了……以外，都……" 　都……"的区别 • "干"和"做"的区别　　　　"干" versus "做" • 复合动词"听见"和"学会"　Compound verbs "听见" and "学会" • "完"字的用法　　　　　　Usage of the character "完" • "就"的作用　　　　　　　Functions of the adverb "就"
六	练习 Exercises
七	读报 Newspaper Reading
八	文化点滴 Culture Notes
九	自我测试 Self Assessment

第六课 你们在中文课上做什么？
What Do You Do in Chinese Class?

一、学习发音 Pronunciation 1

| ua | uo | uai | uang | üan | ün |

Drill 1

j +
- iān （时间）　　iǎn （检）　　iàn （见）
- iāng（江）　　　iǎng（讲）　　iàng（酱）

Drill 2

q +
- iān （千）　　ián （钱）　　iǎn （浅）　　iàn （欠）
- iāng（腔）　　iáng（强大）　iǎng（抢）　 iàng（烟呛）
- ióng（穷）

Drill 3

x +
- iān （先）　　ián （闲）　　iǎn （显）　　iàn （现）
- iāng（香）　　iáng（祥）　　iǎng（想）　　iàng（象）
- iōng（兄）　　ióng（雄）

Drill 4

g +
- uā （瓜）　　　　　　　uǎ （寡）　　uà （挂）
- uāi（乖）　　　　　　　uǎi（拐）　　uài（怪）
- uān（官）　　　　　　　uǎn（管）　　uàn（贯）
- uāng（光）　　　　　　 uǎng（广）　 uàng（逛）
- uō （郭）　　　　　　　uǒ （果）　　uò （过）

Drill 5

h +
- uā （花）　　uá （华）　　　　　　　uà （话）
- 　　　　　　 uái（怀）　　　　　　　uài（坏）
- uān（欢）　　uán（环）　　uǎn（缓）　uàn（换）
- uāng（荒）　 uáng（黄）　 uǎng（晃眼）uàng（晃动）
- uō （豁口）　 uó （活）　　uǒ （火）　 uò （获）

Drill 6

	uā (夸)	uǎ (垮)	uà (跨)
		uǎi (崴)	uài (快)
k +	uān (宽)	uǎn (款)	
	uāng (筐)　uáng (狂)		uàng (况)
			uò (阔)

Drill 7

j	ūn (军)	uān (娟)
q	ún (裙)	uàn (劝)
x	ún (寻)	uǎn (选)

Drill 8

guó (国)	dōu (都)	niáng (娘)	liàng (辆)	mián (棉)
diàn (电)	biǎn (扁)	tiān (天)	xuān (宣)	yuán (员)
yǒng (永)	ruò (若)	huò (或)	luó (罗)	suǒ (所)
shuō (说)	shuāi (衰)	suàn (算)	suān (酸)	cuàn (撺)
duān (端)	nuǎn (暖)	chuān (川)	zhuàng (状)	qián (钱)
juǎn (卷尺)	luàn (乱)	shuāng (双)	kuān (宽)	
kuàng (况)	duǎn (短)	chuǎng (闯)	huān (欢)	

Drill 9

gàn / guǎn (干活 / 馆)	piàn / piào (片 / 票)	duǎn / diǎn (短 / 点)
zuān / zāi (钻 / 栽)	sǎn / sǎng (伞 / 嗓)	yuàn / yàn (愿 / 艳)
tiān / tān (天 / 贪)	bān / biān (般 / 边)	huá / huái (华 / 怀)
niǔ / nǔ (扭 / 女)	nuǎn / niǎn (暖 / 碾)	chuāng / chāng (窗 / 昌)
qián / quán (前 / 全)	shuā / shuō (刷 / 说话)	chuān / chuāi (川 / 揣手)
tián / tuán (田 / 团)	zhuā / zhuō (抓 / 桌)	guā / guō (瓜 / 郭)
suān / suō (酸 / 梭)	zuàn / zuò (攥 / 做)	huán / huáng (环 / 黄)
rù / ruò (入 / 弱)	tuó / tuán (驼 / 团)	guài / guàn (怪 / 贯)

二、课文 Text 2

你们在中文课上做什么？

大家好！我叫黄安竹，是高中一年级的学生。你们问我和我的同学们在中文课上干什么，我现在就告诉你们。

我们在中文初级班，也就是说我们刚刚开始学习这门语言。在每堂中文课上我们都有很多不同的活动。

我们花不少时间学习语音。汉语和英语的发音很不一样，因为汉语有四声。比如，"买"字是第三声；"卖"字是第四声，这两个字的意思是截然不同的。

我们差不多每个星期学习十五至二十个生词。学习生词的时候我们得学会每个生词的发音、书写和用法。

除了学习发音和生词以外，我们还读课文，做对话和练习。有时候老师还教我们唱中国歌。老师给我们每个人起了一个中文名字，要求每个学生尽量多说汉语。

老师几乎每天给我们留作业。每学完一课我们就有一次考试，平时还常常有测验。

我喜欢练习写字

我们天天用中文对话

課文

你們在中文課上做什麼?

大家好!我叫黃安竹,是高中一年級的學生。你們問我和我的同學們在中文課上幹什麼,我現在就告訴你們。

我們在中文初級班,也就是說我們剛剛開始學習這門語言。在每堂中文課上我們都有很多不同的活動。

我們花不少時間學習語音。漢語和英語的發音很不一樣,因為漢語有四聲。比如,"買"字是第三聲;"賣"字是第四聲,這兩個字的意思是截然不同的。

我們差不多每個星期學習十五至二十個生詞。學習生詞的時候我們得學會每個生詞的發音、書寫和用法。

除了學習發音和生詞以外,我們還讀課文,做對話和練習。有時候老師還教我們唱中國歌。老師給我們每個人起了一個中文名字,要求每個學生盡量多說漢語。

老師幾乎每天給我們留作業。每學完一課我們就有一次考試,平時還常常有測試。

我喜歡練習寫字

我們天天用中文對話

LESSON 6

第六课 你们在中文课上做什么?
What Do You Do in Chinese Class?

三、生词 Vocabulary

NOUNS

Huáng Ānzhú 黄安竹 (黃安竹) Andrew Hunt	huáng 黄：yellow, a surname
	ān 安：peaceful, quiet, tranquil
	zhú 竹：bamboo
niánjí 年级 (年級) grade, year	
chūjí 初级 (初級) elementary level	chū 初：elementary, at the beginning of
	jí 级 (級)：rank, grade, level, class
bān 班 (班) class, team	yǔyán 语言 (語言) language
huódòng 活动 (活動) activity	huó 活：alive, living, lively, moving
	dòng 动 (動)：move, act, stir, get moving
shíjiān 时间 (時間) time	yǔyīn 语音 (語音) speech sounds, pronunciation
fāyīn 发音 (發音) pronunciation	fā 发 (發)：to send out
shēng 声 (聲) sound, voice, tone	shēngcí 生词 (生詞) vocabulary, new word
yǔyán 语言 (語言) language	shíhou 时候 (時候) moment	yòngfǎ 用法 (用法) use, usage
kèwén 课文 (課文) text	duìhuà 对话 (對話) dialogue, conversation
liànxí 练习 (練習) practice, exercise	liàn 练 (練)：to practice, train, drill
zuòyè 作业 (作業) homework	zuò 作：to make, write, compose
kǎoshì 考试 (考試) test, examination	kǎo 考：to give or take an examination

cèyàn	huā
测验(測驗) quiz, test	花(花) a surname

VERBS

gàn
干/干 to do, to work

gàosu
告诉/告訴 to tell

kāishǐ
开始/開始 to begin, to start

huā
花/花 to spend

mài
卖/賣 to sell

huì
会/會 to know how, to be able

shūxiě
书写/書寫 to write

xiě
写/寫 to write

dú
读/讀 to read

jiāo
教/教 to teach, to instruct

chàng gē
唱歌/唱歌 to sing

liànxí
练习/練習 to practice, to exercise

qǐ míngzi
起名字/起名字 to name, to give a name ⟶ qǐ
起/起 to begin, to start

liú
留/留 to leave (a message), to assign (homework)

wán
完/完 to finish, to complete

kǎoshì
考试/考試 to test, to give an examination

ADJECTIVES

yíyàng
一样/一樣 alike, same

ADVERBS

gāng (gāng)
刚(刚)/剛(剛) just now, not long ago

chàbuduō
差不多/差不多 almost, nearly

jǐnliàng
尽量/盡量 to the fullest extent, as much as possible

jǐn
尽/盡 to the greatest extent, within the limits of

liàng
量/量 capacity, quantity

LESSON 6

第六课 你们在中文课上做什么？
What Do You Do in Chinese Class?

yǒu shíhou
有时候/有時候 sometimes

jīhū
几乎/幾乎 almost, nearly

jiù
就/就 soon, immediately, right away

píngshí
平时/平時 ordinarily, usually, normally

cháng (cháng)
常(常)/常(常) often, frequently

MEASURE WORDS

táng
堂/堂 for classes or periods at school

PREPOSITIONS

zhì
至/至 to, until

EXPRESSIONS

yě jiù shì shuō
也就是说/也就是說 in other words, that is

jiérán bùtóng
截然不同/截然不同 completely different

chúle …… yǐwài, yě
除了……以外，也 (or 还) / 除了……以外，也 (or 還) in addition to, besides

chúle …… yǐwài, dōu
除了……以外，都/除了……以外，都 except

四、数字复习 Study of Numbers: Addition

★ 练习

1. 两个人一组做这个练习：轮流一个人用中文朗读，一个人听并写下面的数字。
   Work in pairs: take turns to read and write the following numbers using Chinese.

5211	1074	3162	6188	1359	9015	2881	1960	4629	2312
2239	8430	5560	1742	6168	3001	7202	4370	5326	3904
1002	6321	9910	8080	7023	1366	5167	1171	4901	6002
4383	2615	7047	3542	9377	5112	8478	4874	1010	2523

2. 两个人一组：a) 每个人用三至五分钟的时间按照下面的例句准备五道算术题并练习读题；b) 各自用中文把题读给对方听，并请他／她将你的题写下来。
   Work in pairs: a) following the model, use three to five minutes to prepare five arithmetic questions and practice reading them; b) read the questions in Chinese to your partner and ask him / her to write them down.

   Vocabulary: 加（上）jiā: plus, add

   　　　　　　得 dé: result in

   　　　　　　等于 děngyú: equal

   Model:

   　　251 + 2100 = 多少

你的题	对方 (duìfāng: partner) 的题
(1)	(1)
(2)	(2)
(3)	(3)
(4)	(4)
(5)	(5)

c) 然后，互相检查对方写下的题，并用中文告诉他/她：

Afterwards, check each other's written-down questions and tell each other the following using Chinese:

Model:

你写对了三(两、四)道题；写错(cuò: wrong)了一(两、三)道题。

d) 最后，每个人把对方算术题的结果算出来，告诉他／她：

Finally, find out the result for each of the questions you have received and tell your partner the following:

Model:

你的第一道题的得数 (dé shù: result) 是＿＿＿＿＿，第二道题的得数是＿＿＿＿＿，……

五、语法 Grammar

1. 刚(刚)+动词 刚(刚)+verb

The adverb "刚" or "刚刚," when followed by a verb, equals the immediate past in English. It refers to something that has just happened. Please compare the following sentences:

大牛 (niú) 来中国。
Daniel comes to China.

大牛刚刚来中国。
Daniel has just come to China.

我们在学第六课。
We are learning chapter 6.

我们刚学第六课。
We have just started learning chapter 6.

你们学中文多长时间了?
How long have you been learning Chinese?

我们刚刚开始学(中文)。
We have just started (learning it).

练习一

请按照例句做对话。
Make conversation following the model.

 你们学中文多长时间了? 我们刚刚开始学。

(1) 你们学习中文
(2) 他们学习英语
(3) 黄安竹来中国
(4) 贺小音去美国
(5) 赵老师教你们中文
(6) 何老师教你们口语
(7) 张老师教你们写作
(8) 王老师教你们<u>会话</u> (conversation)

2. 除了……以外

The prepositional expression "除了……以外" can be translated into English as "besides," "except," or "in addition to" according to a word that is used in the main clause. For example:

除了文娣(以外)，他们也是我的朋友。
除了文娣(以外)，我还有很多朋友。

In the above two sentences, the words "也" and "还" indicate that 文娣 is my friend; therefore it should be translated as: Besides Wendy, they are also my friends; In addition to Wendy, I also have many other friends. But in the following example,

除了文娣(以外)，他们都是我的朋友。

the main clause "all others are my friends" underlines the meaning that 文娣 is not my friend. The translation would be: They are all my friends except Wendy.

Conclusion:

除了……(以外)，+ 也…… = besides, in addition to
除了英语以外，他也说法语。
He speaks French in addition to English.

除了……(以外)，+ 还…… = besides, in addition to
除了历史课以外，我们还有外语课。
Besides the history class, we also have the foreign language class.

除了……(以外)，+ 都…… = except
除了安竹以外，大家都去北海公园了。
Everyone went to Beihai Park except Andrew.

除了星期二，他每天都很忙。
He is busy every day except Tuesday.

练习二

1. 请按照例句做对话。
   Make conversation following the model.

除了(说)英语以外，你还说什么语？

除了英语以外，我还说法语，你呢？

我只说英语。

(1) (说) 英语 / 法语
(2) (上) 中文课 / 地理课
(3) (有) 数学作业 / 物理作业
(4) (会唱) 美国歌 / 中国歌
(5) (买) 书 / 书包
(6) (喜欢) 法国饭 / 意大利饭
(7) (认识) 江小朋 / 周文亮
(8) (去) 北京 / 上海

2. 一读，二想，三回答 (请用中文)。
Read, think and answer the questions using Chinese.

——读一读—— ——想一想——

(1) 除了星期四以外，我每天都 星期四我有时间吗?
   有时间。
   回答

(2) 除了数学课，我们还有化学课 我们有数学课吗?
   和外语课。
   回答

(3) 除了美国学生以外，我们 我们学校有美国学生吗?
   学校 (xuéxiào: school)也有
   中国、英国和日本学生。
   回答

(4) 除了史小莉，大家都会说英语。 史小莉会说英语吗?
   回答

(5) 除了高英明以外，他们 高英明是我的朋友吗?
   都是我的朋友。
   回答

(6) 除了高英明以外，钟天明 高英明是我的朋友吗?
   和赵文生也是我的朋友。
   回答

(7) 除了我爸爸,他们都是律师。 我爸爸是律师吗?
回答

(8) 除了你和他,还有八个学生 你和他想学法
想学法语。 语吗?
回答

(9) 除了王老师以外,别的 (bié de: other) 我认识王老师吗?
老师我都认识。
回答

(10) 除了第三课,还有哪一课难? 第三课难吗?
回答

3. "干"和"做"的区别 "干" versus "做"

For both verbs "干" and "做," the English equivalent would be "to do." And in some cases, they can be used interchangeably.

你在干什么? or 你在做什么?
What are you doing?

However, sometimes, they are not interchangeable. For instance, when expressing "to do homework" and "to cook," only "做" can be used.

做作业   干作业 ×
做饭   干饭 ×

练习三

请按照例句做对话。
Make conversation following the model.

 你们在干什么?

 我们在做练习。

 做什么练习?

 我们在做语音练习。

(1) 语音   (2) 语法
(3) 写作   (4) 生词
(5) 数学   (6) 英语
(7) 生字   (8) 对话

4. 复合动词"听见"和"学会" Compound Verbs "听见" and "学会"

In the Chinese language, you may often see two verbs (a non-helping verb and a main verb such as: 我想学汉语。他要来中国吗?) combined together. This kind of verb is a "compound verb." Sometimes an English-equivalent translation can be found (for example, "看见" is "to see" and "找到" means "to find," etc.), but this is not always the case. Therefore, it is crucial to understand the principles of the combination of compound verbs. In a compound verb, the second verb normally indicates the result of the action of the first verb.

学生们听到了老师的问题。
Students listened to the professor, and they heard his/her question(s).
Students have heard the professor's question(s).

很快，安娜就学会了做面条。
In no time, Anna has learned how to make noodles.

练习四

请找出每个句子里的名词、动词和量词。
Please identify the different parts of speech (noun, verb and measure words) in each of the following sentences.

Modle：

上个星期我读完了一本小说。

名词：<u>星期、小说</u>

动词：<u>读</u>   量词：<u>本</u>

(1) 他们给妈妈买到了一瓶漂亮的花。

名词：☐

动词：☐   量词：☐

(2) 我们看见了三个孩子。

名词：☐

动词：☐   量词：☐

第六课 你们在中文课上做什么？
What Do You Do in Chinese Class?

(3) 学生们听见了一首(shǒu)中国歌。

名词：☐

动词：☐ 量词：☐

(4) 谁学会了十个新字？

名词：☐

动词：☐ 量词：☐

(5) 老师给我们上完了两节课。

名词：☐

动词：☐ 量词：☐

(6) 我看见他的书包里有六本书。

名词：☐

动词：☐ 量词：☐

(7) 他们找到了好几张老照片。

名词：☐

动词：☐ 量词：☐

(8) 学生们解完了五道数学题。

名词：☐

动词：☐ 量词：☐

5. "完"字的用法 Usage of the Character "完"

In modern Chinese, "完" is often combined with a verb to indicate the completion of the action of the verb.

你看完那本书了吗？
Have you finished reading that book?

我们还没学完第十二课。
We did not finish (learning) chapter 12 yet.

你们什么时候做完练习？
When are you going to finish doing the exercises?

练习五

请按照例句做对话。
Make conversation following the model.

 在中文课上，你们学什么了？

 我们学了第五课的语法。

 你们学完了吗？

 学完了。

 学会了吗？

 学会了，不过我们还得做练习。

(1) 语法 (2) 生词
(3) 四声 (4) 对话
(5) 课文 (6) 名词 (noun)
(7) 动词 (verb) (8) 量词 (measure word)

6. "就"的作用 Functions of the Adverb "就"

As an adverb, the character "就" is used to:

a) stress the quickness and the earliness of an action;

我马上 (mǎshàng) 就来。
I'm coming right now.

饭(马上)就好了。
The meal will be ready soon.

b) indicate that the action of the verb happened earlier than expected;

他昨天就做完作业了。
He finished his homework (as early as) yesterday.

我们早就知道了。
We have already learned about it.

第六课 你们在中文课上做什么?
What Do You Do in Chinese Class?

c) express that one action occurs right after another. For example:

上完课他就回家了。
He went home right after class.

回到家她就开始做饭。
She started cooking as soon as she got home.

练习六

请按照例句做对话。
Make conversation following the model.

 你什么时候做作业?   吃完饭我就做作业。

(1) 去公园、吃饭
(2) 做练习、学发音
(3) 考试、学语法
(4) 听写 (dictation)、学习生词
(5) 找 (zhǎo: to look for)工作、上大学
(6) 上化学课、上数学课
(7) 读课文、做对话
(8) 去上海、过新年
(9) 上大学、上高中
(10) 上高级班、上中级班

六、练习 Exercises

模式练习 Model exercises

1. 请按照例句做对话。
Make conversation following the model.

生词：初中(初级中学：junior school)、高中(高级中学：high school)

 你是初中(学)生还是高中(学)生？

 我是高中生。

 你是高中几年级的学生？

 我是高(中)二(年级)的学生。

(1) 你朋友　　(2) 你们
(3) 他们　　　(4) 你哥哥
(5) 你姐姐　　(6) 你弟弟
(7) 你妹妹　　(8) 她们

2. 请按照例句做对话。
Make conversation following the model.

 妈妈告诉你什么？

 她告诉我："现在五点十分了，我要做晚饭了。"她还告诉我："爸爸今天忙，不回来吃晚饭。"

(1) 妈妈告诉你：现在五点十分了，我要做晚饭了。/爸爸今天忙，不回家吃晚饭。
(2) 老师告诉学生们：做第六课的练习。/明天有一个生词测验。
(3) 爷爷告诉你：我和奶奶都好。/我们很想你和你的弟弟、妹妹。

第六课 你们在中文课上做什么？
What Do You Do in Chinese Class?

(4) 黄安竹告诉他朋友：我来中国半年了，很想家。/ 我打算有时间的时候回美国去看看我的家人。

(5) 你告诉哥哥：这个星期六是姥姥的生日。/ 你想想我们怎么给姥姥过生日。

(6) 大卫告诉你们：我在汉语课上学会了一支中文歌。/ 歌的名字叫"大中国"。

(7) 律师告诉你：今天我很忙。/ 明天也没有时间。

(8) 贺小音告诉你：我的第一节课八点钟开始。/ 今天我有两个考试。

(9) 大牛 (dàniú: Daniel)告诉你们：我爸爸在中国做买卖 (business)。/ 我本人 (myself) 也想去中国看看。

(10) 你们告诉老师：我们喜欢这个练习。/ 在这个练习里我们学会了好几个新词。

3. 请按照例句做对话。
   Make conversation following the model.

 这个学期你在上数学初级班吗？

 不，我在上中级班。

 你什么时候上数学高级班？

 下个学期。

(1) 数学课　　　　　(2) 英语语法课
(3) 英文课　　　　　(4) 法语课
(5) 汉语语法课　　　(6) 法语口语 (spoken language)课
(7) 汉语写作 (writing)课　(8) 日语会话 (conversation)课

4. 请按照例句1和2做下面的练习。如有不懂的词请问老师。
   Do the exercises following models 1 and 2. Ask your instructor if you encounter unfamiliar words.

   Model 1: "一个星期"和"一个学期"

   "一个星期"和"一个学期"的意思截然不同。

Model 2: "中文"和"汉语"
"中文"和"汉语"的意思一样。

(1) "买"和"卖"

(2) "上课"和"下课"

(3) "一周"和"一个星期"

(4) "对我说"和"告诉我"

(5) "语法"和"法语"

(6) "今天"和"今日"

(7) "吃饭"和"用餐"

(8) "妈"和"吗"

(9) "一堂课"和"一节课"

(10) "哥"和"歌"

5. 请按照例句做对话。

Make conversation following the model.

 你妹妹在哪儿读书 (or: 上学)?

第六课 你们在中文课上做什么?
What Do You Do in Chinese Class?

 她在大理第一小学读书 (or: 上学)。

 她是几年级的学生?

 我妹妹刚刚开始读小学,她是一年级的学生。

(1) 你妹妹 / 大理第一小学
(2) 钟大利的哥哥 / 北京外国语 (or: 外语: foreign language) 大学
(3) 江小平的女朋友 / 中文大学
(4) 你最小的弟弟 / 文安中学
(5) 周新竹 / 北京理工大学
(6) 乐明的姐姐 / 上海美术学院 (institute)

6. 两个人一组:轮流提问并用"几乎"和"差不多"回答问题。
   Work in pairs: take turns to ask and answer the following questions using the expressions "几乎" or "差不多."

   (1) 现在几点钟了?
   (2) 在物理课上,你们多长时间有一次考试?
   (3) 在你们学校 (xuéxiào: school),每个学生都有体育活动吗?
   (4) 学生们天天有作业吗?
   (5) 你天天和安竹在一起学习中文吗?
   (6) 在中文课上,你们一个星期学多少个生词?
   (7) 你现在认识多少个中文字?
   (8) 每个外国人来中国都去长城吗?
   (9) 你们多长时间学完一课?
   (10) 在你们学校 (xuéxiào: school),每个学生都得学习一门外语吗?

7. 请按照例句做对话。
   Make conversation following the model.

    你周末做什么?

    我有(的)时候去奶奶家,有(的)时候去姥姥家。

   (1) 你和朋友们在一起做什么 / 听音乐、唱歌

(2) 你们家几点钟吃晚饭 / 六点半、七点钟
(3) 你在家里说什么语言 / 英语、法语
(4) 在<u>学校</u> (xuéxiào: school)你常和谁一起吃中午饭 / <u>黄安竹</u>、<u>高大同</u> (Denton Gay)、<u>谢文娣</u> (Wendy Sherwood)
(5) 你们在中文课上做什么 / 学习生词、练习发音、读课文
(6) 那个老师教什么 / 语法、写作
(7) 你每天几点钟到<u>学校</u> (xuéxiào: school) / 差十分钟八点、差一刻八点
(8) 朋友们什么时候来你家 / 星期六、星期日

8. **两个人一起做这个练习：轮流一个人读，一个人听。然后两个人一起试试<u>理解</u> (understand) 每个句子的意思；<u>如果</u> (rúguǒ: if)不理解再用中文问老师。**
Work in pairs: take turns to read and listen to the sentences first. Afterwards, work together to understand the meaning of each sentence. Ask your instructor questions using Chinese if you have any.

(1) 老师常常告诉学生们学习语言听、说、读、写都很<u>重要</u> (zhòngyào: important)。
(2) 我们家常去餐馆吃意大利饭，因为全家人都喜欢吃，可是没有人会做意大利饭。
(3) 我常常给朋友们过生日，因为每次我过生日的时候他们都来。他们给我买花，买生日卡，祝我生日快乐。
(4) 我听说学生们常在一起做作业，说汉语，有时候还唱中国歌。
(5) 老师要求我们尽量多说汉语。
(6) 你常常读小说吗？读英文小说还是中文小说？
(7) 在经济课上，你们常常考试吗？
(8) 他常常去<u>汉江</u> (place name) 看他的爸爸妈妈吗？
(9) <u>高平</u> (place name)是我的<u>老家</u> (hometown)，我常常回去看看。
(10) 我的爷爷奶奶老了，不常来看我们。不过我们常常去看他们。

9. **参照下列例句采访两个同学 (采访的同时要做笔记)。让他们告诉你三至五件去年和今年学会的事以及一、两件他们打算明年学会做的事。**
First, following the model sentences, interview two classmates and take notes during the interviews. Ask them to tell you three to five things they have learned to do during the last two years and one to two things that they plan to learn next year.

第六课 你们在中文课上做什么?
What Do You Do in Chinese Class?

Model：
    A. 今年你学会了做什么？
    B. 今年我学会了说汉语，学会了写汉字，还学会了唱中国歌。
    A. 明年你打算学会什么？
    B. 我打算学会做饭和照照片。
    A. 你打算和谁学做饭？
    B. 和我爸爸学，他做饭很好。

去年和今年学会做的事	打算明年学会做的事
第一个同学	
第二个同学	

10. 请用中文回答下列问题。
Answer the following questions using Chinese.

(1) 你爸爸妈妈教你做饭吗？

(2) 你的老师每天教几节课？每门课教多少个学生？

(3) 哪个同学的爸爸/妈妈是老师？他/她在哪里教书 (to teach)？

(4) 你小的时候 (When you were little)，谁教你说话 (to talk)？

(5) 今天在中文课上，老师教你们什么了？

(6) 有人 (is there anyone) 教你唱意大利歌吗？

(7) 老师教你们学习知识；谁教你们怎么做人 (to conduct oneself, to behave)？

(8) 谁教会了你们写汉字？

11. 请按照例句做对话。
Make conversation following the model.

 我在汉语初级班。

 也就是说你刚刚开始学汉语。
or: 这么说你刚刚开始学汉语。

(1) 我在汉语初级班 / 刚刚开始学汉语
(2) 我没有哥哥，也没有姐姐 / 你是你们家的老大
(3) 明天我很忙 / 你没有时间来我家
(4) 除了五门课以外我还有很多活动 / 你很忙
(5) 他每次考试都考90多分、100 分 / 他是一个好学生
(6) 我在学校 (xuéxiào: school) 说英语和法语，在家里说汉语 / 你会好几门语言
(7) 这是我们家人在一起照的照片 / 这是你们家的全家福
(8) 学生们都喜欢这个老师 / 他[她]教课不错
(9) 我去了两次长城，还想再去一次 / 你很喜欢长城
(10) 我是高中四年级学生 / 明年你就要上大学了

12. 谁在给你(们)提建议？
Who is giving you suggestions?

(1) 你们要尽量多说汉语。　　　　　　　老师

第六课 你们在中文课上做什么?
What Do You Do in Chinese Class?

(2) 你尽量五点半回到家。

(3) 你去中国的时候尽量多照几张照片。

(4) 请你尽量做完作业。

(5) 你们要尽量多参加 (cānjiā: to participate) 体育活动。

(6) 你要尽量多和爷爷奶奶说话 (to talk)。

(7) 你们要尽量多做练习，因为明天有一个测验。

(8) 你尽量回家来吃晚饭吧!

(9) 你要尽量多解题。

(10) 他们尽量一个星期学会十五个汉字。

13. 请读下面的对话，然后用中文回答问题。
    Read the following dialogue and answer questions using Chinese.

贺开文：老师，"留"字是什么意思？我不太 (tài) 明白 (I'm not quite clear)。

老　师：" 留"字有好几个意思。第一个意思是"to stay"。比如 (bǐrú: for example)，朋友来你家的时候你可以说："请你留下和我们一起吃饭吧!"你明白吗？

贺开文：我明白了。您再给我一个句子 (jùzi: sentence)，好吗？

老　师：好。再比如"留学"的意思是"to stay abroad and study"。

贺开文：太好了 (Wonderful)！老师，我想去中国留学。

老　师：什么时候？

贺开文：明年。

老　师：到那个时候 (by then) 你就是"留学生"。

贺开文：对，明年我就是留学生了！可是，老师，"留"字在我们的课文里不是这个意思。

老　师：好，现在我告诉你"留"字的第二个意思："to leave"。比如："留言"的意思是"to leave a message"。现在你明白"老师给学生留作业"是什么意思了吗？

贺开文：明白了，谢谢王老师。
老　师：不谢。再见！
贺开文：老师再见！

(1) 贺开文有什么问题？他问谁？

(2) 老师说"留"字有几个意思？

(3) "留学生"是什么意思？

(4) 贺开文打算去中国留学，你呢？

(5) "留言"是什么意思？

14. 画线的字是什么意思？

What is the meaning of the underlined word?

(1) 今天上午你们花了多长时间做练习？半个小时还是四十分钟？（　　）
    a. flower　　　　　　b. to spend
    c. surname　　　　　d. colorful

(2) 每次我的朋友们来我们家，我爸爸妈妈都留他们吃饭。
（　　）
    a. to stay　　　　　　b. to ask to stay
    c. to study abroad　　d. to leave

(3) 我们花了和你们一样长的时间学习中文语音和四声。（　　）
    a. flower　　　　　　b. to spend
    c. surname　　　　　d. colorful

(4) 我姓花，叫花音然。我知道是我的爷爷奶奶给我起的这个名字。（　　）
    a. flower　　　　　　b. to spend
    c. surname　　　　　d. colorful

(5) 这所大学有五十多个留学生。(　　)
　　a. to stay　　　　　　　b. to ask to stay
　　c. to study abroad　　　d. to leave

(6) 你打算去哪个国家留学？(　　)
　　a. to stay　　　　　　　b. to ask to stay
　　c. to study abroad　　　d. to leave

(7) 她生日那天，我们给她买了一大瓶花(　　)。
　　a. flower　　　　　　　b. to spend
　　c. surname　　　　　　d. colorful

(8) 今天老师给我们留了一点点作业，我马上就能做完。(　　)
　　a. to stay　　　　　　　b. to ask to stay
　　c. to study abroad　　　d. to leave

(9) 我最好的朋友叫花小莉。(　　)
　　a. flower　　　　　　　b. to spend
　　c. surname　　　　　　d. colorful

(10) 他二〇〇八年来到中国，在这里花了六年时间上学。现在有了工作，他打算留在中国了。(　　)
　　a. to stay　　　　　　　b. to ask to stay
　　c. to study abroad　　　d. to leave

实况演练 Real situation exercises

1. 两个同学一起：互相提问，共同完成下面的任务。
   Work in pairs: ask each other questions and together complete the following task.

   你爸爸妈妈和老师要求你做什么？

	我爸爸妈妈要求我	我的老师们要求我
(1)		
(2)		
(3)		

(4) _____   _____

(5) _____   _____

2. 小作文。
Mini-composition.

请你用 (yòng: to use) 中文说一说你学中文的经历 (experience)。你什么时候开始学中文的？你喜欢不喜欢学？你怎么学习中文？课上课下 (during and after class) 你做什么？你怎么练习听、说、读、写？现在你学会了多少个汉字？你打算今年学多少个？明年呢？你打算去中国学汉语吗？

_____
_____
_____
_____
_____

3. 用中文回答下面的问题。
Answer the following questions using Chinese.

(1) 你见过这个人吗？
_____

(2) 你知道她是哪国人吗？
_____

(3) 她姓什么？叫什么名字？
_____

(4) 她有哥哥、姐姐吗？
_____

(5) 她是大学生吗？
_____

第六课 你们在中文课上做什么?
What Do You Do in Chinese Class?

七、读报　Newspaper Reading

How Many Characters Do You Know?

1. Read the following article.
2. While reading, underline the characters you know.

小留学生

王恩科

美国中学一般不设固定的课堂和班级,而是以学科定教室。学生每节课都要到不同的教室上课,因此要不间断地往返于栋栋大楼之间,甚至两个校区。她说,这种环境的不断转换,在某种程度上提高了学生的学习兴趣,激发了学生的精神状态和注意力。不会像在中国那样一整天待在一个教室里,一个座位上,课上到最后产生昏昏欲睡的感觉。美国的教室只有中国的一半大小,每班只有十几个人,这有利于教师关注每个学生的学习状态,学生也会有更多的发言机会,锻炼自己的思维和表达能力。

小何说,美国学生很热情、真诚、大方。她初来时,有一次找不到上课的教室,向路边的一个学生问路,对方热情地帮她找教室,一路上像老朋友一样侃侃而谈,完全没有陌生的感觉。

学校经常举行集会。一次感恩节集会,主持人对台下的同学说:"如果谁想对爱你的人或你爱的人说说话,可以上台作感恩演讲。"同学们都争先恐后地上台发言。由于人多,主持人只能叫他们依次排队发言。演讲的同学从容镇定,真情实感,表达了自己对同学、老师、父母、亲人和朋友的爱。事例生动,感人肺腑,不少演讲者激动得哽咽起来……在数百人的集会上,争着上台发言,在中国几乎是不可能的,没有准备的会,肯定会冷场的。

她说学校的作文课很有特色,很少做记叙文,以议论为主,老师往往给学生几个题目,让学生自由选择。作文题写在一张纸上,上面老师的目的要求写得很详尽,还附有提示性的问题,便于在构思时参考。完成一篇作文的过程很"复杂",必须先列提纲,然后用一节课让学生切磋讨论,提纲的顺序是否合乎逻辑? 内容是否切题? 在此基础上写出初稿,初稿完成后再用一节课分组评估,要求每个同学朗读自己的作文,同时每人发一张评估书,要求对其他同学写出3个优点3个缺点,并说出理由,完了,把评估书交给文章作者。作者再根据同学的意见修改后交给老师。老师再用一节课时间评讲。为了鼓励学生敢想敢说的精神,老师一般不否定论点,只分析其论据是否有说服力。经过这些程序,同学的作文水平都有很大提高。

美国学校非常重视学生的身体素质,每天下午3点放学后,全体同学必须参加体育锻炼,成绩计入学分。每人每学期选择一项,每项都配有教练,训练强度很大,如参加长跑的每天必须跑完10000米,参加游泳的每天要求游完1500米,参加划船、篮球、足球等项目的每天要训练三四小时。通过训练,同学的身体素质都会大幅度提高。

选自: 新民晚报 日期: 2009年4月13日

3. Pronounce the characters you have recognized.
4. Tell the meaning of each character to your class (or study group).

八、文化点滴　Culture Notes

Why is the "福" Character Upside-down?

During the Lunar New Year, the most important holiday for the Chinese, the "福" character is posted everywhere. The meaning of this character is luck, blessing, happiness and good fortune. The character can be brush written or cut on red square paper; it is not only meaningful but also decorative.

One may be surprised to see that sometimes the "福" character is posted upside-down. Actually, this is to lead people to say "Fu is reversed" when they see the poster; "Fu is reversed," or "Fú dào le（福到了）" in Chinese, is the homophone meaning "Good fortune has come" or "Fortune is here."

The story about the upside-down "福" character comes from the Qing Dynasty (1644-1911). While preparing for the Lunar New Year, the steward of a prince had brush-written several large "福" characters and asked one of the pages to post them out on the gates and doors. Because the page was illiterate, he accidentally put the character in the upside-down position. The princess was so upset that she ordered the page to be punished. At this moment, the steward, who wanted to protect the young man, kneeled and said to his mistress: "My respectful princess, don't you think that this reversed "福" character is even more meaningful?" "How?" asked the princess. "When our guests see this character, they would certainly say: "Fu is upside-down!" That sounds like: Gook luck and happiness are here. Don't you think this is a clever way to post the '福' character?"

The prince, who had just arrived, heard the conversation, loved the steward's explanation, and rewarded both the steward and the page for the beautiful mistake which has become a tradition that remains part of Chinese culture to this day.

第六课 你们在中文课上做什么?
What Do You Do in Chinese Class?

九、自我测试 Self Assessment

1. 谁在说话?
   Who is speaking?

(1) 周末你来我家，我们一起做中文对话，好吗?
　　　　　　　　　　　　　_____在说话。

(2) 孩子们，快点! 现在都七点半了，我们得去学校了。
　　　　　　　　　　　　　_____在说话。

(3) 下个星期三我给你们一个小测验；你们有问题吗?
　　　　　　　　　　　　　_____在说话。

(4) 安竹，你什么时候来北卡 (North Carolina)? 我和你爷爷都想你!
　　　　　　　　　　　　　_____在说话。

(5) 文娣，你有时间和我一起做这个练习吗?
　　　　　　　　　　　　　_____在说话。

(6) 老师，现在您有时间吗? 我想问您两个问题。
　　　　　　　　　　　　　_____在说话。

(7) 哥哥，今天是你的生日，我和爸爸妈妈祝你生日快乐!
　　　　　　　　　　　　　_____在说话。

(8) 现在我做饭，你去做作业。你做完作业我们就吃晚饭，好不好?
　　　　　　　　　　　　　_____在说话。

2. 请用中文回答下列问题。
　 Answer the following questions using Chinese.

(1) 在学校 (xuéxiào: school)，除了上课以外你们还有很多活动吗?

(2) 请你想一想，"课外活动"是什么意思?

(3) 你平时每天花多长时间学习汉语？有考试的时候你花多长时间？

(4) 你们平常 (or: 平时) 多长时间去一次爷爷奶奶家？

(5) 我听说王海生要来北京，你知道他哪天来，几点钟到，和谁一起来吗？

3. 对不对？
   Read the question (A) and the answer (B). Check "对" if you think the answer is logical with respect to the question or check "不对" otherwise.

(1) A. 我们学校高中一年级有一百八十二个学生；二年级有一百四十五个；三年级有一百一十一个学生。哪个年级学生最多？
    B. 高中一年级学生最多。   对_____ 不对_____

(2) A. 你妹妹是初中生还是高中生？
    B. 她是初中三年级的学生。   对_____ 不对_____

(3) A. 老师告诉你们什么？
    B. 我们告诉老师我们喜欢学习中文。   对_____ 不对_____

(4) A. 你们的中文课是高级班吗？
    B. 对，我们班有二十个学生。   对_____ 不对_____

(5) A. 你知道"学年"是什么意思吗？
    B. 知道，一个学年有两个学期。   对_____ 不对_____

(6) A. 我想卖这本书，你想买这本书吗？
    B. 想买，那我们两个人做一次买卖吧。   对_____ 不对_____

(7) A. 她花了多少钱 (qián: money) 买花？
    B. 这瓶花很漂亮。   对_____ 不对_____

(8) A. 老师要求我们做三个练习，
    这个要求高吗？
    B. 我看这个要求不高。　　　　对_____ 不对_____

(9) A. 今天的测验难吗？
    B. 不容易。我花了五十分钟做完的。对_____ 不对_____

(10) A. 他的工作是<u>写作</u> (creative writing)，
     这么说他是一个<u>作家</u> (writer)？
     B. 你说对了。　　　　　　　　对_____ 不对_____

4. 阅读下列段落之后用中文回答问题。
   Answer the question using Chinese after reading the following paragraph.

   我<u>认为</u> (rèn wéi: to think, to consider) <u>花小莉</u> (Shirley Howell) 是我们汉语课上最好的学生。和我们一样，今年是她第一年学习汉语。现在她差不多认识三百个汉字。她的中文发音很好；她写的汉字也漂亮。除了在中文课上以外，她课下也常常和同学们说汉语。有时候她给朋友<u>留言</u> (to leave message) 也<u>用</u> (yòng: to use) 中文。花小莉本人说："我天天花很多时间学习汉语，因为我喜欢学习这门语言。我打算明年去中国留学。"老师和同学们都说她是一个好学生。

   为什么"我"认为花小莉是一个好学生？请说出三个理由。
   Why do "I" think Shirley Howell is a good student? Give out three reasons.

   _____
   _____
   _____

5. 小作文：请你在下面的三个题目中选择一个，写一个一百字左右的小作文。
   Mini-composition: choose one from the following topics and write a mini-composition of (about) 100 characters.

   (1) 你们在中文课上做什么？
   (2) 请你说说你这个学期的课。
   (3) 明年你要去中国学习汉语，<u>将</u> (jiāng: will) 住在黄新明家里。现在请你用中文给他写<u>一封信</u> (yī fēng xìn: a letter)。

我的题目 (My topic):

_____

_____

_____

_____

_____

_____

_____

_____

_____

_____

第七课
LESSON SEVEN

下课以后
After Class

学习目的
Learning Objectives

听懂老师留作业	To understand homework assignments
请求允许	To ask for permission
回敬谢意	To respond to "thank you"
向别人借东西用	To borrow things from people
用"以前"和"以后"叙事	To express "before" and "after"

本课学习内容 Contents of the chapter

一	发音复习 Pronunciation Review	
二	课文：下课以后 Text: After Class	
三	生词 Vocabulary	
	■ 名词 nouns：铃、词汇、听写、故事、蓝冬冬、办公室、事、问题、马可明、乒乓球、手机、早上、威利、电话、昨天、图书馆、前、篮球、号码	
	■ 动词 verbs：下课、响、复习、回答、交、可以、找、问、等、玩儿、走、能、用、出门、忘、带、约、接、比赛、怕、记住、应该、让	
	■ 代词 pronouns：自己、咱们	
	■ 形容词 adjectives：口头、笔头、糟糕	
	■ 副词 adverbs：另外、急忙、按时、可能、只好	
	■ 介词 prepositions：后面、以前（之前）、以后（之后）	
	■ 连词 conjunctions：不然	
	■ 词句 expressions：课下、不客气、怎么办	
四	数字复习 Study of Numbers: Review	
五	语法 Grammar	
	■ 动词"会"	The verb "会"
	■ "以前"和"以后"（"之前"和"之后"）	"以前" and "以后" ("之前" and "之后")
	■ 代词"自己"	The pronoun "自己"
	■ "让"、"不让"和"没让"的用法	The usage of "让," "不让" and "没让"
	■ 再谈副词"就"	More about the adverb "就"
	■ 动词"找"	The verb "找"
六	练习 Exercises	
七	读报 Newspaper Reading	
八	文化点滴 Culture Notes	
九	自我测试 Self Assessment	

第七课 下课以后
After Class

一、语音复习 Pronunciation Review

Drill 1

b +
ái (白)	àng (棒)	ǎo (饱)	ēi (杯)	èn (笨)
ǐ (笔)	iān (边)	iǎo (表)	īn (宾)	īng (兵)
ō (波)	ù (不)	iē (憋)	èng (蹦)	ǎn (板)

Drill 2

c +
ā (擦)	āi (猜)	án (残)	áng (藏身)	ǎo (草)
è (册)	ēn (参差)	éng (曾经)	í (词)	ōng (匆)
òu (凑)	ū (粗)	uì (脆)	ùn (寸)	uō (搓)
uàn (篡)	āng (苍)	ì (次)	èng (蹭)	ūn (村)

Drill 3

ch +
à (岔)	āi (拆)	án (蝉)	àng (唱)	āo (超)
ē (车)	én (陈)	éng (成)	ī (吃)	ǒng (宠)
óu (仇)	ú (除)	uài (踹)	uān (川)	uǎng (闯)
ūn (春)	óng (虫)	uí (垂)	uò (辍)	è (撤)
ū (出)	ǐ (尺)	ún (纯)	uī (吹)	á (茶)
ǎo (吵)	uàn (串)	ù (处)	ǒu (丑)	óng (虫)

Drill 4

d +
á (达)	ǎi (歹)	ān (担保)	ǎng (档)	ào (到)
é (得失)	ěi (得亏)	ēng (灯)	í (敌)	iàn (电)
iǎ (嗲)	iǎn (点)	iào (掉)	ié (蝶)	ǐng (鼎)
iū (丢)	ǒng (懂)	ōu (都是)	ú (独)	uǎn (短)
uì (对)	ùn (顿)	uō (多)	āi (呆)	de (的)

Drill 5

ā (阿姨)	āi (哎)	ǎn (俺)	áng (昂)	ào (傲)
ē (阿胶)	é (额)	ě (恶心)	è (饿)	
ēn (恩)	ér (儿)	ěr (耳)	èr (二月)	

二、课文 Text

下课以后

老　师：同学们，下课铃响了，今天的课就上到这里。课下请你们自己复习词汇，明天我给你们听写。另外，你们的口头作业是读一百零二页的小故事；笔头作业是回答故事后面的问题。明天上课之前交笔头作业。

蓝冬冬：老师，今天下午您有时间吗？我可以去您的办公室吗？
(Winter Lamb)

老　师：三点半以后我会在办公室的。你找我有什么事？

蓝冬冬：我想问您几个问题。

老　师：好，你来吧，我等你。

蓝冬冬：谢谢老师！

老　师：不客气。

第七课 下课以后
After Class

马可明：冬冬，咱们去玩儿乒乓球，怎么样？
(Kim Maas)

蓝冬冬：走吧。

马可明：我能不能用一下儿你的手机？

蓝冬冬：你的(手机)呢？

马可明：今天早上我急急忙忙出门，忘了带手机。我想给我弟弟威利(Willie)打一个电话。

蓝冬冬：你有什么急事？

马可明：昨天我们约好在图书馆门前等妈妈来接我们。可是我刚想起来今天我有篮球比赛，不能按时回家，我怕他和妈妈等我。

蓝冬冬：给你，我的手机，你打吧！

马可明：糟糕，他的电话号码在我的手机里，我没记住。怎么办？

蓝冬冬：你不应该叫马可明，应该叫马大哈！让我看看，我的手机里可能有他的号码。不然，你只好给你妈妈打电话了。

課文

下課以後

老　　師：同學們,下課鈴響了,今天的課就上到這裏。課下請你們自己復習詞匯,明天我給你們聽寫。另外,你們的口頭作業是讀一百零二頁的小故事;筆頭作業是回答故事後面的問題。明天上課之前交筆頭作業。

藍冬冬 (Winter Lamb)：老師,今天下午您有時間嗎?我可以去您的辦公室嗎?

老　　師：三點半以後我會在辦公室的。你找我有什麼事?

藍冬冬：我想問您幾個問題。

老　　師：好,你來吧,我等你。

藍冬冬：謝謝老師!

老　　師：不客氣。

第七课 下课以后
After Class

馬可明：冬冬，咱們去玩兒乒乓球，怎麼樣？
(Kim Maas)

藍冬冬：走吧。

馬可明：我能不能用一下兒你的手機？

藍冬冬：你的(手機)呢？

馬可明：今天早上我急急忙忙出門，忘了帶手機。我想給我弟弟威利(Willie)打一個電話。

藍冬冬：你有什麼急事？

馬可明：昨天我們約好在圖書館門前等媽媽來接我們。可是我剛想起來今天我有籃球比賽，不能按時回家，我怕他和媽媽等我。

藍冬冬：給你，我的手機，你打吧！

馬可明：糟糕，他的電話號碼在我的手機裏，我沒記住。怎麼辦？

藍冬冬：你不應該叫馬可明，應該叫馬大哈！讓我看看，我的手機裏可能有他的號碼。不然，你祇好給你媽媽打電話了。

三、生词 Vocabulary

NOUNS

líng 铃 (鈴) bell	cíhuì 词汇 (詞匯) vocabulary
tīngxiě 听写 (聽寫) dictation	gùshi 故事 (故事) story, tale
Lán Dōngdong 蓝冬冬 (藍冬冬) Winter Lamb	dōng 冬：winter
	lán 蓝 (藍) blue, indigo plant, a surname
bàngōngshì 办公室 (辦公室) office	bàngōng 办公 (辦公) to handle business, to work in an office
	shì 室：room
shì 事 (事) matter, affair, thing, business	wèntí 问题 (問題) question
Mǎ Kěmíng 马可明 (馬可明) Kim Maas	mǎ 马 (馬) horse, a surname
pīngpāngqiú 乒乓球 (乒乓球) table tennis, ping-pong	
shǒujī 手机 (手機) mobile phone, cell phone	shǒu 手：hand
	jī 机 (機) machine, engine
zǎoshang 早上 (早上) early morning	wēilì 威利 (威利) Willie
diànhuà 电话 (電話) telephone	diàn 电 (電) electricity, power
zuótiān 昨天 (昨天) yesterday	
túshūguǎn 图书馆 (圖書館) library	guǎn 馆 (館) accommodation for guests, shop, a place for cultural activities

第七课 下课以后
After Class

qián 前 (前) front, ahead	
lánqiú 篮球 (籃球) basketball	lán 篮 (籃)：basket
hàomǎ 号码 (號碼) number	mǎdàhā 马大哈 (馬大哈)：a careless person, a forgetful person

VERBS

xià kè
下课/下課 to finish attending (or teaching) a class

xiǎng
响/響 to ring, to make sound

fùxí
复习/復習 to review

huídá
回答/回答 to answer, to respond

jiāo
交/交 to hand over, to turn in

kěyǐ
可以/可以 may, can, to be able

wèn
问/問 to ask

děng
等/等 to wait, to wait for

wánr
玩儿/玩兒 to play, to have fun

zǒu
走/走 to walk, to go, to go away

néng
能/能 to be able, can

yòng
用/用 to use, to employ

chūmén
出门/出門 to be away from home, to go out

wàng
忘/忘 to forget

dài
带/帶 to take with, to bring with

yuē
约/約 to make an appointment

jiē
接/接 to meet, to receive, to pick up

bǐsài
比赛/比賽 to compete

pà
怕/怕 to be afraid of, to fear

jìzhù
记住/記住 to remember, to bear in mind

yīnggāi
应该/應該 should, ought

ràng
让/讓 to let, to allow

239

zìjǐ
自己/自己 self, oneself

zánmen
咱们/咱們 we (dialect: including both the speaker and listener)

ADJECTIVES

kǒutóu
口头/口頭 oral

bǐtóu
笔头/筆頭 written

zāogāo
糟糕/糟糕 terrible, too bad

ADVERBS

lìngwài
另外/另外 besides, in addition to

jímáng
急忙/急忙 in a hurry, hastily

ànshí
按时/按時 on time, on schedule

kěnéng
可能/可能 probably

zhǐhǎo
只好/祇好 to have to

PREPOSITIONS

hòumian
后面/後面 behind, at the back

zhīqián (yǐqián)
之前 (以前)/之前 (以前) before, prior

yǐhòu (zhīhòu)
以后 (之後)/以後 (之後) after, hereafter

CONJUNCTIONS

bùrán
不然/不然 if not, otherwise

EXPRESSIONS

kèxià
课下/課下 after class

bù kèqi (bié kèqi)
不客气 (别客气)/不客氣 (別客氣) you are welcome

zěnmebàn
怎么办/怎麼辦 what to do

四、数字复习 Study of Numbers: Review

1. 请用中文读下面的数字。
   Read the following numbers using Chinese.

2508	1136	8271	4055	1938
2991	7089	3295	1001	9999

2. 请读下面的句子。
   Read the following sentences.

   (1) 今年是二零一二年。
   (2) 张大千是一八九九年生人。
   (3) 我是一九九六年生人。
   (4) 《九三年》是一本法国小说 (novel)。
   (5) 长城有两千多年历史了。

3. 请用中文回答下面的问题。
   Answer the following questions using Chinese.

   1) 今年是哪(一)年?

   2) 你是哪年出生的?

   3) 你爸爸是哪年出生的?

   4) 你妈妈呢?她是哪年出生的?

五、语法 Grammar

1. 动词 "会" The Verb "会"

As a verb, the word "会" can be used in two different situations and expresses different meanings.

A. when followed by a verb with or without an object, "会" means "to know how to do something;"

我会打篮球。
I know how to play basketball.

他不会做蛋糕。
He doesn't know how to make a cake.

你会写汉字吗?
Do you know how to write Chinese characters?

我会写。
Yes, I do.

他们会_____。

她会 _____。

第七课 下课以后
After Class

她们会 ＿＿＿＿＿＿＿＿＿＿＿＿。

B. When followed by a verb (with or without an object) or a prepositional phrase and the particle "的" (except in a question) at the very end of the sentence, the word "会" indicates a kind of certainty.

你们会帮助 (bāngzhù) 他吗?
Are you going to help him?

我们会帮助他的。
We will help him for sure.

可明会来上海吗?
Will Kim come to Shanghai?

他会来的。
He will come.

他会告诉你吗?
Will he tell you.

他不会告诉我的。
He won't tell me.

练习一

1. 请按照例句做对话。
   Make conversation following the model.

    你会打 (or: 玩儿) 篮球吗?

    会打 (or: 玩儿)。

你常常打 (or: 玩儿) 吗?

 我一个星期打 (or: 玩儿) 三次。

 你常常和谁一起打 (or: 玩儿)?

 我有时候和朋友一起打 (or: 玩儿)，有时候和同学一起打 (or: 玩儿)。

如果你不会打篮球：

 你会打篮球吗?

 我不会打。你能教我吗?

 没问题。

开文在玩儿足 (zú: foot) 球。

(1) 篮球
(2) 乒乓球
(3) 网 (wǎng) 球 tennis
(4) 高尔夫 (gāo'ěrfū) 球 golf
(5) 保龄 (bǎolíng) 球 bowling

2. 请按照例句做对话。
   Make conversation following the model.

 你打算买这本书吗?

 我会买的。

 你打算什么时候买?

 我打算下个星期买。

第七课 下课以后
After Class

(1) 你打算上物理课吗？　　　　　　（下个学期）
(2) 你打算做蛋糕吗？　　　　　　　（明天）
(3) 你朋友打算来北京学汉语吗？　　（明年）
(4) 你们打算去长城吗？　　　　　　（下个星期六）
(5) 你打算做长寿面吗？　　　　　　（爷爷生日那天）
(6) 你打算做这个练习吗？　　　　　（现在）

2. "以前"和"以后"（"之前"和"之后"） "以前" and "以后" ("之前" and "之后")

"以前" and "以后" are prepositions meaning "before" and "after" respectively. Unlike the two prepositions in English, they are always preceded by a noun, a verb, or a sentence to express time or order.

A. noun + "以前" or "以后"

新年之前妈妈买了很多贺年卡。
Mom bought a lot of greeting cards before the New Year.

爸爸十二点钟以后吃中午饭。
Dad has lunch after twelve o'clock.

B. verb + "以前" or "以后"

打电话以前我得问一下他的号码。
I have to ask his number before I make the phone call.

下课之后请你们交作业。
Please turn in your homework after class.

C. sentence + "以前" or "以后"

他来我家之前给我打了一个电话。
He called me before coming to my home.

她去中国以后我给她写了两封信(fēng xìn)。
I wrote her twice after she went to China.

练习二

请按照例句做对话。
Make conversation following the model.

 你上课之前还是上课之后给你妈妈打电话？

我上课之前打,因为上课以后老师不让学生们打电话。

(1) 你吃饭以前还是吃饭以后做作业?
(2) 你们三点钟以前还是三点钟以后打乒乓球?
(3) 你们打算学习语法之前还是学习语法之后读课文?
(4) 你们听写之前还是听写之后做练习?
(5) 你下课之前还是下课之后问老师问题?
(6) 你打开书以前还是打开书以后回答问题?
(7) 你回家以前还是回家以后给我打电话?
(8) 你们去北京之前还是去北京之后找这个人?
(9) 你们考试之前还是考试之后去图书馆?
(10) 你们十点钟以前还是十点钟以后有时间?

3. 代词"自己" The Pronoun "自己"

自己吃　　　　　自己唱　　　　　自己玩儿

The word "自己" is the pronoun "oneself" and at the same time the equivalent to the possessive adjective "one's own" in English. The only way to identify which definition of the word is to see what follows the word "自己."

A. 自己 + verb = pronoun

他可以自己去西安(Xī'ān)。
He can travel to Xi'an by himself.

我自己还不知道,怎么告诉你?
I don't even know (it) myself, so how can I tell you?

你自(己)学英语?
You study English yourself?

B. 自己 + 的 + noun = possessive adjective

这是安娜自己的打算。
This is Anna's own plan.

这不是图书馆的书,是我自己的。
This is not the library's book; it's my own.

练习三

1. 请按照例句做对话。
   Make conversation following the model.

    你和谁一起做练习?

    我自己做。

    "自己做"是什么意思?

    "自己做"的意思是"我一个人做"。

   (1) 去北京　　　　(2) 写作业
   (3) 练习生词　　　(4) 吃晚饭
   (5) 做蛋糕　　　　(6) 听音乐
   (7) 找律师　　　　(8) 去长城

2. 请采访两个同学:问他们喜欢自己做什么事。然后把你和两个同学都喜欢自己做的事用中文写下来。
   Interview two of your classmates to find out the things that they enjoy doing themselves and then write out using Chinese the common things that the three of you enjoy doing yourselves.

   我们三个人都喜欢自己做的事:

   (1) _____ (2) _____

   (3) _____ (4) _____

   (5) _____ (6) _____

3. 请按照例句做对话。
   Make conversation following the model.

    这是学校的篮球吗？ 不是，这是我自己的篮球。

   (1) 你姐姐的书　　　(2) 你爸爸妈妈的想法 (idea, opinion)
   (3) 大家的事　　　　(4) 图书馆的书
   (5) 你朋友的手机　　(6) 你同学的笔记本 (notebook)
   (7) 老师的笔　　　　(8) 你哥哥的看法 (viewpoint, way of thinking)
   (9) 你弟弟的作业　　(10) 马可明的回答

4. "让"、"不让"、"没让"的用法　The Usage of "让," "不让" and "没让"

The verb "让" in the affirmative form means "to ask someone to do something."

妈妈让我给她打电话。
Mom asks / asked me to call her.

老师让我们做练习。
The teacher asks / asked us to do exercises.

你让他干什么？
What do / did you ask him to do?

The negative form "不让" means "to not allow someone to do something."

老师不让我们说英语，所以我们只能说汉语。
The teacher does not allow us to speak English, so we can only speak Chinese.

他们不让我去上海。
They do not allow me to go to Shanghai.

"没让" can mean "did not ask" or "did not allow." One should examine the context before making the translation.

我妈妈没让我去她的办公室。
My mom did not ask me to go to her office.
My mom did not allow me to go to her office.

Note that when the context is clear, "不让" can be used instead of "没让" to

express the meaning "did not allow or did not ask."

今天上午你为什么没来我家?
Why didn't you come to my home this morning?

因为我妈妈没让我来。or: 因为我妈妈不让我来。
Because my mother didn't allow me to come.

练习四

1. 请按照例句做对话。
   Make conversation following the model.

    昨天你为什么没来和我们打篮球?

    因为我妈妈没 (or: 不) 让我来。

   (1) 你没打开书　　　　　(2) 昨天你没来我家
   (3) 你没用他的手机　　　(4) 他们没用英文写作业
   (5) 你没有买电话卡　　　(6) 下课以后同学们没打乒乓球
   (7) 你没去老师的办公室　(8) 你不去北京学习中文
   (9) 你不用中文回答问题　(10) 你们为什么不给我打电话

2. 上中文课的时候老师让你们做什么? 不让你们做什么? 请你和一个同学一起把每种情况列举三件。
   In Chinese class, what does your teacher ask (or allow) you to do? What does he/she not allow you to do? Work with a classmate to find and write out three examples for each case.

老师让我们	老师不让我们
(1)	(1)
(2)	(2)
(3)	(3)

249

5. 再谈副词 "就" More about the Adverb "就"

"就" is a multi-function word. It can be used as an adverb, conjunction or preposition. Even as an adverb, "就" is still different from other adverbs because an adverb normally is used to indicate one of the following: manner, time, place, and degree, etc., while "就" can be used to stress more than one of those factors. For example:

Manner

我弟弟吃饭就是快。
My brother eats really fast.

他们就大声说话,你怎么办?
They speak loud no matter what, what can you do (about it)?

Time

今天的课就上到这里。
We stop here (with our class) today.

我现在就告诉你。
I can tell you right now.

你什么时候来?
When will you come?

我马上就来。
I'm coming right now.

Place

练习五在哪儿?
Where is exercise five?

就在第三十页。
It's right on page 30.

问题在哪里?
Where is the problem?

问题就在这里。
The problem is right here.

练习五

1. 请重写每个句子,并把"就"字加在正确的地方。
   Rewrite each sentence by adding the character "就" in the right place.

第七课 下课以后
After Class

(1) 我们现在做练习。

(2) 他明天去上海。

(3) 这是我们的问题。

(4) 今天的练习我们做到这儿。

(5) 我们明天期末 (end of semester) 考试。

(6) 图书馆在那儿。

(7) 下个星期一是何文英的生日。

(8) 孩子们马上来。

(9) 我找你。

(10) 练习二在四十五页。

6. 动词 "找" The Verb "找"

Although the direct meaning for the verb "找" is "to look for," "to want to see," or "to seek," sometimes these may not be the best translation. The following sentences will help better understand the verb under different situations.

To look for

你在找什么？
What are you looking for?

我在找我的笔。
I'm looking for my pen.

你在找谁?
Whom are you looking for?

我在找我朋友。你知道他去哪了吗?
I'm looking for my friend. Do you know where he went?

To want to see

谁找我?
Who wants to see me?

律师。
The lawyer.

您找我爸爸? 对不起,今天他不在家。
You want to see my father? Sorry, he is not home today.

To come to somebody

你找他做什么?
What led you to him?

我找他做练习。
I come to do the exercises with him.

你找我有什么事?
What can I do for you?

练习六

请按照例句做对话。
Make conversation following the model.

 请问,<u>小姐</u> (miss, young lady),您找谁?

 我找李文能<u>先生</u> (xiānsheng: mister),他在吗?

 您和他约好了吗?

 我昨天打电话和他约好了,今天上午九点一刻在他的办公室见面。

 请问,您<u>贵姓</u> (guì xìng: surname)?

 我姓谢,叫谢小英。

第七课 下课以后
After Class

 好，请您等一下。

 谢谢您。

(1) 我是谢小英 / 我找李文能先生
(2) 我是史冬明 / 我找贺赛莉小姐 (miss, young lady)
(3) 我是马文会 / 我找钟一复先生
(4) 我是王育美 / 我找习文之先生
(5) 我是张以来 / 我找江会新小姐
(6) 我是李天容 / 我找蓝自书先生
(7) 我是安习艺 / 我找马小妹女士 (nǚshì: lady, madam. A polite way to address a woman, married or unmarried.)
(8) 我是何思亮 / 我找刘之利先生
(9) 我是贺同政 / 我找马可明先生
(10) 我是刘来喜 / 我找周文娣女士

请问，您找谁？   请问，何先生在吗？

请问，您是周女士吗？

六、练习 Exercises

模式练习 Model exercises

1. 请你读下面的句子，想一想每个句子里的"问题"是什么意思；然后用中文解释。如果句子是一个问题，请用中文回答问题。
   Read the following sentences, try to understand, and explain using Chinese the meaning of the word "问题" in each. If the sentence is a question, answer it using Chinese.

   (1) 在中文课上，哪个学生老是 (always) 有很多问题？

   (2) 你有没有手机？没有手机是不是一个大问题？

   (3) 有问题的时候你们去老师的办公室吗？

   (4) 他们今天有一个小问题，明天有一个小问题；小问题多了就是大问题。

   (5) 我想问您几个问题，可以吗？没问题，你问吧。

   (6) 同学们，请你们用中文回答我的问题。

   (7) 大学四年级的学生们开始想找工作的问题。

   (8) 你们之间 (between, among) 有问题吗？

   (9) 外国人学习中文，语音是一个大问题吗？

第七课 下课以后
After Class

(10) 昨天的历史课考试有五个大问题,有多少个小问题?

2. 请三个同学一组,按照下面的两个步骤完成任务。
   Work in groups of three: complete the task by following the two steps.

   a) 问左边的组员下面的问题,同时把他／她的回答记下来;
   Ask the group member to your left the following questions and take note of his / her answers;

   (1) 你觉得上课的时候可以打电话吗?

   (2) 你认为 (to think) 听写的时候可以看同学写的字吗?

   (3) 你觉得做作业的时候可以听音乐吗?

   (4) 上课的时候可以问老师问题吗?可以做笔记 (take notes) 吗?可以和同学说话吗?可以看照片吗?可以不听老师说话吗?可以不回答老师的问题吗?

   (5) 你觉得在图书馆里可以打电话吗?可以唱歌吗?

   (6) 你认为考试的时候可以看笔记吗?可以看书吗?

   (7) 作为 (as) 一个学生,你可以天天都不来上课吗?你可以不交作业吗?

   (8) 考试之前你可以自己复习吗?

(9) 我来你家之前不打电话，可以吗？

(10) 你可以在地理课上看中文课的书吗？

b) 然后用第三人称把左边同学的回答告诉右边的同学。
and then report the information you collected from the answers to the classmate to your right using a third person subject (he or she).

Model:

他 / 她觉得……

3. 请按照例子做小对话。
Compose mini-dialogues following the model.

A. 你常常忘记做什么事？
B. 我常常忘记带书和笔。

(1) 看篮球比赛   (2) 给朋友们回电话
(3) 写日记 (diary)   (4) 交作业
(5) 带电话   (6) 做自我介绍 (self introduction)
(7) 做作业   (8) 复习生词
(9) 问问题   (10) 在书上写我的名字

4. (做这个活动的时候你们可以打开手机) 四个同学一组完成下面的任务：每个人都问自己左边的同学有没有手机，如果有，问他 / 她的电话号码是多少。听的时候请把号码记下来。然后把这个号码告诉 (请不要给他 / 她看) 你右边的同学，并让他 / 她用这个号码打一个电话。
(You are allowed to use your mobile phone during this exercise): Work in groups of four: take turns to ask the group member to your left whether he / she has a mobile phone, and if so, what his or her phone number is. Take note of the phone number you hear. Then, tell (not show) the number to the group member to your right and ask him / her to call this number.

Note that in a phone, room or street number, number 1 is pronounced 'yāo' instead of 'yī.'

Model:

问你左边的同学 Ask the classmate to your left:

A. 安娜，你有手机吗？

B. 我有手机。

A. 你能不能告诉我你的手机号码是多少？

B. 我可以告诉你。我的号码是：243 - 178 - 1511

A. 谢谢你。

告诉你右边的同学 Tell the classmate to your right:

A. 大卫，请你记一下，安娜的手机号码是：243 - 178 - 1511

B. 我记下来了 (I got it)。

A. 现在请你给安娜打一个电话。

B. 好，我试试。

5. 请你用下面的问题采访一个同学，并把他 / 她的回答写下来。
Interview one classmate with the following questions and write down his / her answers using Chinese.

(1) 你记住我的名字了吗？

(2) 你记住了几个中国地名 (places' names)?

(3) 你朋友在哪里接你？时间、地点 (place) 你都记住了吗？

(4) 你记住我的电话号码了吗？

(5) 你一天能记住多少个生词？

(6) 那个医生说什么了？你记住了吗？

(7) 老师给咱们留什么作业了？谁记住了吗？

(8) 我告诉你了我家有几口人，你记住了吗？

(9) 你记住朋友的生日了吗？是几月几号？

(10) 这一课的生词你记住了多少个？

6. 和一个同学一起做下面的练习：请你们轮流读下面的问题 (A) 与回答 (B)，然后两个人一起决定每个回答是否正确。如果你们的选择是"不对"，请说出正确的答案。
Work in pairs: take turns to read the question (A) and the answer (B) and together decide whether each answer is logical with respect to the question. Find the correct answer if you check "不对."

(1) A. 下课以后你去哪儿？
　　B. 我去图书馆。
　　　　　　　　　　　　　　　　　　对__✓__ 不对____

(2) A. 你每次出门都带你的手机吗？
　　B. 我很喜欢我的手机。
　　　　　　　　　　　　　　　　　　对____ 不对____

(3) A. 明天你们有篮球比赛？
　　B. 对。所以今天我们得练习(篮球)。
　　　　　　　　　　　　　　　　　　对____ 不对____

(4) A. 你几点钟去老师的办公室问问题？
　　B. 我和老师约好了。
　　　　　　　　　　　　　　　　　　对____ 不对____

(5) A. 你忘了带手机？
　　B. 没忘。你看，我的手机在这儿。
　　　　　　　　　　　　　　　　　　对____ 不对____

(6) A. 昨天你用了多长时间做经济课的作业?
　　B. 我用了五十多分钟。
　　　　　　　　　　　　　对_____ 不对_____

(7) A. 你怕谁?
　　B. 我怕我的数学课老师。
　　　　　　　　　　　　　对_____ 不对_____

(8) A. 这是你自己的书还是图书馆的书?
　　B. 图书馆里有很多书。
　　　　　　　　　　　　　对_____ 不对_____

实况演练 Real situation exercises

你觉得这个人现在应该打手机吗?

1. 两个人一组：从下面的十个题中选择五个按照例句完成任务：我应该怎么办？请你用中文告诉我。
   Work in pairs to accomplish the tasks for five of the following ten questions: tell me what I should do in this situation using Chinese.

Model:
　　明天我有数学考试，我怕考不好。
　　今天你应该好好复习；有问题问老师，明天你会考好的。

(1) 明天我要给朋友过生日，我怕做蛋糕做不好。
请你告诉我：

(2) 我和马可明约好今天下午 4:20 打篮球。可是我有很多作业，不能去，我怕他等我。
请你告诉我：

(3) 上个星期我告诉奶奶这个周末我去看她。可是这个周末我有一个活动，不能去看奶奶了，我怕她不<u>高兴</u> (gāoxìng: happy)。
请你告诉我：

(4) 今天老师给我们留了很多作业，我怕做不完。
请你告诉我：

(5) 今天在中文课上老师教了二十个生词，我怕明天有听写。
请你告诉我：

(6) 我应该三点十分在图书馆<u>门前</u> (in front of) 和我的同学们见面。现在三点二十了，我还没到。我怕他们不等我。
请你告诉我：

第七课　下课以后
After Class

(7) 今天我们有物理课，可是我忘了带书。我怕老师说 (to blame, to scold) 我。

请你告诉我：

(8) 今天我的中文生词听写得 (dé: to obtain, to get) 了50分，我怕妈妈说我。

请你告诉我：

(9) 老师让我们用中文做自我介绍，我怕说不好。

请你告诉我：

(10) 我想和蓝冬冬、马可明交朋友 (to make friends)，可是我怕他们不喜欢我。

请你告诉我：

9. 比赛。

Competition.

(1) 两个学生一组，按照下面的步骤进行比赛：
Work in pairs and participate in the competition by following each of the steps:

第一步：从下面的题目中选择一个，用五分钟写一个小对话。
Step1: Use five minutes to write a mini-dialogue on one of the following topics:

(1) 上课铃响了
(2) 下课铃响了
(3) 电话铃响了
(4) 门铃 (doorbell) 响了

第二步：用五分钟大声练习你们的小对话。
Step 2: Use five minutes to practice your dialogue aloud.

第三步：在全班人面前表演你们的对话。
Step 3: Present your dialogue in front of the class.

第四步：你们觉得哪个组的对话最好？按照下面的例句说说为什么。
Step 4: Work in pairs again: decide which dialogue you think is the best and explain why following the model sentences below.

我们觉得第一（二、三……）个对话最好，因为……
(1) 这个对话最长
(2) 这个对话的词汇量大 (large vocabulary)
(3) 这个对话的语法没有问题
(4) 这个对话有意思
(5) 这两个对话人的中文发音好
(6) 他们的对话很容易，我们都能听明白

10. 两个人一组：用中文讲故事："谁是马大哈？"先按照下面的问题写自己的故事，然后把你的故事讲给对方听。
Work in pairs: tell a story in Chinese: "谁是马大哈？" First, write out your own story by answering the following questions and then tell it to your partner.

你认识一个马大哈吗？这个马大哈是谁？是你哥哥？姐姐？弟弟？妹妹？还是你自己？这个马大哈常常忘什么事？他/她忘大事还是忘小事？他/她是不是大事小事都忘？请你用中文告诉大家这个马大哈的故事。

七、读 报　Newspaper Reading

How Many Characters Do You Know?

1. Read the following article.
2. While reading, underline the characters you know.

手机没电之后

赵 朋

周末，约好去朋友家聚会，忘了她家的具体地址，到了那片儿，我赶紧掏出手机打电话："我快到了，你家在几号……"话还没说完，手机没电了。

还好路边一个报摊上摆着一部电话。卖报的是个老头儿，我连忙上去："大爷，我用一下电话。"谁知老头儿拿了张报纸就把电话盖上了："这电话不能用。"我心中一愣，明明电话摆在这嘛，我只好堆起满脸的笑："大爷，我真有急事，我知道你这不是公用电话。这样，我给您双倍的钱打一个行不？"不料，老头儿腾地站起来，怒气冲冲道："你这是干啥？以为我在勒索你？告诉你，这儿没电话！"

正吵着，过来一位包着头巾的姑娘，袅袅婷婷地走到老头儿跟前，娇声道："大爷，我打个电话！"老头儿本来怒气冲冲的脸一下子像盛开的菊花，立马把报纸从电话机上拿开，连声道："好好，你打，你打。"说完，从桌边绕出来，还搬了个凳子给姑娘。那姑娘坐在桌边拿起电话就聊开了："喂，老公啊，今晚，我给你做红烧肉吃啊，我用小火给你慢慢地炖，炖到八成熟，我再给你放作料，什么葱啊，姜啊，香菜啊，对了，你不愿吃太烂的，我早早给你盛出来，等你回来吃，你说好不好……"那姑娘打起电话没完没了，我在边上把肚子都气炸了，这叫什么事，明明有电话，不让我打，见了人家姑娘就眉开眼笑，还搬凳子给人家坐，这个老头是不是有点儿那个呀。

姑娘啰啰嗦嗦总算打完了，却还是坐在桌边不走，好像还有什么事情忘了说。我一个箭步上去就按住了电话："大爷，您也别太那个了吧，你不能让姑娘打，不让男人打啊！"老头儿腾地一下红了脸："你个小子，想哪儿去了？好好，你打你打！"我心下不由微微得意，不抓着他痛处今儿这电话肯定打不成了。我抓起电话，咦，连拨号音都没有！一看电话机根本没有电话线！

"那这姑娘……"我结结巴巴地问老头儿，老头儿长叹了一口气："她是个疯子！她每天晚上都要上这儿来打电话，这部电话就是为她准备的！"

姑娘的丈夫是个消防战士，在一次救火中牺牲了。丈夫是在一次晚饭前接到命令的，那晚，她为丈夫做了他最爱吃的红烧肉，因为那天是丈夫的生日。可惜丈夫这一走，就再也没有回来。受到刺激的她一下子神经失常了，原先这个地方的报摊确实有个公用电话，她的新家就离报摊不远，有时候她会在这里给丈夫打电话，自从丈夫走了，她几乎每天晚上都来这儿打电话，而且内容永远都是红烧肉……

老头儿抹抹眼角："以后这报摊儿的主人也去干别的了，我就接了他的报摊，为的就是这位姑娘，只不过电话没线而已，我是害怕她再伤心……"我张大嘴："大爷，您是怎么知道她这些事的？"老大爷叹了口气："因为我就是她公公！自从她疯了后，就不认识我了，这孩子，心重，丈夫那晚没有吃上红烧肉，她疯了，还惦记着……"

选自：新民晚报　日期：2008年11月12日

3. Pronounce the characters you have recognized.
4. Tell the meaning of each character to your class (or study group).

八、文化点滴　Culture Notes

The Great Wall

The Great Wall of China, one of the greatest wonders of the world, is the symbol of China. Learning about the Great Wall will help you to learn a lot about Chinese history and culture. Please use an encyclopedia or websites as resources to find the answers to the following questions:

1. Who started building the Great Wall and why?
2. At what periods of time in the Chinese history had the Great Wall been rebuilt and restored?
3. Where is the starting point of the Great Wall and where does it end?
4. What is the length of the Great Wall?
5. What kind of materials were used to build the Great Wall?
6. What is the shape of the Great Wall? Make a drawing of the monument if you can.
7. Who is Meng Jiangnu (Mèng Jiāngnǚ:孟姜女)? And what does this person have to do with the Great Wall?
8. Can you find one or more poems in which the Great Wall has been mentioned?
9. Where can you go to visit the Great Wall in the Beijing area?
10. What is the literary translation of the word "长城"?

第七课 下课以后 After Class

九、自我测试 Self Assessment 9

1. 这是口头作业还是笔头作业？
Is this oral or written homework?

(1) 老师让我们读课文
这是 _____ 。

(2) 老师让大家写一个小对话
这是 _____ 。

(3) 老师让每个人讲 (jiǎng: to tell) 一个故事
这是 _____ 。

(4) 老师让每个学生说上个周末干什么了
这是 _____ 。

(5) 老师让我们用五分钟给朋友写一张生日卡
这是 _____ 。

(6) 老师让我们说说这个学期有什么课
这是 _____ 。

(7) 老师让每个学生说这个周末的打算
这是 _____ 。

(8) 老师让我们写作文 (composition)："你喜欢长城吗？"
这是 _____ 。

2. 请用"另外"把每个练习里的成分连成一个完整的句子。
For each of the following exercise, use "另外" to link the elements into a complete sentence.

(1) 下课以后我要去买书 / 找同学 / 去老师的办公室

(2) 爸爸生日那天 / 我给他买了生日卡 / 蛋糕 / 买了一本他喜欢的书

(3) 我打算去上海看家人 / 朋友 / 回学校去看看我的老师们

(4) 和我们一起去长城的有马可明 / 蓝冬冬 / 马可明的女朋友

(5) 在今天的中文课上 / 我们学了五个名词 / 三个动词 / 三个量词

3. 对不对？

   Read the question (A) and the answer (B). Check "对" if you think the answer is logical with respect to the question or check "不对" otherwise.

   (1) A. 你们找老师有什么事？
       B. 老师很忙。　　　　　　　　　　　　对＿＿＿　不对＿＿＿

   (2) A. 昨天你为什么没给我打电话？
       B. 对不起，我忘了。　　　　　　　　　对＿＿＿　不对＿＿＿

   (3) A. 明天你能按时来我的办公室吗？
       B. 我记住了。　　　　　　　　　　　　对＿＿＿　不对＿＿＿

   (4) A. 谁在图书馆门口等你？
       B. 我在那里等我弟弟。　　　　　　　　对＿＿＿　不对＿＿＿

   (5) A. 我能不能用一下你的手机？
       B. 对不起，你不能用，因为我的
          手机没有电了。　　　　　　　　　　对＿＿＿　不对＿＿＿

   (6) A. 你喜欢玩儿篮球还是乒乓球？
       B. 篮球和乒乓球我都喜欢玩儿。　　　　对＿＿＿　不对＿＿＿

   (7) A. 同学们，你们打开书第二十二
          页了吗？
       B. 糟糕！我忘了带书。　　　　　　　　对＿＿＿　不对＿＿＿

   (8) A. 你怕什么？
       B. 我怕我的物理课老师。　　　　　　　对＿＿＿　不对＿＿＿

第七课 下课以后
After Class

4. 在这些情况下你说什么？

Using Chinese, what would you say in each of the following situations?

(1) 你的同学们想和你一起打篮球，可是你没有时间。

(2) 你想用一下朋友的手机。

(3) 你想让同学们告诉你练习五在第几页。

(4) 你想知道同学的电话号码。

(5) 你想去老师的办公室问问题。

(6) 今天下午你要和同学一起打球。现在你想知道你的同学几点钟、在哪里等你。

5. 读下面的对话，然后用中文回答问题。

Read the following dialogue and answer questions using Chinese.

A. 你认识"时"和"刻"这两个字吗？

B. 认识。

A. 好。现在我们学习一个新词。

B. 什么新词？

A. "时刻"。

B. "时刻"是什么意思？

A. "时刻"的意思是"at anytime, always"。比如，我们时刻可以问老师问题。也可以说，我们时时刻刻能问老师问题。

B. 有意思。我们再学一个新词，怎么样？

A. 好。现在我问你认不认识这两个字："说话"？

B. 认识，"说话"的意思是"to talk, to speak"。

A. 那请你想一想"说大话"是什么意思。

B. 可能和英文一样，"说大话"的意思是"talk big"，对吗。

A. 对。你再想想下面的话是什么意思："他说话不算话。"
B. 我不知道这是什么意思。你告诉我吧。
A. 好。这句话的意思是："He doesn't keep his word."
B. 那可以说"他说话算话"吗?
A. 可以说。现在我问你：你说话算话吗?
B. 我说话算话。你呢?
A. 我也说话算话。今天我们就到这里吧 (Let's stop here today)，下次再学。
B. 好，谢谢你。再见!
A. 不谢。下次见!

(1) "时刻"和"时时刻刻"的意思一样吗?

(2) "说话"和"说大话"的意思一样吗?

(3) 你认识一个喜欢说大话的人吗?

(4) 你想做"说话不算话"的人吗?

(5) 在这个对话里你学会了几个词? 什么词?

第八课
LESSON EIGHT

我的理想
My Dream: What I Want to Become in the Future

学习目的
Learning Objectives

做加法题	To solve math (addition) problems
请求别人告诉你某事	To ask people to tell you something
夸奖别人	To praise others
谈论自己的理想	To talk about your dream for the future
描述过去的事	To describe past events
对人和事进行比较	To compare people and things

本课学习内容 Contents of the chapter

一	发音复习 Pronunciation Review
二	课文：我的理想 Text: My Dream: What I Want to Become in the Future
三	生词和生字 Vocabulary
	● 名词 nouns：理想、英安迪、周伟石、作文、题目、科学家、文学家、家庭、演员、事业、厨师、会计师、工程师、邮递员、飞行员、警察、军官、社会、白珍妮、画、作品、海明威、赛珍珠、道理、作家 ■ 动词 verbs：当、成家、结婚、立业、画、解释、分析、造、理解、改变、比、明白 ■ 代词 pronouns：这些 ■ 形容词 adjectives：早、认真、有用、别、出色 ■ 副词 adverbs：当然、认真、到底、总、因此、当时、不再 ■ 介词 prepositions：作为、与、比、对、从 ■ 连词 conjunctions：或者 ■ 虚词 particles：得 ■ 量词 measure words：篇、部、位 ■ 词句 expressions：了不起、有的……有的、不但……而且
四	数字复习 Study of Numbers: Review
五	语法 Grammar
	■ "有的"的用法 Usage of "有的" ■ 比较句 Comparative sentences with "比" ■ 连词"或(者)"的用法 Usage of the conjunction "或(者)" ■ 虚词"得" The particle "得" ■ 词语"是……的" The expression "是……的" ■ "明白"和"理解"的区别 "明白" versus "理解"
六	练习 Exercises
七	读报 Newspaper Reading
八	文化点滴 Culture Notes
九	自我测试 Self Assessment

第八课 我的理想
My Dream: What I Want to Become in the Future

一、语音复习 Pronunciation Review

练习

1. 哪个字是这样发音?
   Which character has this pronunciation?

   Model: dà ( ) → dà (大)

rén ( )	lái ( )	ba ( )	gè ( )	èr ( )
bǐ ( )	sān ( )	lǎo ( )	wǒ ( )	liú ( )
dōu ( )	bù ( )	hé ( )	yīn ( )	lán ( )
wǔ ( )	hǎo ( )	dì ( )	shǐ ( )	jiā ( )
de ( )	wèn ( )	xí ( )	nín ( )	yě ( )
nǐ ( )	duì ( )	xiè ( )	mén ( )	xué ( )
tú ( )	nà ( )	yǒu ( )	shū ( )	zài ( )
xīn ( )	lǐ ( )	kàn ( )	lù ( )	rì ( )
jiǔ ( )	zhǐ ( )	gěi ( )	nǎ ( )	suǒ ( )
mǎi ( )	kǒu ( )	yé ( )	nán ( )	yào ( )
huā ( )	kāi ( )	tǐ ( )	zì ( )	hàn ( )
cí ( )	qiú ( )	kè ( )	rán ( )	jí ( )
huà ( )	pà ( )	kǒu ( )	dǎ ( )	le ( )
ān ( )	gāo ( )	yǐ ( )	gù ( )	zěn ( )
jī ( )	nǚ ( )	fǎ ( )	dài ( )	yuē ( )

2. 哪个字是这样发音?
   Which character has this pronunciation?

   Model: yīng ( ) → yīng (英)

shēng ( )	tóng ( )	líng ( )	néng ( )
zhāng ( )	yuán ( )	xīng ( )	huáng ( )
yàng ( )	dòng ( )	yòng ( )	zhōng ( )
qǐng ( )	zhōng ( )	péng ( )	děng ( )
míng ( )	cháng ( )	lìng ( )	xiǎng ( )
píng ( )	gāng ( )	liàng ( )	chéng ( )

3. 这两个音节是什么词?

   What is the word corresponding to the two syllables?

   Model: dàxué (　　) → (大学)

   xiànzài (　　)　　shǒujī (　　)　　yǔfǎ (　　)
   lùshī (　　)　　dìlǐ (　　)　　měiguó (　　)
   dǎsuàn (　　)　　jièshào (　　)　　rènshi (　　)
   jīngjì (　　)　　suǒyǐ (　　)　　xuéqī (　　)
   kǎoshì (　　)　　bùguò (　　)　　tǐyù (　　)
   jīntiān (　　)　　yīnyuè (　　)　　yāoqiú (　　)
   shēngcí (　　)　　kāishǐ (　　)　　chúle (　　)
   liànxí (　　)　　gàosu (　　)　　chànggē (　　)
   yìsi (　　)　　shùxué (　　)　　shēngwù (　　)
   fāyīn (　　)　　shíjiān (　　)　　zhèngzhì (　　)
   wèntí (　　)　　ménkǒu (　　)　　wénhuà (　　)
   hànyǔ (　　)　　yīyuàn (　　)　　zhàopiàn (　　)
   dàngāo (　　)　　shēngrì (　　)　　gōngzuò (　　)
   háizi (　　)

4. 这四个音节是什么意思?

   What does each group of four syllables represents?

   Model: běijīng dàxué　　→　　北京大学

   (1) xiōng (兄) dì jiěmèi　→
   (2) shēngrì kuàilè　→
   (3) dàxué lǎoshī　→
   (4) lánqiú bǐsài　→
   (5) zìwǒ jièshào　→
   (6) qīmò kǎoshì　→
   (7) tǐyù huódòng　→
   (8) yǔfǎ liànxí　→
   (9) jiérán bùtóng　→
   (10) tīngshuō dúxiě　→

第八课 我的理想
My Dream: What I Want to Become in the Future

5. 两个人做这个练习：请轮流读下面每一个句子的发音，并一起写出中文句子。

   Work in pairs: take turns to pronounce each sentence and together write out the sentence using Chinese.

   Model: wǒ shì běi jīng dà xué de xué sheng

   我是北京大学的学生。

   (1) Shéi shì nǐ de huà xué kè lǎo shī?

   (2) Wǒ zuì xǐ huan de tǐ yù huó dòng shì pīng pāng qiú.

   (3) Xiàn zài jǐ diǎn zhōng?

   (4) Zuó tiān māma mǎi le yì běn shū hé yì zhāng shēng rì kǎ.

   (5) Nǐ shì běi jīng rén hái shì shàng hǎi rén?

   (6) Qǐng tóng xué men àn shí jiāo zuò yè.

   (7) Wǒ men xǐ huān zài tú shū guǎn li kàn shū, xiě zuò yè.

   (8) Kè xià dà jiā děi fù xí, yīn wèi míng tiān yǒu kǎo shì.

   (9) Dìdi jí jí máng máng chū mén le; wàng le dài shǒu jī.

   (10) Xià kè yǐ hòu nǐ men néng zài tú shū guǎn mén kǒu děng wǒ ma?

二、课文 Text

我的理想

周伟石 (Stoney Joel) 的理想

英安迪：伟石，你在用中文写什么？能告诉我吗？
周伟石：当然可以。我在写一篇作文。
英安迪：用中文写作文？你花了多长时间学这些汉字？
周伟石：我是一年半以前开始学习汉语的。
英安迪：了不起！作文的题目是什么？
周伟石：题目是：我的理想。
英安迪：你的理想？我真想听听你的理想是什么。
周伟石：作为学生，我们每个人都有自己的理想。有的人想当科学家，有的人想当文学家，也有的人想当演员，当体育明星。早一点成家立业也是很多人的理想。
英安迪："成家立业"是什么意思？
周伟石："成家"就是结婚，成立一个家庭；"立业"就是有自己的事业。
英安迪：我明白了。谢谢你的解释。你接着说你的理想吧。
周伟石：与同学们比，我的理想不高。我要求自己认真学习文化知识，将来当厨师、会计师、工程师，当邮递员、飞行员，或者当警察、军官都可以。

第八课 我的理想

My Dream: What I Want to Become in the Future

英安迪：那你在作文里写什么？你的理想到底是什么？

周伟石：做一个对社会有用的人，这就是我的理想。

白珍妮 (Jenny Bailey) 的理想

我上小学的时候很喜欢画画儿。美术老师总说我比别的孩子画得好。因此，我当时的理想是当画家。

上中学的时候我有一个出色的英语老师。他不但教会了我怎样分析和造句子，而且教会了我怎样理解文学作品。我从海明威的《老人与海》和赛珍珠的《大地》这两部作品中学到了很多人生的道理。可以说，是这位老师改变了我的人生理想。

我不再想当画家；当作家是我最新的理想。

課文

我的理想

周偉石 (Stoney Joel) 的理想

英安迪：偉石，你在用中文寫什麼？能告訴我嗎？
周偉石：當然可以。我在寫一篇作文。
英安迪：用中文寫作文？你花了多長時間學這些漢字？
周偉石：我是一年半以前開始學習漢語的。
英安迪：了不起！作文的題目是什麼？
周偉石：題目是：我的理想。
英安迪：你的理想？我真想聽聽你的理想是什麼。
周偉石：作為學生，我們每個人都有自己的理想。有的人想當科學家，有的人想當文學家，也有的人想當演員，當體育明星。早一點成家立業也是很多人的理想。
英安迪："成家立業"是什麼意思？
周偉石："成家"就是結婚，成立一個家庭；"立業"就是有自己的事業。
英安迪：我明白了。謝謝你的解釋。你接着說你的理想吧。
周偉石：與同學們比，我的理想不高。我要求自己認真學習文化知識，將來當廚師、會計師、工程師，當郵遞員、飛行員，或者當警察、軍官都可以。

第八課 我的理想
My Dream: What I Want to Become in the Future

英安迪：那你在作文裏寫什麼？你的理想到底是什麼？

周偉石：做一個對社會有用的人，這就是我的理想。

白珍妮 (Jenny Bailey) 的理想

我上小學的時候很喜歡畫畫兒。美術老師總說我比別的孩子畫得好。因此，我當時的理想是當畫家。

上中學的時候我有一個出色的英語老師。他不但教會了我怎樣分析和造句子，而且教會了我怎樣理解文學作品。我從海明威的《老人與海》和賽珍珠的《大地》這兩部作品中學到了很多人生的道理。可以說，是這位老師改變了我的人生理想。

我不再想當畫家；當作家是我最新的理想。

三、生词 Vocabulary

NOUNS

lǐxiǎng 理想 (理想) ideal	yīng āndí 英安迪 (英安迪) Andy Yoon
Zhōu Wěishí 周伟石 (周偉石) Stoney Joel	shí 石：stone, rock, a surname
	wěi 伟 (偉)：big, great
zuòwén 作文 (作文) composition	
tímù 题目 (題目) title, topic	mù 目：eye, item, a list of, catalogue
kēxuéjiā 科学家 (科學家) scientist	kēxué 科学 (科學)：science
	jiā 家：a specialist in a certain field
wénxuéjiā 文学家 (文學家) writer, man of letters	jiātíng 家庭 (家庭) family, household
yǎnyuán 演员 (演員) actor, actress	shìyè 事业 (事業) cause
chúshī 厨师 (廚師) cook, chef	chú 厨：kitchen
	shī 师 (師)：a person skilled in a certain profession
kuàijìshī 会计师 (會計師) accountant	
gōngchéngshī 工程师 (工程師) engineer	gōngchéng 工程：project
yóudìyuán 邮递员 (郵遞員) postman	yóu 邮 (郵)：post, mail, to send
	dì 递 (遞)：to hand over, to pass
	yuán 员 (員)：a person engaged in some field of activity

第八课 我的理想
My Dream: What I Want to Become in the Future

fēixíngyuán 飞行员 (飛行員) pilot	fēixíng 飞行 (飛行): to fly	
jǐngchá 警察 (警察) police	jūnguān 军官 (軍官) military officer	shèhuì 社会 (社會) society
Bái Zhēnnī 白珍妮 (白珍妮) Jenny Bailey	bái 白：white, a surname	
	zhēn 珍：treasure, precious, valuable	
	nī 妮：girl	
huà 画 (畫) drawing, painting	zuòpǐn 作品 (作品) work (artistic and literary)	
Hǎimíngwēi 海明威 (海明威) Hemingway	Sàizhēnzhū 赛珍珠 (賽珍珠) Pearl S. Buck	
dàolǐ 道理 (道理) principle, reason	zuòjiā 作家 (作家) writer	

VERBS

dāng
当/當 to serve as, to work as

chéng jiā
成家/成家 to marry (for a man)

jié hūn
结婚/結婚 to marry

lì yè
立业/立業 to start a career

huà
画/畫 to draw, to paint

jiěshì
解释/解釋 to explain

fēnxi
分析/分析 to analyze

zào
造/造 to make, to manufacture

lǐjiě
理解/理解 to understand, to comprehend

gǎibiàn
改变/改變 to change, to alter, to transform

bǐ
比/比 to compare

míngbai
明白/明白 to understand

PRONOUNS

zhèxiē
这些/這些 these, those

bié
别/別 other, else

ADJECTIVES

zǎo
早/早 early

rènzhēn
认真/認真 carefully, seriously

yǒuyòng
有用/有用 useful

chūsè
出色/出色 outstanding, remarkable

ADVERBS

dāngrán
当然/當然 of course

dàodǐ
到底/到底 after all, finally

zǒngshì
总是/總是 always, invariably

yīncǐ
因此/因此 therefore, consequently

dāngshí
当时/當時 at that time, at once

bùzài
不再/不再 no more, no longer

PREPOSITIONS

zuòwéi
作为/作爲 as

yǔ
与/與 and, together with

bǐ
比/比 compared to

duì
对/對 to

cóng
从/從 from

CONJUNCTIONS

huòzhě
或者/或者 or, either... or

第八课 我的理想
My Dream: What I Want to Become in the Future

PARTICLES

de
得/得

MEASURE WORDS

piān
篇/篇 for papers, articles

bù
部/部 for books, works, films

wèi
位/位 for people (polite form)

EXPRESSIONS

liǎo bu qǐ
了不起/了不起 amazing, terrific, extraordinary

yǒude……yǒude
有的……有的/有的……有的 some... some others

bùdàn……érqiě
不但……而且/不但……而且 not only... but also

四、数字复习 Study of Numbers: Review

两个人一起做下面这三个练习：

1. 第一个人用中文读下面的五道题；第二个人把听到的题写下来。
   The first person reads the following five questions using Chinese, and the second person writes down the questions he/she hears.

   Model: 2 + 3 = ?
   二加 (jiā) 三等于 (děngyú) 多少？

   1. 2810 + 603 =
   2. 1009 + 4106 =
   3. 375 + 8200 =
   4. 6104 + 1000 =
   5. 2035 + 4214 =

2. 第二个人用中文读下面的五道题；第一个人把听到的题写下来。
   The second person reads the following five questions using Chinese, and the first person writes down the questions he/she hears.

   6. 3005 + 798 =
   7. 1683 + 2220 =
   8. 2099 + 1020 =
   9. 7072 + 150 =
   10. 4601 + 2003 =

3. 各自把题算出来，然后用中文把答案告诉对方。
   Each person solves the problems and tells each other the results using Chinese.

   Model: 2 + 3 = 5
   二加 (jiā) 三等于 (děngyú) 五。
   或者：
   2 + 3 = 5
   二加 (jiā) 三得 (dé) 五。

第八课 我的理想
My Dream: What I Want to Become in the Future

五、语法 Grammar

1. "有的"的用法 Usage of "有的"

The pronoun "有的" is the equivalent of the indefinite pronoun "some" in English.

有的学生学法语，有的(学生)学意大利语。
Some students learn French and some Italian.

有的书有意思，有的(书)没有意思。
Some books are interesting, some are not.

However, the difference is that "some" can be used as both subject and object in English while the noun that follows "有的" has to be at the beginning of the sentece when it functions as an object in Chinese.

这些学生有的我认识，也有的我不认识。
I know some of these students, but not all of them.

那些书有的我喜欢，有的我不喜欢。
I like some of those books, but not all of them.

练习一

1. 请按照例句做对话。
   Make conversation following the model.

 这些活动你都喜欢吗？

 有的我喜欢，有的我不喜欢。

(1) 那些都是汉语老师吗？
(2) 这些人都成家了吗？
(3) <u>所有的人</u> (all, everybody) 都喜欢吃面条吗？
(4) 大家都觉得历史课有意思吗？
(5) 那些发音练习都有用吗？
(6) 每个学生都有手机吗？
(7) 人人都打算结婚吗？
(8) 所有的比赛都好看吗？

2. 请按照例句做对话。
Make conversation following the model.

 你总是去图书馆看书吗？

 我有(的)时候去，有(的)时候在家看书。

(1) 你总是吃中国饭吗？
(2) 你总是给朋友们打电话吗？
(3) 你出门总是忘带手机吗？
(4) 老师总是给你们留很多作业吗？
(5) 你总是和大伟一起打乒乓球吗？
(6) 你爷爷奶奶总是住在北京吗？
(7) 他们总是来这个餐馆吃饭吗？
(8) 你总是听法国音乐吗？

2. 比较句　Comparative Sentences with 比

姚明 (Yáo Míng) 比学生们高。

There are basically three ways to use the character "比" in comparative sentences:

A. A 比 B + adjective

大明比二明高。
Daming is taller than Erming.

第八课 我的理想
My Dream: What I Want to Become in the Future

爸爸比我忙。
Dad is busier than I am.

这个公园比那个公园漂亮。
This park is prettier than the other one.

B. A 和 B 比，A or B 更 + adjective

这个回答和那个回答比，这个回答更糟糕。
Comparing these two answers, this one is worse.

政治课和经济课比，经济课更难。
Comparing the political and economic classes, the latter is more difficult.

这两个字比，哪个更难记住？
Comparing these two characters, which one is harder to remember?

C. 和 B 比，A 更 + adjective

和他的书比，我的书更新。
Compared to his book, mine is newer.

和打乒乓球比，打篮球更难学。
Compared to ping-pong, basketball is harder to learn.

和昨天比，今天我的课更多。
Compared to yesterday, I have more classes today.

练习二

1. 三个人一组做这个练习：
   Work in groups of three:

   a) 轮流提问每个人父母的<u>岁数</u> (age)，同时每个人都要在图表(1)里做记录；
   Take turns to ask the age of everybody's parents, and at the same time, each of the group members should take notes using Table 1;

   图表 Table (1)

学生姓名	爸爸的岁数	妈妈的岁数

b) 按照图表中的内容，每个人用比较级造五个句子。
   Based on the information from Table (1), each member should make five comparative sentences.

   Model： 大卫的爸爸比大牛的爸爸大三岁。
   　　　　 大卫的妈妈比文娣的妈妈小两岁。
   　　　　 文娣的妈妈和大卫的妈妈岁数一样大。

   (1) _____
   (2) _____
   (3) _____
   (4) _____
   (5) _____

c) 每个人轮流说出自己的句子。一个人说的时候另外两个人认真听；如有不对的地方要指出问题。
   Take turns to give out your sentences. When one person is speaking, the other two should listen carefully and indicate problems in case there are any.

d) 最后，三个人一起回答下面的问题。
   Finally, answer the following questions together.

   (1) 谁的爸爸岁数最大？
   _____

   (2) 谁的妈妈岁数最大？
   _____

   (3) 谁的爸爸岁数最小？
   _____

   (4) 谁的妈妈岁数最小？
   _____

2. 请用中文回答下列问题。
   Answer the following questions using Chinese.

第八课 我的理想
My Dream: What I Want to Become in the Future

(1) 篮球和乒乓球比，你更喜欢哪种 (zhǒng: kind) 体育活动？

(2) 你觉得中文比英文更难学吗？为什么？

(3) 和你的同学们比，你看书更多还是更少？

(4) 和中国饭比，你更喜欢吃什么饭？法国饭、日本饭还是意大利饭？

(5) 这个星期和下个星期比，你哪个星期更忙？

(6) 美术课和音乐课比，你觉得哪门课更有意思？

(7) 语音练习和语法练习比，做哪种练习花的时间更多？

(8) 今天和昨天比，你哪天的作业更多？

3. 连词"或（者）"的用法 Usage of the Conjuction "或者"

Like the conjunction "or" in English, "或(者)" is used to indicate an alternative, a synonymous or equivalent expression, and an indefiniteness in the Chinese language. As a conjunction, "或(者)" can be used to link two or more nouns, pronouns, verbs, and expressions.

A. An alternative

我们应该给她打个电话，或(者)今天，或(者)明天。
Either today or tomorrow, we should call her.

或者你，或者我得打这个电话。
Either you or I should make this phone call.

祝贺生日的<u>方法</u> (method, way) 很多：或者买<u>礼物</u> (lǐwù: gift)，或者打电话，或者写生日卡。
There are many ways for wishing someone Happy Birthday: buy a gift, make a phone call, or write a card.

B. A synonymous or equivalent expression

中国人说的语言叫中文，或者汉语。
The language that the Chinese people speak is called Chinese or Han language.

北大，或者说北京大学，是一个有很长历史的学校。
Beida, or Peking University, is a school with a long-standing history.

C. An indefiniteness

请给我几张纸，四张或(者)五张都可以。
Please give me some sheets of paper, four or five would be okay.

你想看哪天的<u>篮球比赛</u>？
Which day's game do you want to watch?

今天的或(者)明天的都可以。
Today's or tomorrow's, either one would be fine.

Note that unlike the word "or" in English, "或(者)" cannot be used to ask a question. Another conjunction, "还是" is used instead of "或(者)" (introduced in Chapter Three) in this case.

咱们在哪儿学习，我去你家还是你来我家？
Where are we going to study? Should I go to your home or you come to mine?

你来我家，或(者)我去你家，都没问题。
Either way will not be a problem.

他叫<u>比尔</u> (ěr) 还是<u>威廉</u> (wēilián)？
Is his name Bill or William?

你可以叫他比尔或(者)威廉，哪个名字都行。
You can call him Bill or William; either name will be fine.

练习三

1. 请按照例句做对话。

Make conversation following the model.

你想几点钟去图书馆？三点钟还是四点钟？

第八课 我的理想
My Dream: What I Want to Become in the Future

 三点钟或者四点钟都可以。

(1) 去哪个公园 / 长城公园还是北海公园

(2) 做什么饭 / 米饭 (mǐfàn: rice) 还是面条

(3) 买哪张卡 / 这张还是那张

(4) 用谁的手机打电话 / 我的还是他的

(5) 解哪道题 / 第一题还是第二题

(6) 用哪个词造句子 / "复习"还是"考试"

(7) 和谁一起打乒乓球 / 大卫还是大牛

(8) 在哪里等你的同学 / 这里还是那里

2. 填空：用"或者"，还是用"还是"？
   Fill in the blanks: which one would you use: "或者" or "还是?"

   (1) 他叫马可明 _____ 叫马大哈？

   (2) 你打算在比赛以前 _____ 比赛以后给他打电话？

   (3) 这是我们家的两个电话号码。
       这么说我打这个号码 _____ 那个号码都可以，是吗？

   (4) 你们叫我高二明 _____ 高老二都可以。

   (5) 你们有问题的时候，_____ 问我，_____ 王老师都可以，明白了吗？

   (6) 你来 _____ 不来？来 _____ 不来，都告诉我一下，知道了吗？

   (7) 他想参加 (cānjiā: to participate) 一种活动，_____ 唱歌，_____ 打球。

   (8) 我今天 _____ 明天给他打电话，好不好？

3. 请你参考下面的例句准备五个问题，然后用这五个问题采访两个同学。
   Use the following model sentences to make five questions with which you will interview two classmates.

   (1) 将来你想做什么工作？当老师还是当工程师？

   (2) 你觉得什么人对社会更有用？厨师、邮递员、飞行员还是作家？

   (3) 如果你可以当演员或者体育明星，你想当什么？

你的五个问题:

1) _____
2) _____
3) _____
4) _____
5) _____

采访之后，两个人一组，互相提问并回答下列问题。
After the interview, work in pairs to ask each other and answer the following questions.

(1) 你第一个采访 (cǎifǎng: to interview) 了谁?
(2) 你问了他／她几个问题？第一个问题是什么?
(3) 他／她是怎么回答你的问题的?
(4) 第一和第二个问题比，哪个问题他／她回答得更好?
(5) 哪个问题他／她回答得最好？哪个问题回答得最不好?

(1) _____
(2) _____
(3) _____
(4) _____
(5) _____

4. 虚词 "得" The Particle "得"

The particle "得" normally appears between a verb and an adjective or a verbal phrase: verb + 得 + adjective or verbal phrase. It can be considered as an adverb marker because the function of the particle is to indicate the manner or result of the action of the verb.

他学汉语学得好 (adjective)。
He studies Chinese well.

老师说英语说得快: kuài: fast (adjective)。
The teacher speaks English fast.

第八课 我的理想
My Dream: What I Want to Become in the Future

我累 (lèi) 得不想去学校了 (verbal phrase)。
I'm so tired that I don't want to go to school.

In the first two examples above, since the two verbs (学 and 说) are identical, the first one is optional for this reason.

他 (学) 汉语学得好。
老师 (说) 英语说得快。

Note that "怎么样" is the interrogative expression one should use in order to ask a question about the part of 得 + adjective (or verbal phrase).

他(说)英语说得好。
He speaks English well.
他(说)英语说得怎么样?
How does he speak English?

他忙得没有时间吃饭。
He is so busy that he has no time to eat.
他忙得怎么样?
How heavy is he?

雨 (yǔ: rain)下得很大。
It's raining heavily.
雨下得怎么样?
How heavy is the rain?

练习四

1. 请按照例句做对话。
   Make conversation following the model.

 何文利 (打) 乒乓球打得怎么样?

 他打得不错。可是他弟弟比他打得更好。

(1) 史汉生 (学) 英语学得怎么样? / 他的女朋友
(2) 这位厨师 (做) 意大利饭做得怎么样? / 那位厨师
(3) 祝小英 (写) 生日卡写得怎么样? / 她姐姐
(4) 周理明考试考得怎么样? / 李长江

(5) 容一新 (写) 作文写得怎么样？/ 钟莉莉

(6) 马小亮唱歌唱得怎么样？/ 他哥哥

(7) 谢老师 (教) 数学教得怎么样？/ 高老师

(8) 时伟 (回答) 问题回答得怎么样？/ 刘小明

2. 在汉语课上，什么是你的强项和弱项？请你用下列词语 (你也可以加进更多的词语) 自我鉴定一下你在汉语课上的表现。

What are your strong and weak points in Chinese class? Use the provided expressions (and feel free to add more if you can) to make self-evaluations about your performance in Chinese class.

发音、理解语法、记生词、读课文、造句子、分析句子、做练习、听、说、读、写、考试、做对话、写作文、回答问题

很糟糕、很不好、不太 (tài) 好 (not very good)、不怎么样 (not very good)、不错、还可以 (passable, not bad)、很不错、好、很好、很出色、好极 (jí) 了 (super good)、最好

在汉语课上，我发音发得还可以，……

_____

_____

_____

_____

_____

5. 词语 "是……的" The Expression "是……的"

The expression "是……的" represents another way to state past events besides using the past tense markers "了" and "过" introduced in Chapter Four. However, the difference between the two usages is that this expression is instead used to explain the time and place of the action of a certain verb that was accomplished as well as the manner in which the action of the verb was carried out in the past. In other words, "是……的" is used to ask and answer questions that start with the interrogative words such as when, where, and how.

第八课 我的理想
My Dream: What I Want to Become in the Future

Time

你们是什么时候开始学中文的?
When did you start learning Chinese?

我们是一年以前开始学的。
We started one year ago.

您是哪年开始在这个律师所工作的?
When did you start working at this law firm?

我已经 (yǐjīng: already)在这里工作五年了。
I've being working here for five years.

Place

你是在哪里买到这本书的?
Where did you buy this book?

我是在新明书店 (diàn: store) 买到的。
It was from Xinming Book Store that I bought it.

你是在哪儿找到你的手机的?
Where did you find your cell phone?

我是在我的书包里找到的。
I found it in my book bag.

Manner

你是怎么找到你的手机的?
How did you find you cell phone?

是同学帮 (bāng: to help) 我找到的；他打了一下我的手机号码。
My classmate helped me to find it by calling my number.

你的中文这么好! 你是怎么学的? 是和谁学的?
Your Chinese is so good. How did you learn it? Who taught you?

Note that in all above sentences, the character "是" is optional in the expression "是……的," and the character "的" can be placed either directly after the verb or after the object.

练习五

两个人一组做这个练习：互相提问下面的问题，并把对方的回答用中文写下来。
Work in pairs: ask each other the following questions and write down your partner's answers using Chinese.

(1) 你(是)什么时候认识贺文新的？你在哪里认识她的？

(2) 你昨天几点钟吃的晚饭？和谁一起吃的？在哪里吃的？

(3) 你是在哪里出生 (to be born) 的？

(4) 你昨天在哪儿做的作业？在图书馆，还是在家？

(5) 上个周末你看篮球比赛了吗？是和家人一起看的，还是和朋友们一起看的？

(6) 你去过北卡 (North Carolina) 吗？你是哪年去的？和谁一起去的？

(7) 你读过《老人与海》和《大地》这两部小说吗？什么时候读的？

(8) 你用中文写过作文吗？什么时候写的？作文的题目是什么？

6. "明白"和"理解"的区别 "明白" versus "理解"

Although the two words "明白" and "理解" may both be translated as "understand" in English, there are some major differences that one should be aware of.

a) while the word "明白" functions as both an adjective and a verb, "理解" may be used as a noun and a verb. For example:

这个解释很明白，因此很容易理解。
This explanation is very clear; therefore it's really easy to understand.

我明白你的意思，(所以)你不用再多说了。
I understand what you mean; therefore you don't need to say more.

第八课 我的理想
My Dream: What I Want to Become in the Future

你理解这个句子的意思吗?
Do you understand the meaning of this sentence?

你们的理解很对，因此我不用多讲 (jiǎng: to explain) 了。
You have an accurate understanding; therefore I don't need to explain further.

b) the verb "理解" can be used in the context of understanding people while "明白" would be inappropriate in this case.

你觉得谁最理解你?
Who do you think understands you the best?

他是一个会理解别人的人。
He is someone who understands others.

练习六

请用"理解"或"明白"填空。
Fill in the blanks with "理解" or "明白."

(1) 你都不＿＿＿＿我，谁还能＿＿＿＿我?

(2) 我不＿＿＿＿他为什么说话不算话。

(3) 这道题，有的学生＿＿＿＿，有的学生不＿＿＿＿。

(4) 我爸爸妈妈不＿＿＿＿我；我也不＿＿＿＿他们。

(5) 你们＿＿＿＿这个句子的意思吗?

(6) 我们＿＿＿＿了老师的解释。

(7) 你解释了很多，现在大家都＿＿＿＿你了。

(8) "兄"和"哥"这两个字有什么不一样? 我不＿＿＿＿。

六、练习 Exercises

模式练习 Model exercises

1. 请用中文口头回答下列问题。
Answer the following questions orally using Chinese.

(1) 这个学生是从哪个国家来的？英国还是法国？
(2) 你从第八课里学会了多少个词？
(3) 从今天开始，在中文课上你能不能只说汉语？
(4) 用中文，你可以从一数 (shǔ: to count) 到多少？
(5) 你是从什么时候开始学中文的？
(6) 谁<u>从来都</u> (always) 是你的好朋友？
(7) 在你家，谁<u>从来不</u> (never) 做饭？
(8) <u>从现在起</u> (from now on)，你打算天天去图书馆看书吗？

2. 请按照例句做对话。
Make conversation following the model.

 贺小飞为什么谢你？

 他用了我的手机，因此谢谢我。

(1) 贺小飞用了我的手机，因此谢谢我。
(2) 张大牛想当工程师，因此他要上很多数学和物理课。
(3) 白文新想给刘威打电话，因此来电话问我有没有刘威的电话号码。
(4) 易小生打算将来学习法国文学，因此他每个学期都上法语课。
(5) 学生们在中文课上都说中文，因此老师很<u>满意</u> (pleased)。
(6) 大家都不理解这个孩子，因此他很少说话。
(7) 这个老师中文课教得好，因此他的学生们听、说、读、写<u>样样</u> (all) 好。
(8) 我今天没来上课，因此不知道今天的作业是什么。

第八课 我的理想
My Dream: What I Want to Become in the Future

3. 在这样的情况下说什么？
What would one say in the following cases?

了不起！　　　这有什么了不起？　　　这没什么了不起。

Model:
周伟石能用中文写作文。　　　了不起！
今天他们学了两个新字。　　　这有什么了不起？

(1) 一个七岁的孩子会说四种语言。

(2) 那个学生解了两道数学题。

(3) 今天我们做了六个练习。

(4) 一位八十岁的老奶奶上了长城。

(5) 五十个人打乒乓球比赛，他得了第一名。

(6) 我们明白了这个字的意思。

(7) 一个十五岁的女孩子当二十个小学生的老师。

(8) 那个考试很难，只有他一个人得了一百分 (yībǎi fēn: 100%)。

4. 两个人一组按下列步骤做这个练习。
Do this exercise in pairs by following the steps.

A. 先请你自己想一想，在你的家人和朋友中谁是，或者谁想当：
First, think about who is (or who wants to be) the following among your family members and friends:

	谁是	谁想当
(1) 厨师		厨师	?
(2) 律师		律师	?
(3) 警察		警察	?
(4) 军人		军人	?
(5) 老师		老师	?
(6) 医生		医生	?
(7) 会计师		会计师	?
(8) 工程师		工程师	?
(9) 邮递员		邮递员	?
(10) 飞行员		飞行员	?

B. 如有可能，请你们每人问十个同学将来他们想当什么。然后回答下面的问题。

If possible, each of you should ask ten of your classmates what they want to be in the future and answer the following questions afterwards.

在你的同学中，将来谁想当……

(1) 厨师？

(2) 律师？

(3) 警察？

(4) 军人？

(5) 老师？

(6) 医生？

(7) 会计师？

第八课 我的理想
My Dream: What I Want to Become in the Future

(8) 工程师？

(9) 邮递员？

(10) 飞行员？

C. 根据A和B部分收集到的信息，两个人互相问问题。比如：
Two students should ask each other questions about the information collected for A and B. For example:

(1) 在你的家人和朋友(当)中，谁是厨师？
(2) 在我们的同学(当)中，谁想当工程师？
(3) 在我们的同学(当)中，想当老师的人多还是想当律师的人多？

5. 请用中文笔头回答下列问题。注意：回答问题时请不要用"到底"。
Write out the answers using Chinese for the following questions. Do not use "到底" in the answers.

(1) 他今天说李明是他的朋友，明天说王军是他的朋友；到底谁是他的朋友？

(2) 英语、法语和意大利语，你到底想学哪种 (zhǒng: kind) 语言？

(3) 你到底喜欢哪门课？

(4) 她/他到底是你的同学还是你的女/男朋友？

(5) 老师刚刚让我们打开书22页，现在又说32页，到底多少页？你知道吗？

(6) 你说这本书好，他说那本书好。你们到底觉得哪本书最好？

(7) 他介绍了半天，我还是不明白这个人到底怎么样。你明白吗？

(8) 你到底想和谁一起做练习？和我还是和他？

6. 请按照例句做对话。
Make conversation following the model.

 "成家立业"是什么意思？你能给我解释一下吗？

 当然可以。这个词语的意思是"to marry and embark on a career。"

 我明白了。两年以前，我哥哥上完大学就成家立业了。谢谢你的解释。

 没什么，不用谢。

(1) "成家立业"是什么意思？/ to marry and embark on a career / 两年以前，我哥哥上完大学就成家立业了。
(2) "兄(xiōng:哥哥)弟姐妹"是什么意思？/ siblings / 我的好朋友家有兄弟姐妹六个。
(3) "欢欢喜喜"是什么意思？/ merrily / 下个星期大家就可以欢欢喜喜过年了。
(4) "半天"是什么意思？/ half day, a long time / 我说了半天，你们到底明白了吗？
(5) "白花时间"是什么意思？/ to spend time in vain / 我们白花了半天时间等他，他到底还是没来。
(6) "来回"是什么意思？/ to make a round trip / 从北京去上海，来回要花多长时间？
(7) "天不怕，地不怕"是什么意思？/ to fear nothing at all / 这个孩子天不怕，地不怕。
(8) "周年"是什么意思？/ anniversary / 我爸爸妈妈结婚二十二周年了。
(9) "打听"是什么意思？/ to ask about, to inquire about / 我想和您打听一个人，您认(识)不认识王大伟？

(10) "早（早）晚（晚）"是什么意思？/ sooner or later / 我弟弟说他早早晚晚要当画家。

7. 两个人一组：用中文轮流提问并回答下列问题。
Work in pairs: take turns to ask and answer the following questions using Chinese.

(1) 你是一个认真的学生吗？在学校你做什么事认真？做什么事不认真？
(2) 和你的兄弟姐妹比，你是一个更认真的人吗？在家里你做什么事认真？做什么事不认真？
(3) 如果你不是最认真的人，你的家人(当)中，谁是？
(4) 在你们的英文课上，你觉得谁是最认真的学生？和多数 (most of) 学生比，这个学生做什么事更认真？
(5) 上中文课的时候，所有的学生都认真听老师讲课 (jiǎng kè: teaching) 吗？
(6) 你觉得学习不认真，做事也不认真的人能当医生吗？能当厨师吗？能当警察吗？
(7) 我现在没有家庭医生，想找一个。你认识一个做事认真的医生吗？他/她姓什么？叫什么名字？能给我介绍一下吗？
(8) 中国人常说："认认真真做事，老老实实shí (honest, well-behaved) 做人。"你是这样要求自己的吗？

8. 请按照例句做对话。
Make using conversation following the model.

  刘大伟还是中山 (shān) 大学的学生吗？

  他不再是中山大学的学生了。

(1) 刘大伟还是中山大学的学生吗？
(2) 谢文莉家还在上海住吗？
(3) 周小朋的爷爷还在这家医院工作吗？
(4) 他还在学日语吗？
(5) 王老师还是你们的历史老师吗？
(6) 在中文课上，你们还用英语上课吗？
(7) 你还每天去图书馆看书吗？
(8) 这个孩子还喜欢画画吗？

9. 比赛：两个人一组。

Competition: work in pairs.

第一步：从下面的题目中选择一个，用五分钟写一个小对话。

Step 1: Use five minutes to write a mini-dialogue on one of the topics you chose from the following list.

(1) 了不起！
(2) 兄弟姐妹
(3) 有的时候……，有的时候……
(4) 为了理想

第二步：用五分钟大声练习你们的小对话。

Step 2: Use five minutes to practice your dialogue aloud.

第三步：在全班人面前表演你们的对话。

Step 3: Present your dialogue in front of the class.

第四步：你们觉得哪个对话最好？按照下面的例句说说为什么。

Step 4: Work in pairs again. Decide which dialogue you think is the best and explain why following the model sentences below.

第八课 我的理想
My Dream: What I Want to Become in the Future

我们觉得第一个对话最好，因为……
1) 这个对话最长
2) 这个对话的词汇量大 (large vocabulary)
3) 这个对话的语法没有问题
4) 这个对话有意思
5) 这两个对话人的中文发音好
6) 他们的对话很容易，大家都能听明白
7) ……

10. 请按照例句用中文完成下面的句子。
Complete the sentences following the model.

Model:
那本小说我还没读完，我还得接着读。

(1) 这篇作文我还没写完，_____。
(2) 第八课的语法我们还没学完，_____。
(3) 小明的数学作业还没做完，_____。
(4) 这个问题你们还没回答完，_____。
(5) 那些练习学生们还没做完，_____。
(6) 篮球比赛大家还没看完，_____。
(7) 那张画我还没画完，_____。
(8) 这个句子你还没造完，_____。

11. 请按照例句做对话。
Make conversation following the model.

你为什么上这么多英语课？

因为我想将来当作家，所以英语课对我很有用。

(1) 上这么多英语课 / 当作家
(2) 上这么多数学和物理课 / 当工程师

(3) 上这么多生物课 / 当医生
(4) 上这么多政治课 / 当律师
(5) 上这么多经济课 / 当会计师
(6) 上这么多历史课 / 当历史老师
(7) 上这么多的美术课 / 当画家
(8) 上这么多音乐课 / 当音乐家

12. 阅读练习：请认真阅读每个段落，然后用中文回答问题。
Reading exercise: read carefully each paragraph before answering the questions using Chinese.

A. "早"字有很多意思；比如：morning, good morning, early, in advance, long ago, 等等 (etc.)。请你读下面的小对话，想一想每一个"早"字是什么意思。

史冬明：老师早[1]！
老师：史冬明，你早[2]！今天你怎么来得这么早[3]？

(1) 在这句话里，"早"是什么意思？

(2) "你早！"是什么意思？

(3) 第三个"早"和第二个一样吗？这个"早"字是什么意思？

B. 现在请你读下面的对话，认真看看上下文 (context)，再理解一下"早上"和"早饭"是什么意思。

何复思：刘大伟，你每天早上几点钟起床 (qǐ chuáng: to get up)？
刘大伟：我每天早上六点半起床。你呢？
何复思：我比你起床起得早[4]；我六点钟起床。你每天几点钟吃早饭[5]？
刘大伟：我差不多七点钟吃早饭。可是我有时候吃早饭，有时候不吃，因为我早上[6]很忙。

(4) 这个"早"字是什么意思？

(5)"早饭"是什么意思?

(6)"早上"呢? 是什么意思?

C. 在下面这个小对话里也有两个"早"字。请你读一读,想一想,"早晚"这两个字在一起的时候是什么意思;"早"和"就"两个字在一起的时候是什么意思? 请从上下文里找意思。

马小妹：妈妈,去英国的事我早晚⁷得告诉爸爸,您说是不是?
妈　妈：你不用和他说了,我早就⁸告诉他了。
马小妹：爸爸同意 (to agree) 我去吗?
妈　妈：你爸爸当然同意你去,他只是怕……
马小妹：怕什么? 我都过了二十岁的生日,不再是孩子了,早就是大人了。

(7) 在这个对话里,"早晚"的意思你理解吗? 你会用这个词了吗?

(8) "早就"的意思好理解吗? 这两个字在一起是什么意思?

实况演练 Real situation exercises

这个人是做什么工作的?
_____。

1. 先个人，后分组完成下面的任务。
Work on your own first and then in groups to achieve the following task.

A. 每个人从下面的题目中选择一个，用三至五分钟写出自己的看法；
Each student chooses one from the following topics and writes out his / her opinions about it;

(1) 谁是对社会有用的人？谁是对社会没有用的人？为什么？

(2) 有人说"社会是一个大家庭"。你觉得这样说对吗？为什么对？为什么不对？

(3) 你们是学生，现在你们可以做对社会有用的事吗？

(4) 作为学生，现在你们做什么将来能成为 (chéngwéi: to become) 一个对社会有用的人？

(5) 你认为 (to believe, think that) 什么人能改变社会？为什么？

第八课 我的理想
My Dream: What I Want to Become in the Future

B. 三个选择了不同题目的人一组，每个人介绍自己的题目及看法，并在别人介绍时做笔记。选出最好的一个代表你们组在全班发言；
Three students (who have worked on different topics) should work together to introduce his / her own topic. Each one should speak about his / her opinions and take notes when other group members speak. Finally, select the best one to represent the group and present in front of the entire class.

C. 各组代表在全班发言。大家认真做笔记；不明白的时候可以问问题。
Presentation of each group in front of the class. Everyone should take good notes and ask questions when you do not understand.

D. 用中文回答下列问题。
Answer the following questions using Chinese.

(6) 你认为谁<u>发言</u> (fā yán: speech)的时候中文发音最好？

(7) 谁的发言里用的句子漂亮？

(8) 谁的发言最长？

(9) 谁的发言里<u>说出的想法</u> (ideas expressed)最好？<u>比如</u> (for example)…

(10) <u>总的来说</u> (in summary, in short)，谁的发言最好？为什么？

2. 三个人一组谈论自己的理想。
Work in groups of three to talk about your dreams for the future.

你上小学的时候有什么理想？上中学时候的理想是什么？现在呢？和小的时候比，你的理想改变了吗？

上小学的时候

上中学的时候

现在

你为什么改变了理想

等我长大了，我想去中国学习中文，也想去德国学习工程。我想在NASA工作。工程师有意思，也很好玩。在中国学中文也有意思，因为我能学习很多。

戴开文
Kevin Davis

等我长大了我想当一个语言老师。我想去中国，西班牙和意大利。我很喜欢学生和语言。

戴丹妮
Danielle Daley

第八课 我的理想
My Dream: What I Want to Become in the Future

等我长大了我想在中国工作。我想每天说中文。我想先参观中国,看她的漂亮的景色。然后我想在中国当一个生意人。

卢侯骏
Jose Luna

等我长大了,我想当一个很有名的医生。我想去中国和外国工作,因为我觉得我可以帮助别的人。对我来说,医生的工作很有意思。

苏南欧
Neel Swami

等我长大了,我想在中国当明星。我现在学中文,所以我可以是中国明星。我想在中国有名,因为中国的人口是最多的,在中国有很多人想听我唱歌。

魏佩木莫
Palmer Withers

七、读报 Newspaper Reading

How Many Characters Do You Know?

1. Read the following articles.
2. While reading, underline the characters you know.

想起海明威
李国文

　　海明威，是人所共知的硬汉了，读过《老人与海》的读者，通常会把他和作品中那个与鲨鱼作殊死战的桑地雅哥等同起来。因为他是一位强者，一位文学的强者，一位奔赴世界各地，总处于第一线的记者、作家、战士。

　　其实，再强的强者，年龄也会一天天地老起来。也许他永远不想知道自己在老的事实，也许在他这样强者的辞典里，压根就没有老的概念。所以，在这样良好的自我感觉下，他一生曾经毫不疲倦地结过四次婚，其中三位的年龄都大大小于他。说他是一位爱娶少妇的文学大师，这个评价大抵是不会错的。如果说《老人与海》的主人公桑地雅哥在海上，是与鲨鱼搏斗的话，那么，这位文学大师的一生，至少要用很多力气对付他身边的这一个和那一个，或者，这两个和那两个少妇。

　　所以这位自以为雄风不减，金枪不倒的海明威，居然信口开河地"告诉查尔斯（巴克）·兰汉姆将军，经过一段时间的冷落，安抚玛丽·韦尔什是件很容易的事……海明威死后，兰汉姆将军偶然间向那第四位太太玛丽·韦尔什求证这个问题，她叹息着说：'那要是真的该多好！'"（据保罗·约翰逊的《知识分子》）读到这里，我突然觉得在古巴寓居的海明威，最后饮弹自杀，其中一个很重要的因素，恐怕是这个硬汉，终于不得不承认自己老了。显然，他接受不了事实，于是，他用硬汉的手段，结束了生命。

　　这位伟大的作家不明白，老是一种必然，也是一门学问。人过花甲，应该追求一种成熟的美。进入古稀之年，更应该体现出一种智慧的美。但实际上，要做到这种程度，又是谈何容易。所以，最难得者：六十岁时清醒，七十岁时更清醒，八十岁时彻底清醒，那就达到上善若水的至美境界了。

选自：新民晚报　日期：2008年7月19日

为苏老拍照
陈继超

　　苏步青是杰出的数学家、教育家、著名的社会活动家。为这样的名人拍照，说实话，我觉得有点又敬又怕的感觉。

　　1992年《新民晚报》计划出专版报道"健康老人"。听说已90岁高龄的苏步青校长，仍坚持每天锻炼身体，我觉得是个好选题。怕苏老不接受采访拍摄，于是抱着试试的想法，请我的好友、复旦大学宣传部的杨光亮联系。结果，让我喜出望外：苏老不但同意拍照，而且为此专门安排了一整天时间。

　　那天早上，我在约定时间之前到达苏老的办公室，可他早已从家里步行到办公室等我。我告诉他，我姓陈，名继超，复旦新闻系毕业。他笑吟吟握着我的手说："你要继承赵超，超过赵超老。"他见我一愣，说："你们新民晚报社长不是叫赵超构吗？"我说："是的。总编辑是丁法章。"他说："回去告诉丁法章，要办好报，不要为复旦丢脸。"一番对话，顿时打消我怕名人的顾虑。

　　苏老简单谈了他一天生活，并主动提出可以从智、体、艺术等方面的健身进行拍摄。他告诉我，上午他在数学研究所看书做习题；午睡后，他在家里养花、室外运动、写书法和听音乐。

　　我跟随苏校长来到数学研究所。苏校长先翻了一会儿外文资料，然后选了一则数学题，坐在朝阳的窗口桌子上看题，很快就拿起一支笔在纸上聚精会神地做题，遨游在数学的王国里。阳光漫射在苏校长充满智慧的光光的脑袋上，随着脑袋的晃动，光亮在其头顶闪烁，智慧在其头脑中涌动。我轻手轻脚，选择角度，抓拍了这位被国际数学界赞誉为"东方国度升起的灿烂数学明星"。

　　我顺利完成余下几个镜头的拍摄，又亲眼目睹老一天的健康生活，十分愉快。

选自：新民晚报　日期：2008年5月13日

3. Pronounce the characters you have recognized.
4. Tell the meaning of each character to your class (or study group).

第八课 我的理想
My Dream: What I Want to Become in the Future

八、文化点滴　Culture Notes 8

About the Chinese Characters

繁體字　简体字

There are two sets of Chinese characters: traditional 繁体字 and simplified 简体字. The latter are characters based on the traditional set officially simplified by the Chinese Characters Reform Commission, (established in December 1952; in December 1985, the name of this institution was changed to State Language Work Committee) under the government of the People's Republic of China in an attempt to promote literacy.

The understanding of the principles applied in simplifying the characters provide a key to recognize the two different writing systems. Comparison is perhaps the best way to learn how to read and write one set while being able to recognize the other.

1. Radical part simplification:

Traditional Characters	Simplified Characters
語	语
說	说
紅	红
給	给
鐘	钟
錢	钱

2. Pronunciation part simplification:

馬	马
媽	妈
嗎	吗
見	见
現	现
硯	砚

長　　　　　　　　　　　　长
張　　　　　　　　　　　　张

3. Parts of the characters have been dropped:

號　　　　　　　　　　　　号
幹　　　　　　　　　　　　干
習　　　　　　　　　　　　习
麼　　　　　　　　　　　　么
裏　　　　　　　　　　　　里

学生们在练习毛笔字。／學生們在練習毛筆字。
Courtesy of Indiana University

Currently, the simplified characters are used in Mainland China, Malaysia and Singapore while in Hong Kong, Macao, Taiwan and most overseas Chinese communities, traditional characters are still in use.

第八课 我的理想
My Dream: What I Want to Become in the Future

九、自我测试　Self Assessment

1. 用中文回答下列问题。
Answer the following questions using Chinese.

(1) 钟思文和钟思明兄弟两个比，谁说英语说得更好？

(2) 你是什么时候开始学习汉语的？汉语对你有什么用？

(3) 大家都理解这一课的语法吗？

(4) 你们到底是这个周末还是下个周末去长城？

(5) 在你的同学中，谁用中文写作文写得最出色？

(6) 作为学生，你可以做对家庭或者对社会有用的事吗？

(7) 你读过海明威的作品吗？什么作品？你喜欢吗？

(8) 在中文课上，你们总是说汉语吗？

(9) 你能不能用英文给我解释一下"成家立业"这个词语的意思？

(10) 你能不能用"不但……而且"造一个句子？

2. 请用适当的量词填空。
Fill in the blanks with appropriate measure words.

(1) 老师让我们用中文写一 _____ 作文。

(2) 那是一 _____ 科学家。

(3) "三国"是一 _____ 有名的中国文学作品。

(4) 这 _____ 题好解吗?

(5) 大家都觉得这 _____ 书很有用。

3. 对不对?
Read the question (A) and the answer (B). Check "对" if you think the answer is logical with respect to the question or check "不对" otherwise.

(1) A. 这位警察是你同学的爸爸?
　　B. 对,我爸爸是警察。
　　　　　　　　　　　　　　　　对_____ 不对_____

(2) A. 谁理解他?
　　B. 只有他朋友理解他。
　　　　　　　　　　　　　　　　对_____ 不对_____

(3) A. 这位先生(Mister)是做什么工作的?
　　B. 他是邮递员。
　　　　　　　　　　　　　　　　对_____ 不对_____

(4) A. 当军官是你的理想?
　　B. 这个军官有理想。
　　　　　　　　　　　　　　　　对_____ 不对_____

(5) A. 周文娣做事认真吗?
　　B. 认真。她是一个很认真的人。
　　　　　　　　　　　　　　　　对_____ 不对_____

(6) A. 这个人是马大哈?
　　B. 对,他姓马。
　　　　　　　　　　　　　　　　对_____ 不对_____

第八课 我的理想
My Dream: What I Want to Become in the Future

(7) A. 这本书对你很有用吗？
　　B. 是，我常常用这本书。

　　　　　　　　　　　　　　对_____ 不对_____

(8) A. 我听说你成家了，是吗？
　　B. 对，我是去年结婚的。

　　　　　　　　　　　　　　对_____ 不对_____

(9) A. 你分析一下这个句子，好吗？
　　B. 我不理解这个句子，因此不会分析。

　　　　　　　　　　　　　　对_____ 不对_____

(10) A. 飞行员会飞吗？
　　 B. 飞行员不会飞，会<u>开飞机</u> (to pilot)。

　　　　　　　　　　　　　　对_____ 不对_____

4. 请用适当的词填空。
   Fill in the blanks with appropriate words.

   作文、作业、作品、作家、作为

   (1) 这部小说是谁的　　　　　　　。
   (2) 　　　　　　朋友，我很理解你。
   (3) 星期二考试的时候，老师让我们写一篇　　　　　　。
   (4) 你的　　　　　　是写作文还是造句子？
   (5) 我很喜欢这位　　　　　　的作品。

   理解、理想、道理、物理

   (6) 看完这部小说我明白了很多　　　　　　。
   (7) 谁没有　　　　　　？
   (8) 这个词语是什么意思？我不　　　　　　。
   (9) 在　　　　　　课上你为什么总是不说话？

5. 请用"不但……而且"这个词语将每个练习的两部分连成一句话。
Combine the two parts of each exercise into one sentence using the expression "不但…… 而且."

Model：
　　这个学生学习英文，也学习中文。
　　这个学生不但学习英文，而且学习中文。

(1) 我认识这个词语，还会用这个词语造句子。

(2) 当警察是他的理想，也是他弟弟的理想。

(3)《老人与海》这部小说容易读，容易理解，也很有意思。

(4) 我爸爸会做饭，也做得很好。

(5) 马可明忘了带手机，也忘了他弟弟的电话号码。

(6) 我们理解这道题，也会分析(这道题)。

第二单元 结尾活动
Second Unit End Activities

说说唱唱学中文
Learning Chinese in singing and speaking

 听歌曲：《长大后我就成了你》
Listen to the song: I Became You

作词：宋青松
作曲：王佑贵

长大后我就成了你

1. 小时候我以为你很美丽，领着一群小鸟，飞来飞去。小时候我以为你很神气，说上一句话也惊天动地。长大后我就成了你，才知道那间教室放飞的是希望，守巢的总是你。长大后我就成了你，才知道那块黑板写下的是真理，擦去的是功利。

2. 小时候我以为你很神秘，让所有的难题，成了乐趣。小时候我以为我很有力，你总喜欢把我们高高举起。长大后我就成了你，才知道那支粉笔画出的是彩虹，洒下的是泪滴。长大后我就成了你，才知道那个讲台举起的是别人，奉献的是自己。

长大后我就成了你，我就成了你，我就成了你。

词汇源
Vocabulary Support

zhǎngdà
长大/長大 to grow up

měilì
美丽/美麗 beautiful

qún
群/群 crowd, group

shénqì
神气/神氣 spirited, vigorous

(biàn)chéng
(变)成/(變)成 to become, to change to

fàng
放/放 to let go, to set free, to release

shǒu
守/守 to guard, to defend

kuài
块/塊 piece, lump, chunk

zhēnlǐ
真理/真理 truth

gōnglì
功利/功利 material gain

suǒyǒu
所有/所有 all

yǒulì
有力/有力 strong

zhī
支/支 measure word for stick-like things

cǎihóng
彩虹/彩虹 rainbow

lèi
泪/泪 tear

fèngxiàn
奉献/奉獻 to offer as a tribute

yǐwéi
以为/以爲 to believe, to think

lǐng
领/領 to lead

niǎo
鸟/鳥 bird

jīng tiān dòng dì
惊天动地/驚天動地 earthshaking

jiàoshì
教室/教室 classroom

xīwàng
希望/希望 to hope

cháo
巢/巢 nest

hēibǎn
黑板/黑板 blackboard

cā
擦/擦 to erase, to wipe out

shénmì
神秘/神秘 mysterious

lèqù
乐趣/樂趣 fun, joy, pleasure

jǔqǐ
举起/舉起 to lift, to hold up

fěnbǐ
粉笔/粉筆 chalk

sǎ
洒/灑 to sprinkle, to spray

dī
滴/滴 drop

jiǎngtái
讲台/講臺 platform

Unit 2 第二单元 结尾活动
Second Unit End Activities

这是什么地方？
这是 _____。

⭐ 练 习

1. 请用中文填空。

Fill in the blanks using Chinese.

长大后我就成了你

小时候 _____ 以为你 _____ 美丽
领着一群 _____ 鸟 _____ 来 _____ 去
_____ 时候我以 _____ 你很神气
_____ 上一句 _____ 也惊 _____ 动地

长 _____ 后我 _____ 成了你
才 _____ 那间教室
放飞的 _____ 希望守巢的总是 _____
长大 _____ 我就成了 _____
才知道 _____ 块黑板
_____ 下的是真理擦 _____ 的是功利

小 _____ 我 _____ 为你很神秘
让所有的 _____ 题成了 _____ 趣
_____ 时候我以 _____ 你很 _____ 力
你总 _____ 把我们高高举 _____

长大 _____ 我就成 _____ 你

才知道 _____ 支粉 _____

_____ 出的是彩虹洒 _____ 的是泪滴

长 _____ 我就成 _____

才知道 _____ 讲台举起的是 _____

奉献 _____ 是 _____

_____ 我就成了你

我就 _____

2. 多种选择题：歌词的意思是什么？两个人一组：轮流一个人读题一个人找出答案。

Multiple choice questions: which one represents the best meaning of the lyrics? Work in pairs: take turns to read the questions and make choices.

(1) 小时候我以为你很<u>美丽</u> (měilì: beautiful)

这句话的意思是……

a. 我小的时候很美丽
b. 你小的时候很美丽
c. 我小的时候觉得你很美丽
d. 你小的时候觉得我很美丽

(2) 领着一群小鸟飞来飞去

"一群小鸟"是什么意思？

只 (zhī: measure word for bird here)

a. 一群小鸟是很多小鸟
b. 一群小鸟是一只小鸟
c. 一群小鸟是两只小鸟
d. 一群小鸟是一只大鸟和一只小鸟

(3) 小时候我以为你很<u>神气</u> (shénqì: spirited, vigorous)

这句话的意思是……

a. 我小的时候觉得你很神气　　b. 你小的时候觉得我很神气
c. 我小的时候很神气　　　　　d. 你小的时候很神气

Unit 2 第二单元 结尾活动

(4) 说上一句话也惊天动地
　　这是一句什么样的话？
　　　a. 这句话很难理解　　　　b. 这句话很长
　　　c. 这句话很有意思　　　　d. 这句话很有力

(5) 长大后我就成了你
　　这句话的意思是……
　　　a. 我长大以后也是一只小鸟
　　　b. 你长大以后也是一只小鸟
　　　c. 我长大以后和你做一样的工作
　　　d. 你长大以后和我做一样的工作

(6) 长大后我就成了你，才知道那块黑板写下的是真理擦去的是功利
　　谁在黑板上写真理？
　　　a. 我　　　　　　　　　　b. 你
　　　c. 他　　　　　　　　　　d. 她

(7) 小时候我以为你很神秘，让所有的难题成了乐趣
　　为什么"难题"变成了"乐趣"？因为……
　　　a. "你"不喜欢难题　　　b. "我"不做难题
　　　c. "你"让我理解了难题　d. "你"忘了给我难题

(8) 你总喜欢把我们高高举起
　　这是因为……
　　　a. 我们喜欢你　　　　　　b. 你喜欢我们
　　　c. 我们认识你　　　　　　d. 你认识我们

(9) 画出的是彩虹洒下的是泪滴
　　"你"用什么画彩虹？
　　　a. 泪滴　　　　　　　　　b. 粉笔
　　　c. 难题　　　　　　　　　d. 乐趣

(10) 长大后我就成了你，才知道那个讲台举起的是别人奉献的是自己
　　　"奉献自己"是什么意思？
　　　　a. 喜欢自己　　　　　　b. 介绍自己
　　　　c. 做对自己有用的事　　d. 做对别人有用的事

321

3. 请用中文回答问题。
Answer the questions using Chinese.

(1) 歌词中的"你"是谁？

(2) "小鸟"是谁？

(3) "巢"的直接 (zhíjiē: direct, immediate) 英文意思是什么？
在这首歌中真正 (zhēnzhèng: real, true) 的意思是什么？

(4) 谁总是"守巢"？为什么？

(5) 什么是真理？请你用中文给一个例子 (lìzi: example)。

(6) 你什么时候觉得解难题是一种 (yī zhǒng: a kind of) 乐趣？

(7) 你小的时候觉得谁最有力气 (yǒu lìqi: strong)？

(8) 你喜欢用粉笔在黑板上写字吗？

(9) 你小的时候喜欢画彩虹 (cǎihóng: rainbow) 吗？现在呢，还喜欢画吗？

(10) 歌中的"你"做的工作是你的理想工作吗？

看电影学中文
Learning Chinese while watching movie

看电影：《一个都不能少》
Movie screening: Not One Less

看电影之前
Before watching the movie

词汇源
Vocabulary Support

Wèi Mǐnzhī 魏敏芝/魏敏芝	Zhāng Huìkē 张慧科/張慧科
shuǐquán 水泉/水泉 name of the village	cūn(zi) 村(子)/村(子) village
shāncūn 山村/山村 mountain village	cūnzhǎng 村长/村長 village head
shuì jiào 睡觉/睡覺 to sleep	dài kè 代课/代課 to substitute an absent teacher
bān 搬/搬 to carry away, to move	zhuān 砖/磚 brick
qián 钱/錢 money	kěkǒu kělè 可口可乐/可口可樂 Coca Cola
rìjì 日记/日記 diary, journal	dǎ gōng 打工/打工 to work (temporary)
chāo 抄/抄 to copy by hand	chēpiào 车票/車票 train or bus ticket
xúnrén qǐshì 寻人启示/尋人啟示 missing person	niánqīng 年轻/年輕 young
chénglǐ 城里/城裏 in town, inside the city	diànshìtái 电视台/電視臺 TV station
táizhǎng 台长/臺長 station manager	xuéshēngzhèng 学生证/學生證 student ID
qióng 穷/窮 poor	yào fàn 要饭/要飯 to beg (for food or money)
bìng 病/病 sick	hē 喝/喝 to drink

练习

1. 请阅读下面的段落，然后用中文回答问题。
   Answer the questions using Chinese after reading the following paragraph.

   这是一部中国电影，一九九九年拍摄 (pāishè: to make a film)。电

影导演 (dǎoyǎn: director)叫张艺谋 (Zhāng Yìmóu)。

在中国的北方(běifāng: north)有一个小山村 (shāncūn: mountain village)，叫水泉村。这个村子里有一所学校，名字叫"水泉小学"。因为这个学校里只有一个老师 (这位老师姓高)，所以高老师当老师，也当校长。高老师在这个学校教书很多年了；他很喜欢他的学生们。

有一天，村长请来了一位新老师，这是一位年轻 (nián qīng: young) 漂亮的女老师。这位女老师姓什么？叫什么？她多大？她为什么来水泉小学？她来了高老师干什么工作？等你们看了电影《一个都不能少》就可以用中文回答这些 (zhèxiē: these, those) 问题了。

(1) 水泉村在哪儿？

(2) 水泉村是一个什么样的村子？

(3) 这个村子里有几所学校？

(4) 这所小学的名字叫什么？

(5) 这所小学有几个老师？

(6) 谁是这所小学的校长？

(7) 高老师是新老师吗？

(8) 村长请来了什么样的新老师？

(9) 你想在看电影的时候知道什么？

(10) 你觉得这个电影会有意思吗？

看电影之后
After watching the movie

2. 看完电影后请用中文回答问题。
Answer the questions using Chinese after the screening of the movie.

(1) 代课的老师姓什么？叫什么名字？

(2) 高老师为什么不能给学生们上课了？

(3) 高老师有多少个学生？

(4) 魏老师代课多长 (duō cháng: how long) 时间？

(5) 高老师给了魏老师多少支 (zhī: measure word) 粉笔？

(6) 村长说给魏老师多少钱？

(7) 上课的时候魏老师让她的学生们做什么？

(8) 晚上学生们在哪里睡觉？

(9) 谁是张慧科？

(10) 学生们为什么搬砖 (bān zhuān: to carry bricks)？

(11) 魏老师买了几瓶可口可乐？

(12) 二十六个学生和一个老师怎么喝可口可乐？

(13) 魏老师为什么去城里？

(14) 魏老师为什么买纸 (zhǐ: paper) 和笔？

(15) 在城里，魏老师去哪里找张慧科？她找到这个学生了吗？

3. 比赛。

   Competition.

   (1) 请按照下面的每一步完成任务。

   Complete the task by following each of the steps.

   A. 两个人一组：轮流读题，并在二十分钟内用中文回答下列问题。答题的时候每个人都要把答案写下来。

   Work in pairs: within twenty minutes, take turns to read the questions and find the answers. Each of you should write down the answers using Chinese.

   1) 在你的国家 (country) 魏老师可以当老师吗？为什么？

   2) 你们的学校和"水泉小学"有什么一样？有什么不一样？

   3) "水泉小学"的学生们上课的时候做什么？你们上课的时候做什么？

4) 你们怎么喝 (hē: to drink) 可口可乐？山村的孩子们怎么喝？

5) 魏老师一天可以用几支 (zhī: measure word) 粉笔？你们的老师呢？

6) 你没有钱 (qián: money) 的时候怎么办？"水泉小学"的学生们没有钱的时候做什么？

7) 在这个电影里，谁病了 (bìng le: to be sick)？谁要饭了？谁在外面 (outside)睡觉了？谁上电视 (to be on TV) 了？谁哭 (kū: to cry) 了？

8) 在电视里，魏老师对她的学生说什么？

9) 魏老师、张慧科和谁一起回村子了？

10) 在电影的结尾 (jiéwěi: end)，学生们在黑板上写了什么字？他们写的字你们认识几个？

B. 用十分钟的时间口语练习以上的问题与答案。
Use ten minutes to orally practice the above questions and answers.

C. 在全班面前表演。
Present in front of the class.

D. 用中文讨论：哪个组得第一名，哪个组第二名。说说为什么。
   Discuss using Chinese: which group wins first place and which one second. Explain why.

E. 每个组用中文向全班汇报你们的讨论结果。
   Using Chinese, each group should report the results of your discussion to the entire class.

F. 老师用中文宣布比赛结果。
   The instructor announces the results of the competition using Chinese.

4. 请按照例句做练习。
   Do the exercise following the model.

请你想一想这是什么意思？

Model: 校长 — principal

(1) 村长

(2) 班长

(3) 家长

(4) 银行行长

(5) 律师所所长

(6) 医院院长

(7) 电视台台长

(8) 体育馆馆长

(9) 美术学院院长

(10) 北京大学校长

Index
生词索引

1UE: First Unit End Activities
2UE: Second Unit End Activities

Chinese — English

Chinese		English	Function	Lesson
A				
ān	安/安	a surname	proper noun	3
Ānnà	安娜/安娜	Anna	proper noun	3
ànshí	按时/按時	on time, on schedule	adverb	7
B				
ba	吧/吧		particle	2
bā	八/八	eight	numeral	2
bāshí	八十/八十	eighty	numeral	4
bàba	爸爸/爸爸	dad, daddy	noun	3
bái	白/白	white	adjective	8
Bái	白/白	a surname	proper noun	8
bǎi	百/百	hundred	numeral	5
Bái Zhēnnī	白珍妮/白珍妮	Jenny Bailey	proper noun	8
bān	班/班	class, team	noun	6
bān	搬/搬	to carry away, to move	verb	2UE
bàn	半/半	half, semi-	noun	5
bàn	办/辦	to handle, to manage	verb	7
bàngōng	办公/辦公	to handle business, to work in an office	verb	7
bàngōngshì	办公室/辦公室	office	noun	7
bāngzhù	帮助/幫助	to help	verb	1UE
bāo	包/包	bag	noun	5
Běijīng	北京/北京	Beijing	proper noun	2
Běijīng Dàxué	北京大学/北京大學	Peking University	proper noun	2

331

běn	本/本		measure word	5
bǐ	比/比	to compare	verb	8
bǐ	比/比	compared to	preposition	8
biàn	变/變	to change	verb	1UE
biànchéng	变成/變成	to change into, to turn into	verb	1UE
bié	别/別	other, else	pronoun	8
bìng	病/病	sick	adjective	2UE
bǐsài	比赛/比賽	to compete	verb	7
bǐtóu	笔头/筆頭	written	adjective	7
bù	不/不	no, not	adverb	1
bù	部/部		measure word	8
bùdàn……érqiě	不但……而且/ 不但……而且	not only... but also	expression	8
bùguò	不过/不過	but, however	conjunction	5
bùkèqì	不客气/不客氣	you are welcome	expression	7
bùrán	不然/不然	if not, otherwise	conjunction	7
bùzài	不再/不再	no more, no longer	adverb	8

C

cā	擦/擦	to erase	verb	2UE
cǎihóng	彩虹/彩虹	rainbow	noun	2UE
cānguǎn	餐馆/餐館	restaurant	noun	4
cèyàn	测验/測驗	quiz, test	noun	6
chà	差/差	short of	adjective	5
chàbuduō	差不多/差不多	almost, nearly	adverb	6
cháng	长/長	long	adjective	4
cháng (cháng)	常(常)/(常常)	often, frequently	adverb	6
Chángchéng	长城/長城	the Great Wall	proper noun	4
chànggē	唱歌/唱歌	to sing	verb	6
Chángjiāng	长江/長江	the Yangtze River	proper noun	4
chángshòu	长寿/長壽	longevity	noun	4
chāo	抄/抄	to copy by hand	verb	2UE

cháo	巢/巢	nest	noun	2UE
chēpiào	车票/車票	train or bus ticket	noun	2UE
chéngjiā	成家/成家	to marry (for a man)	verb	8
chénglǐ	城里/城裏	in town, in the city	expression	2UE
chī	吃/吃	to eat	verb	4
chuán	船/船	boat, ship	noun	1UE
chūjí	初级/初級	elementary level	noun	6
chúle……yǐwài, dōu	除了……(以外),都/除了……(以外),都	except	preposition	6
chúle……yǐwài, yě (or: hái)	除了……(以外),也(or: 还)/除了……(以外),也(or: 還)	in addition to, besides	preposition	6
chūmén	出门/出門	to be away from home, to go out	verb	7
chūsè	出色/出色	outstanding, remarkable	adjective	8
chúshī	厨师/厨師	cook, chef	noun	8
chūn (tiān)	春(天)/春(天)	spring	noun	1UE
cíhuì	词汇/詞匯	vocabulary	noun	7
cì	次/次	time (recurring instances)	measure word	4
cóng	从/從	from	preposition	8
cóngcǐ	从此/從此	from now on	adverb	1UE
cūnzhǎng	村长/村長	village head	noun	2UE
cūnzi	村子/村子	village	noun	2UE
cuò	错/錯	wrong	adjective	4

D

dǎgōng	打工/打工	to work (temporarily)	verb	2UE
dǎkāi	打开/打開	to open	verb	2
dǎsuan	打算/打算	to plan, to intend	verb	4
dà	大/大	big, large, great	adjective	2
dàjiā	大家/大家	everybody	pronoun	1UE
dàxué	大学/大學	university	noun	2
dài	带/帶	to bring, to take with	verb	7
dàikè	代课/代課	to substitute an absent teacher	verb	2UE

dàngāo	蛋糕/蛋糕	cake	noun	4
dāng	当/當	to serve as, to work as	verb	8
dāngrán	当然/當然	of course	adverb	8
dāngshí	当时/當時	at that time, at once	adverb	8
dǎoyǎn	导演/導演	director (of a film or play)	noun	1UE
dào	到/到	to arrive	verb	4
dàochù	到处/到處	everywhere	adverb	1UE
dàodǐ	到底/到底	after all, finally	adverb	8
dàolǐ	道理/道理	principle, reason	noun	8
de	的/的		particle	1
de	得/得		particle	8
děi	得/得	to have to	verb	5
děng	等/等	to wait, to wait for	verb	7
dī	滴/滴	drop	noun	2UE
dì	第/第	ordinal number marker	particle	2
dì	地/地	earth, land, soil	noun	5
dìdi	弟弟/弟弟	younger brother	noun	3
dìfang	地方/地方	place	noun	1UE
dìlǐ	地理/地理	geography	noun	5
diǎn	点/點	dot, point	noun	5
diǎntóu	点头/點頭	to nod one's head	verb	1UE
diàn	电/電	electricity, power	noun	7
diànhuà	电话/電話	telephone	noun	7
diànshìtái	电视台/電視臺	TV station	noun	2UE
diànyǐng	电影/電影	movie	noun	1UE
dōng	冬/冬	winter	noun	7
dōu	都/都	both, all, already	adverb	5
dú	读/讀	to read	verb	6
duì	对/對	correct, yes, right	adjective	5
duì	对/對	to	preposition	8

duìbuqǐ	对不起/對不起	sorry	expression	5
duìhuà	对话/對話	dialogue, conversation	noun	6

E

èr	二/二	two	numeral	2
èrshí	二十/二十	twenty	numeral	3
èrshíyī	二十一/二十一	twenty one	numeral	3

F

fāyīn	发音/發音	pronunciation	noun	6
fǎ	法/法	law, method, way	noun	2
fàn	饭/飯	meal, food	noun	4
fàng	放/放	to let go, to set free, to release	verb	2UE
fēi	飞/飛	to fly	verb	8
fēixíngyuán	飞行员/飛行員	pilot	noun	8
fēnxi	分析/分析	to analyze	verb	8
fēnzhōng	分钟/分鐘	minute	noun	5
fěnbǐ	粉笔/粉筆	chalk	noun	2UE
fèngxiàn	奉献/奉獻	to offer as a tribute	verb	2UE
fùxí	复习/復習	to review	verb	7
fùxí	复习/復習	review	noun	7

G

gǎibiàn	改变/改變	to change, to alter, to transform	verb	8
gàn	干/幹	to do, to work	verb	6
gāng (gāng)	刚(刚)/剛(剛)	just now, not long ago	adverb	6
Gāo	高/高	a surname	proper noun	2
gāo	高/高	tall, high	adjective	2
Gāo Yīngmíng	高英明/高英明	a person's name	proper noun	2
gàosu	告诉/告訴	to tell	verb	6
gè	个/個		measure word	2
gēcí	歌词/歌詞	lyrics	noun	1UE
gēge	哥哥/哥哥	elder brother	noun	3

gē (qǔ)	歌(曲)/歌(曲)	song	noun	1UE
gěi	给/給	to give	verb	3
gěi	给/給	to, for	preposition	3
gōng	公/公	public	adjective	4
gōngyuán	公园/公園	park	noun	4
gōnglì	功利/功利	material gain	noun	2UE
gōngchéngshī	工程师/工程師	engineer	noun	8
gōngzuò	工作/工作	work, job	noun	3
gōngzuò	工作/工作	to work	verb	3
gǒu	狗/狗	dog	noun	1UE
gùshi	故事/故事	story, tale	noun	7
guǎn	馆/館	accomodation for guests, shop, a place for cultural activities	noun	7
guó	国/國	country, nation	noun	2
guò	过/過	to spend, to pass, to go through	verb	4

H

hái	还/還	also, still	adverb	3
háishì	还是/還是	or	conjunction	3
háizi	孩子/孩子	child	noun	3
hǎi	海/海	ocean, sea	noun	8
Hǎimíngwēi	海明威/海明威	Hemingway	proper noun	8
Hànyǔ	汉语/漢語	Chinese language	proper noun	2
hǎo	好/好	good, nice, fine	adjective	1
hǎo	好/好	well	adverb	1
hào	号/號	day of the month	noun	4
hàomǎ	号码/號碼	number	noun	7
hē	喝/喝	to drink	verb	2UE
hé	和/和	and, with	conjunction	2
hé	何/何	a surname	proper noun	5
hé……yīqǐ	和……一起/和……一起	together with...	expression	3

hēibǎn	黑板/黑板	blackboard	noun	2UE
hěn	很/很	very, quite, awfully	adverb	4
hóu	猴/猴	monkey	noun	1UE
hòumian	后面/後面	behind, that follows	preposition	7
hòutiān	后天/後天	the day after tomorrow	noun	7
huā	花/花	flower	noun	4
huā	花/花	a surname	proper noun	6
huā	花/花	to spend	verb	6
huà	画/畫	to draw, to paint	verb	8
huà (r)	画(儿)/畫(兒)	drawing, painting	noun	8
Huáng Ānzhú	黄安竹/黄安竹	Andrew Hunt	proper noun	6
huídá	回答/回答	answer, response	noun	7
huídá	回答/回答	to answer, to respond	verb	7
huítóujiàn	回头见/回頭見	see you later, see you soon	expression	5
huì	会/會	to know how, to be able	verb	6
huódòng	活动/活動	activity	noun	6
huò (zhě)	或(者)/或(者)	or, either...or	conjunction	8

J

jī	机/機	machine, engine	noun	7
jīhū	几乎/幾乎	almost, nearly	adverb	6
jímáng	急忙/急忙	in a hurry, hastily	adverb	7
jǐ(gè)	几(个)/幾(個)	how many	adjective	3
jǐhé	几何/幾何	geometry	noun	5
jìzhù	记住/記住	to remember, to bear in mind	verb	7
jiā	家/家	home, family	noun	3
jiā	家/家		measure word	3
jiātíng	家庭/家庭	family, household	noun	8
jiā	加/加	to add	verb	8
jiǎngtái	讲台/講臺	platform	noun	2UE
jiāo	教/教	to teach, to instruct	verb	6

jiāo	交/交	to hand over, to turn in	verb	7
jiào	叫/叫	to call, to be named	verb	1
jiàoshì	教室/教室	classroom	noun	2UE
jiē	接/接	to meet, to receive, to pick up	verb	7
jié	节/節		measure word	5
jiéhūn	结婚/結婚	to marry	verb	8
jiéshí	结识/結識	to become acquainted with	verb	1UE
jiérán bùtóng	截然不同/截然不同	completely different	expression	6
jiějie	姐姐/姐姐	elder sister	noun	3
jiěshì	解释/解釋	to explain	verb	8
jiětí	解题/解題	to solve a problem	verb	5
jièshào	介绍/介紹	to introduce	verb	2
jièshào	介绍/介紹	introduction	noun	2
jiǔ	九/九	nine	numeral	2
jiǔshí	九十/九十	ninety	numeral	4
jiù	就/就	soon, immediately, right away	adverb	6
jīn	金/金	gold, metals	noun	1UE
jìnliàng	尽量/盡量	to the fullest extent, as much as possible	adverb	6
jīngtiān dòngdì	惊天动地/驚天動地	earthshaking	adjective	2UE
jīng	京/京	the capital of a country	noun	2
jīngjì	经济/經濟	economy, economics	noun	5
jìnglǐ	敬礼/敬禮	to salute	verb	1UE
jǐngchá	警察/警察	police	noun	8
jīntiān	今天/今天	today	noun	2
jǔqǐ	举起/舉起	to hold up, to lift	verb	2UE
jù	剧/劇	drama, play, opera	noun	1UE
juéde	觉得/覺得	to feel, to think	verb	4
jūnguān	军官/軍官	military officer	noun	8

K

kǎ	卡/卡	card	noun	4
kāishǐ	开始/開始	to start, to begin	verb	6
kàn	看/看	to look at, to watch	verb	3
kànlái	看来/看來	to seem, to look as if	verb	5
kǎoshì	考试/考試	to test, to give an examination	verb	6
kǎoshì	考试/考試	test, examination	noun	6
kēxuéjiā	科学家/科學家	scientist	noun	8
kěyǐ	可以/可以	may, can, to be able	verb	7
Kěkǒu Kělè	可口可乐/可口可樂	Coca-Cola	proper noun	2UE
kěnéng	可能/可能	probably	adverb	7
kěshì	可是/可是	but, yet, however	conjunction	4
kè	课/課	course, lesson, class	noun	2
kèwén	课文/課文	text	noun	6
kèxià	课下/課下	after class	expression	7
kè	刻/刻	a quarter (of an hour)	noun	5
kǒu	口/口		measure word	3
kǒutóu	口头/口頭	oral	adjective	7
kuài	快/快	fast, quickly, soon	adverb	4
kuài	块/塊		measure word	2UE
kuàijìshī	会计师/會計師	accountant	noun	8
kuàilè	快乐/快樂	happy, joyful	adjective	4

L

lái	来/來	to come	verb	2
Lán Dōngdōng	蓝冬冬/藍冬冬	Winter Lamb	proper noun	7
lánqiú	篮球/籃球	basketball	noun	7
lǎo	老/老	old	adjective	1
lǎobǎn	老板/老板	boss	noun	1UE
lǎolao	姥姥/姥姥	grandmother (maternal)	noun	3
lǎoshī	老师/老師	teacher	noun	1

lǎoye	姥爷/姥爺	grandfather (maternal)	noun	3
le	了/了		particle	4
lèqù	乐趣/樂趣	fun, pleasure, joy	noun	2UE
lèi	泪/泪	tear	noun	2UE
Lǐ	李/李	a surname	proper noun	1
Lǐ Tóngwén	李同文/李同文	a person's name	proper noun	1
lǐ	里/裏	in, inside	preposition	4
lǐjiě	理解/理解	to understand, to comprehend	verb	8
lǐxiǎng	理想/理想	ideal	noun	8
lì	莉/莉	jasmine	noun	5
lìshǐ	历史/歷史	history	noun	5
lìyè	立业/立業	to start a career	verb	8
liǎn	脸/臉	face	noun	1UE
liànxí	练习/練習	practice, exercise	noun	6
liànxí	练习/練習	to practice, to exercise	verb	6
liǎo bu qǐ	了不起/了不起	amazing, terrific, extraordinary	expression	8
líng	零/零	zero	noun	5
líng	铃/鈴	bell	noun	7
lǐng	领/領	to lead	verb	2UE
lìngwài	另外/另外	besides, in addition to	adverb	7
Liú	刘/劉	a surname	proper noun	1
Liú Xiǎomíng	刘小明/劉小明	a person's name	proper noun	1
liú	留/留	to leave (a message), to assign (homework)	verb	6
liúxià	留下/留下	to leave something, to stay	verb	6
liù	六/六	six	numeral	2
liùshí	六十/六十	sixty	numeral	4
lù	路/路	road, way, journey, route	noun	1UE
lǜshī	律师/律師	lawyer	noun	3
lǜshīsuǒ	律师所/律師所	law firm	noun	3

M

| ma | 吗/嗎 | | particle | 1 |

māma	妈妈/媽媽	mom	noun	3
mǎdàhā	马大哈/馬大哈	a careless person, a forgetful person	noun	7
Mǎ Kěmíng	马可明/馬可明	Kim Maas	proper noun	7
mǎi	买/買	to buy	verb	4
mài	卖/賣	to sell	verb	6
mǎn	满/滿	full, filled, packed	adjective	5
máng	忙/忙	busy	adjective	5
méi	没/没	not	adverb	3
měi	美/美	pretty, beautiful	adjective	2
Měiguó	美国/美國	America	proper noun	2
měilì	美丽/美麗	beautiful	adjective	2UE
měishù	美术/美術	fine arts, art	noun	5
měi	每/每	every, each	adjective	5
mèimei	妹妹/妹妹	younger sister	noun	3
mén	门/門		measure word	5
miàntiáo	面条/面條	noodles	noun	4
míng	名/名	name, fame, reputation	noun	1
míngzi	名字/名字	name	noun	1
míng	明/明	bright, brilliant	adjective	1
míngbai	明白/明白	to understand	verb	8
míngtiān	明天/明天	tomorrow	noun	4
míngtiān jiàn	明天见/明天見	see you tomorrow	expression	4

N

nǎgè	哪个/哪個	which	pronoun	3
nǎ (r)	哪(儿)/哪(兒)	where	pronoun	3
nà	那/那	that	pronoun	2
nàlǐ	那里/那裏	there	pronoun	4
nà (me)	那(么)/那(麼)	so, then, in that case	conjunction	4
nà (r)	那(儿)/那(兒)	(informal) there	pronoun	4
nà	娜/娜	grace	noun	3

nǎinai	奶奶/奶奶	grandmother (paternal)	noun	3
nán	难/難	difficult	adjective	1UE
nán	男/男	male	adjective	3
nán péngyou	男朋友/男朋友	boyfriend	noun	4
ne	呢/呢		particle	1
néng	能/能	to be able, can	verb	7
nǐ	你/你	you (singular)	pronoun	1
nǐ duō dà	你多大/你多大	how old are you (used for young people)	expression	3
nǐmen	你们/你們	you (plural)	pronoun	1
nián	年/年	year	noun	3
niánjí	年级/年级	grade, year	noun	6
niánqīng	年轻/年輕	young	adjective	2UE
niǎo	鸟/鳥	bird	noun	2UE
nín	您/您	you (formal)	pronoun	1
nín duō dà suìshù	您多大岁数/您多大歲數	how old are you (used for elder people)	expression	3
nǚ	女/女	female	adjective	3

P

pà	怕/怕	to fear, to be afraid of	verb	7
péngyou	朋友/朋友	friend	noun	2
piān	篇/篇		measure word	8
piàoliang	漂亮/漂亮	pretty	adjective	4
pīngpāngqiú	乒乓球/乒乓球	ping-pong, table tennis	noun	7
píng	瓶/瓶	bottle, vase, jar	noun	4
píngshí	平时/平時	ordinarily, usually, normally	adverb	6

Q

qī	七/七	seven	numeral	4
qīshí	七十/七十	seventy	numeral	4
qī	期/期	term, a period of time	noun	4

qǐ míngzi	起名字/起名字	to name, to give a name	verb	6
qiān	千/千	thousand	numeral	5
qián	钱/錢	money	noun	2UE
qián	前/前	front, ahead	noun	7
qǐng	请/請	to invite, please	verb	2
qǐngwèn	请问/請問	may I ask, please tell me	expression	1
qióng	穷/窮	poor	adjective	2UE
qù	去/去	to go	verb	4
quánjiāfú	全家福/全家福	family picture	noun	3
qún	群/群	crowd, group	noun	2UE

R

ràng	让/讓	to let, to allow	verb	7
rén	人/人	people, person	noun	2
rènshi	认识/認識	to know	verb	2
rènzhēn	认真/認真	careful, serious	adjective	8
rì	日/日	sun, day	noun	3
Rìběn	日本/日本	Japan	proper noun	4
rìjì	日记/日記	diary, journal	noun	2UE
róngyì	容易/容易	easy	adjective	5
rúguǒ	如果/如果	if	conjunction	1UE

S

sǎ	洒/灑	to sprinkle, to spray	verb	2UE
Sài Zhēnzhū	赛珍珠/賽珍珠	Pearl S. Buck	proper noun	8
sān	三/三	three	numeral	3
sānshí	三十/三十	thirty	numeral	3
shān	山/山	mountain	noun	2UE
shāncūn	山村/山村	mountain village	noun	2UE
shàngkè	上课/上課	to attend a class, to teach a class	verb	2
shàngxué	上学/上學	to go to school, to attend school	verb	3
shèhuì	社会/社會	society	noun	8

shéi (or: shuí)	谁/誰	who, whom	pronoun	2
shēng	声/聲	sound, voice, tone	noun	6
shēngcí	生词/生詞	new word, vocabulary	noun	6
shēngrì	生日/生日	birthday	noun	3
shēngwù (xué)	生物 (学)/生物（學）	biology	noun	5
shénme	什么/什麼	what	pronoun	1
shénmì	神秘/神祕	mysterious	adjective	2UE
shénqì	神气/神氣	spirited, vigorous	adjective	2UE
shí	十/十	ten	numeral	2
shíyī	十一/十一	eleven	numeral	3
shíhou	时候/時候	moment	noun	6
shíjiān	时间/時間	time	noun	6
shǐ	史/史	history, a surname	noun	5
shì	是/是	to be	verb	1
shì	试/試	to try, to test	verb	4
shì	室/室	room	noun	7
shì (r)	事 (儿)/事（兒）	matter, affair, thing, business	noun	7
shìyè	事业/事業	cause	noun	8
shǒu	手/手	hand	noun	7
shǒujī	手机/手機	mobile phone, cell phone	noun	7
shǒu	守/守	to guard, to defend	verb	2UE
shū	书/書	book	noun	2
shūbāo	书包/書包	book bag	noun	5
shūxiě	书写/書寫	to write	verb	6
shùxué	数学/數學	mathematics	noun	5
shuí (or: shéi)	谁/誰	who, whom	pronoun	2
shuǐ	水/水	water	noun	2UE
shuǐquán	水泉/水泉	Shuiquan	proper noun	2UE
shuìjiào	睡觉/睡覺	to sleep	verb	2UE
shuō	说/説	to speak, to say	verb	4

sì	四/四	four	numeral	2
Sìchuān	四川/四川	Sichuan Province	proper noun	1UE
sìshí	四十/四十	forty	numeral	3
suì	岁/歲	year, age	noun	3
sūnnǚ	孙女/孫女	granddaughter	noun	1UE
sūnzi	孙子/孫子	grandson	noun	1UE
suǒ	所/所	place	noun	3
suǒ	所/所		measure word	3
suǒyǐ	所以/所以	therefore, thus, as a result	conjunction	5
suǒyǒu	所有/所有	all	pronoun	2UE

T

tā	他/他	he, him	pronoun	2
tā	她/她	she, her	pronoun	2
tāmen	他们/他們	they, them (masculine)	pronoun	2
tāmen	她们/她們	they, them (feminine)	pronoun	2
táng	堂/堂		measure word	6
táizhǎng	台长/臺長	station manager	noun	2UE
tí	题/題	topic, title, problem	noun	5
tímù	题目/題目	topic, title	noun	8
tǐyù	体育/體育	sports, physical education	noun	5
tiān	天/天	sky, heaven, day	noun	2
tiāncì	天赐/天賜	God-send, God's gift	proper noun	1UE
tīng	听/聽	to listen	verb	4
tīngshuō	听说/聽說	to be told, to hear that	verb	4
tīngxiě	听写/聽寫	dictation	noun	7
tóngxué	同学/同學	schoolmate, classmate	noun	1
túshūguǎn	图书馆/圖書館	library	noun	7

W

wá (wa)	娃(娃)/娃(娃)	baby, newborn animal	noun	1UE
wán	完/完	to finish, to complete	verb	6

Wáng	王/王	a surname	proper noun	1
wáng	王/王	king	noun	1UE
wàng	忘/忘	to forget	verb	7
wán (r)	玩(儿)/玩(兒)	to play, to have fun	verb	7
Wēilì	威利/威利	Willie	proper noun	7
wèi	位/位		measure word	8
Wèi Mǐnzhī	魏敏芝/魏敏芝	a person's name	proper noun	2UE
wèishénme	为什么/爲什麽	why	adverb	5
wén	文/文	character, script, writing, language	noun	1
wénhuà	文化/文化	culture	noun	2
Wén Xiǎoyīng	文小英/文小英	a person's name	proper noun	2
wénxué	文学/文學	literature	noun	8
wénxuéjiā	文学家/文學家	writer, man of letters	noun	8
wèn	问/問	to ask	verb	7
wèntí	问题/問題	question	noun	7
wǒ	我/我	I, me	pronoun	1
wǒmen	我们/我們	we	pronoun	1
wòshǒu	握手/握手	to shake hands	verb	1UE
wǔ	五/五	five	numeral	2
wǔshí	五十/五十	fifty	numeral	4
wùlǐ	物理/物理	physics	noun	5

X

xīwàng	希望/希望	to hope	verb	2UE
xǐhuan	喜欢/喜歡	to like, to be fond of	verb	4
xì	戏/戲	drama, play, opera	noun	1UE
xià	下/下	lower, inferior, next	adjective	4
xiàkè	下课/下課	to finish attending (or teaching) a class	verb	7
xiàwǔ	下午/下午	afternoon, P.M.	noun	5
xiānsheng	先生/先生	mister, husband	noun	1
xiànzài	现在/现在	now	adverb	2

xiǎng	想/想	to think, to plan, to want, to miss	verb	4
xiǎng	响/響	to ring, to make sound	verb	7
xiǎo	小/小	small, little	adjective	1
xiào	笑/笑	to smile	verb	1UE
xiě	写/寫	to write	verb	6
xiè	谢/謝	to thank	verb	2
Xiè	谢/謝	a surname	proper noun	2
Xiè Péng	谢朋/謝朋	a person's name	proper noun	2
xièxie	谢谢/謝謝	thanks, thank you	expression	2
xīn	新/新	new	adjective	2
xīn	心/心	heart	noun	1UE
xīngqī	星期/星期	week	noun	4
xīngqīrì	星期日/星期日	Sunday	proper noun	4
xīngqītiān	星期天/星期天	Sunday	proper noun	4
xìng	姓/姓	to be surnamed	verb	1
xìng	姓/姓	surname	noun	1
xué	学/學	to study, to learn	verb	1
xuéqī	学期/學期	semester	noun	4
xuésheng	学生/學生	student	noun	1
xuéshēng zhèng	学生证/學生證	student identification	noun	2UE
xuéxí	学习/學習	to study	verb	2
xún	寻/尋	to seek, to look for	verb	1UE
xúnrén qǐshì	寻人启示/尋人啓示	missing person	expression	2UE

Y

yā (or: ya)	呀/呀	ah, oh	exclamation	1UE
yǎnyuán	演员/演員	actor, actress	noun	8
yào	要/要	to ask, to want	verb	4
yàofàn	要饭/要飯	to beg (for food or money)	verb	2UE

yéye	爷爷/爺爺	grandfather (paternal)	noun	3
yě	也/也	also, too	adverb	1
yě jiù shì shuō	也就是说/也就是說	in other words, that is	expression	6
yè	页/頁	page	noun	2
yī	一/一	one	numeral	2
yībǎi	一百/一百	one hundred	numeral	5
yīhuì (r)	一会儿/一會兒	a little while, very soon	expression	5
yīhuì (r) jiàn	一会儿见/一會兒見	see you soon	expression	5
yīqǐ	一起/一起	together	adverb	3
yīqiān	一千/一千	one thousand	numeral	5
yīshēng	医生/醫生	doctor	noun	3
yīxià (r)	一下(儿)/一下(兒)	quickly, for a short while	expression	2
yīyàng	一样/一樣	alike, same	adjective	6
yīyuàn	医院/醫院	hospital	noun	3
yǐhòu	以后/以後	after, hereafter	preposition	7
yǐqián	以前/以前	before, prior	adverb	7
yǐwéi	以为/以爲	to think, to believe	verb	2UE
yìdàlì	意大利/義大利	Italy	proper noun	4
yìsi	意思/意思	meaning	noun	5
yīncǐ	因此/因此	therefore, consequently	adverb	8
yīnwèi	因为/因爲	because, since, as	expression	5
yīnyuè	音乐/音樂	music	noun	5
yínháng	银行/銀行	bank	noun	3
yīng	英/英	flower (written language)	noun	2
Yīng Āndí	英安迪/英安迪	Andy Yoon	proper noun	8
yīnggāi	应该/應該	should, ought	verb	7
yīngmíng	英明/英明	wise	adjective	2
Yīngyǔ	英语/英語	English	proper noun	2
yǒngyuǎn	永远/永遠	forever, always	adverb	1UE
yòng	用/用	to use, to employ	verb	7

yòngfǎ	用法/用法	use, usage	noun	6
yóudìyuán	邮递员/郵遞員	postman	noun	8
yǒu	有/有	to have	verb	3
yǒude…… yǒude	有的……有的/有的……有的	some... some others	expression	8
yǒulì	有力/有力	strong	adjective	2UE
yǒushí (hou)	有时(候)/有時(候)	sometimes	adverb	6
yǒu yìsi	有意思/有意思	interesting	expression	5
yǒuyòng	有用/有用	useful	adjective	8
yǔ	语/語	language	noun	2
yǔfǎ	语法/語法	grammar	noun	2
yǔyán	语言/語言	language	noun	6
yǔyīn	语音/語音	pronunciation, speech sounds	noun	6
yǔ	与/與	and, together with	preposition	8
yuán	园/園	garden, park	noun	4
yuàn	院/院	yard, public places	noun	3
yuàn	愿/願	to hope, to wish, to desire	verb	1UE
yuē	约/約	to make an appointment	verb	7
yuè	月/月	month, moon	noun	4

Z

zài	在/在	to be in	verb	2
zài	在/在	at, in, on	preposition	2
zàijiàn	再见/再見	goodbye	expression	4
zánmen	咱们/咱們	we (dialect)	pronoun	7
zāogāo	糟糕/糟糕	terrible, too bad	adjective	7
zǎo	早/早	early	adjective	8
zǎofàn	早饭/早飯	breakfast	noun	8
zǎoshang	早上/早上	early morning	noun	7
zào	造/造	to make, to manufacture	verb	8
zěnme	怎么/怎麼	how	adverb	4
zěnmebàn	怎么办/怎麼辦	what to do	expression	7

zěnmeyàng	怎么样/怎麼樣	how, how about	adverb	5
zhāng	张/張		measure word	3
Zhāng	张/張	a surname	proper noun	3
Zhāng Dàwèi	张大卫/張大衛	David Johnson	proper noun	2
Zhāng Huìkē	张慧科/張慧科	a person's name	proper noun	2UE
zhǎngdà	长大/長大	to grow up	verb	2UE
zhǎo	找/找	to look for	verb	1UE
zhǎodào	找到/找到	to find	verb	1UE
Zhào	赵/趙	a surname	proper noun	4
zhàopiàn	照片/照片	photograph, picture	noun	3
zhè	这/這	this	pronoun	2
zhè (r)	这(儿)/這(兒)	here (informal)	pronoun	4
zhèlǐ	这里/這裏	here	pronoun	4
zhèxiē	这些/這些	these, those	pronoun	8
zhēnlǐ	真理/真理	truth	noun	2UE
zhēnzhū	珍珠/珍珠	pearl	noun	8
zhèngzhì	政治/政治	politics	noun	5
zhī	只/隻		measure word	1UE
zhī	支/支		measure word	2UE
zhīdào	知道/知道	to know, to be aware of	verb	4
zhīhòu	之后/之後	after, hereafter	preposition	7
zhīqián	之前/之前	before, prior	preposition	7
zhǐ	只/祇	only	adverb	3
zhǐhǎo	只好/祇好	to have to	adverb	7
zhǐ	纸/紙	paper	noun	2UE
zhì	至/至	to, until	preposition	6
zhōng	钟/鐘	clock	noun	5
zhōng	中/中	center, middle	adjective	1
Zhōngguó	中国/中國	China	proper noun	2
Zhōngwén	中文/中文	Chinese	proper noun	1

zhōngwǔ	中午/中午	noon	noun	5
zhōngxué	中学/中學	middle school	noun	2
zhōu	周/周	week, cycle, a surname	noun	4
Zhōu Wěishí	周伟石/周偉石	Stoney Joel	proper noun	8
zhú	竹/竹	bamboo	noun	6
zhǔtí	主题/主題	theme	noun	1UE
zhǔyào	主要/主要	main, chief, major	adjective	1UE
zhù	祝/祝	to wish	verb	4
zhùhè	祝贺/祝賀	to congratulate	verb	4
zhù	住/住	to live	verb	3
zhuān	砖/磚	brick	noun	2UE
zì	字/字	word, character	noun	1
zìjǐ	自己/自己	self, oneself	pronoun	7
zǒngshì	总是/總是	always, invariably	adverb	8
zǒu	走/走	to walk, to go, to go away	verb	7
zuì	最/最	the most (indicating the superlative)	adverb	2
zuótiān	昨天/昨天	yesterday	noun	7
zuò	做/做	to do, to make	verb	3
zuòcí	作词/作詞	to write lyrics	verb	2UE
zuòjiā	作家/作家	writer	noun	8
zuòpǐn	作品/作品	work (artistic and literary)	noun	8
zuòqǔ	作曲/作曲	composer	noun	1UE
zuòwéi	作为/作爲	as	preposition	8
zuòwén	作文/作文	composition	noun	8
zuòyè	作业/作業	homework	noun	6

English — Chinese

1UE: First Unit End Activities
2UE: Second Unit End Activities

English	Chinese		Function	Lesson
A				
able	能/能	néng	verb	7
(be) able	会/會	huì	verb	6
(be) able	可以/可以	kěyǐ	verb	7
accomodation for guests	馆/館	guǎn	noun	7
accountant	会计师/會計師	kuàijìshī	noun	8
activity	活动/活動	huódòng	noun	6
actor	演员/演員	yǎnyuán	noun	8
actress	演员/演員	yǎnyuán	noun	8
add	加/加	jiā	verb	8
affair	事(儿)/事(兒)	shì (r)	noun	7
(be) afraid of	怕/怕	pà	verb	7
after	之后/之後	zhīhòu	preposition	7
after	以后/以後	yǐhòu	preposition	7
after all	到底/到底	dàodǐ	adverb	8
after class	课下/課下	kèxià	expression	7
afternoon	下午/下午	xiàwǔ	noun	5
age	岁/歲	suì	noun	3
ah	呀/呀	yā (or: ya)	exclamation	1UE
ahead	前/前	qián	noun	7
alike	一样/一樣	yīyàng	adjective	6
all	所有/所有	suǒyǒu	pronoun	2UE
all	都/都	dōu	adverb	5
almost	差不多/差不多	chàbuduō	adverb	6
almost	几乎/幾乎	jīhū	adverb	6
allow	让/讓	ràng	verb	7
already	都/都	dōu	adverb	5

also	还/還	hái	adverb	3
also	也/也	yě	verb	1
alter	改变/改變	gǎibiàn	verb	8
always	永远/永遠	yǒngyuǎn	adverb	1UE
always	总是/總是	zǒngshì	adverb	8
amazing	了不起/了不起	liǎo bu qǐ	expression	8
America	美国/美國	Měiguó	proper noun	2
An	安/安	Ān	proper noun	3
analyze	分析/分析	fēnxi	verb	8
and	与/與	yǔ	preposition	8
and	和/和	hé	conjunction	2
Andrew Hunt	黄安竹/黄安竹	Huáng Ānzhú	proper noun	6
Andy Yoon	英安迪/英安迪	Yīng Āndí	proper noun	8
Anna	安娜/安娜	Ānnà	proper noun	3
answer	回答/回答	huídá	verb	7
answer	回答/回答	huídá	noun	7
arrive	到/到	dào	verb	4
art	美术/美術	měishù	noun	5
as	因为/因爲	yīnwèi	expression	5
as	作为/作爲	zuòwéi	preposition	8
as a result	所以/所以	suǒyǐ	conjunction	5
ask	问/問	wèn	verb	7
ask	要/要	yào	verb	4
assign (homework)	留/留	liú	verb	6
at	在/在	zài	preposition	2
at once	当时/當時	dāngshí	adverb	8
at that time	当时/當時	dāngshí	adverb	8
attend a class	上课/上課	shàngkè	verb	2
attend school	上学/上學	shàngxué	verb	3
(be) aware of	知道/知道	zhīdào	verb	4

(be) away from home	出门/出門	chūmén	verb	7
awfully	很/很	hěn	adverb	4

B

baby	娃(娃)/娃(娃)	wá (wa)	noun	1UE
bag	包/包	bāo	noun	5
Bai	白/白	bái	proper noun	8
bamboo	竹/竹	zhú	noun	6
bank	银行/銀行	yínháng	noun	3
basketball	篮球/籃球	lánqiú	noun	7
be	是/是	shì	verb	1
bear in mind	记住/記住	jìzhù	verb	7
beautiful	美丽/美麗	měilì	adjective	2UE
beautiful	美/美	měi	adjective	2
because	因为/因爲	yīnwèi	expression	5
become acquainted with	结识/結識	jiéshí	verb	1UE
before	之前/之前	zhīqián	preposition	7
before	以前/以前	yǐqián	adverb	7
beg (for food or money)	要饭/要飯	yàofàn	verb	2UE
begin	开始/開始	kāishǐ	verb	6
behind	后面/後面	hòumian	preposition	7
Beijing	北京/北京	Běijīng	proper noun	2
believe	以为/以爲	yǐwéi	verb	2UE
bell	铃/鈴	líng	noun	7
besides	另外/另外	lìngwài	adverb	7
besides	除了……(以外)，也(or: 还)/除了……(以外)，也(or: 還)	chúle……yǐwài, yě (or: hái)	preposition	6
big	大/大	dà	adjective	2
biology	生物(学)/生物(學)	shēngwù (xué)	noun	5
bird	鸟/鳥	niǎo	noun	2UE
birthday	生日/生日	shēngrì	noun	3
blackboard	黑板/黑板	hēibǎn	noun	2UE

boat	船/船	chuán	noun	1UE
boat	书/書	shū	noun	2
book bag	书包/書包	shūbāo	noun	5
boss	老板/老板	lǎobǎn	noun	1UE
both	都/都	dōu	adverb	5
bottle	瓶/瓶	píng	noun	4
boyfriend	男朋友/男朋友	nán péngyou	noun	4
breakfast	早饭/早飯	zǎofàn	noun	8
brick	砖/磚	zhuān	noun	2UE
bright	明/明	míng	adjective	1
brilliant	明/明	míng	adjective	1
bring	带/帶	dài	verb	7
business	事(儿)/事(兒)	shì (r)	noun	7
busy	忙/忙	máng	adjective	5
but	不过/不過	bùguò	conjunction	5
but	可是/可是	kěshì	conjunction	4
buy	买/買	mǎi	verb	4

C

cake	蛋糕/蛋糕	dàngāo	noun	4
call	叫/叫	jiào	verb	1
can	能/能	néng	verb	7
can	可以/可以	kěyǐ	verb	7
capital of a country	京/京	jīng	noun	2
card	卡/卡	kǎ	noun	4
careful	认真/認真	rènzhēn	adjective	8
careless person	马大哈/馬大哈	mǎdàhā	noun	7
carry away	搬/搬	bān	verb	2UE
cause	事业/事業	shìyè	noun	8
cell phone	手机/手機	shǒujī	noun	7
center	中/中	zhōng	adjective	1
chalk	粉笔/粉筆	fěnbǐ	noun	2UE

change	变/變	biàn	verb	1UE
change	改变/改變	gǎibiàn	verb	8
change into	变成/變成	biànchéng	verb	1UE
character	文/文	wén	noun	1
character	字/字	zì	noun	1
cheap	经济/經濟	jīngjì	adjective	5
chef	厨师/厨師	chúshī	noun	8
chief	主要/主要	zhǔyào	adjective	1UE
child	孩子/孩子	háizi	noun	3
China	中国/中國	Zhōngguó	proper noun	2
Chinese	中文/中文	Zhōngwén	proper noun	1
Chinese language	汉语/漢語	Hànyǔ	proper noun	2
class	班/班	bān	noun	6
class	课/課	kè	noun	2
classmate	同学/同學	tóngxué	noun	1
classroom	教室/教室	jiàoshì	noun	2UE
clock	钟/鐘	zhōng	noun	5
Coca-Cola	可口可乐/可口可樂	Kěkǒu Kělè	proper noun	2UE
come	来/來	lái	verb	2
compare	比/比	bǐ	verb	8
compared to	比/比	bǐ	preposition	8
compete	比赛/比賽	bǐsài	verb	7
complete	完/完	wán	verb	6
completely different	截然不同/截然不同	jiérán bùtóng	expression	6
composer	作曲/作曲	zuòqǔ	noun	1UE
composition	作文/作文	zuòwén	noun	8
comprehend	理解/理解	lǐjiě	verb	8
consequently	因此/因此	yīncǐ	adverb	8
conversation	对话/對話	duìhuà	noun	6
cook	厨师/厨師	chúshī	noun	8

correct	对/對	duì	adjective	5
country	国/國	guó	noun	2
course	课/課	kè	noun	2
congratulate	祝贺/祝賀	zhùhè	verb	4
copy by hand	抄/抄	chāo	verb	2UE
crowd	群/群	qún	noun	2UE
culture	文化/文化	wénhuà	noun	2
cycle	周/周	zhōu	noun	4

D

dad	爸爸/爸爸	bàba	noun	3
daddy	爸爸/爸爸	bàba	noun	3
David Johnson	张大卫/張大衛	Zhāng Dàwèi	proper noun	2
day	日/日	rì	noun	3
day	天/天	tiān	noun	2
day after tomorrow	后天/後天	hòutiān	noun	7
day of the month	号/號	hào	noun	4
defend	守/守	shǒu	verb	2UE
desire	愿/願	yuàn	verb	1UE
dialogue	对话/對話	duìhuà	noun	6
diary	日记/日記	rìjì	noun	2UE
dictation	听写/聽寫	tīngxiě	noun	7
difficult	难/難	nán	adjective	1UE
director (of a film or play)	导演/導演	dǎoyǎn	noun	1UE
do	做/做	zuò	verb	3
do	干/幹	gàn	verb	6
doctor	医生/醫生	yīshēng	noun	3
dog	狗/狗	gǒu	noun	1UE
dot	点/點	diǎn	noun	5
drama	剧/劇	jù	noun	1UE
drama	戏/戲	xì	noun	1UE

draw	画/畫	huà	verb	8
drawing	画(儿)/畫(兒)	huà (r)	noun	8
drink	喝/喝	hē	verb	2UE
drop	滴/滴	dī	noun	2UE

E

each	每/每	měi	adjective	5
early	早/早	zǎo	adjective	8
early morning	早上/早上	zǎoshang	noun	7
earth	地/地	dì	noun	5
earthshaking	惊天动地/驚天動地	jīngtiān dòngdì	adjective	2UE
easy	容易/容易	róngyì	adjective	5
eat	吃/吃	chī	verb	4
economics	经济/經濟	jīngjì	noun	5
economy	经济/經濟	jīngjì	noun	5
eight	八/八	bā	numeral	2
eighty	八十/八十	bāshí	numeral	4
either...or	或(者)/或(者)	huò (zhě)	conjunction	8
elder brother	哥哥/哥哥	gēge	noun	3
elder sister	姐姐/姐姐	jiějie	noun	3
electricity	电/電	diàn	noun	7
elementary level	初级/初級	chūjí	noun	6
eleven	十一/十一	shíyī	numeral	3
else	别/別	bié	adjective	8
embassy	使馆/使館	shǐguǎn	noun	7
employ	用/用	yòng	verb	7
engine	机/機	jī	noun	7
engineer	工程师/工程師	gōngchéngshī	noun	8
erase	擦/擦	cā	verb	2UE
English	英语/英語	Yīngyǔ	proper noun	2
every	每/每	měi	adjective	5

everybody	大家/大家	dàjiā	pronoun	1UE
everywhere	到处/到處	dàochù	adverb	1UE
examination	考试/考試	kǎoshì	noun	6
except	除了……(以外)，都/除了……(以外)，都	chúle……yǐwài, dōu	preposition	6
exercise	练习/練習	liànxí	verb	6
explain	解释/解釋	jiěshì	verb	8
extraordinary	了不起/了不起	liǎo bu qǐ	expression	8

F

face	脸/臉	liǎn	noun	1UE
fame	名/名	míng	noun	1
family	家/家	jiā	noun	3
family	家庭/家庭	jiātíng	noun	8
family picture	全家福/全家福	quánjiāfú	noun	3
fast	快/快	kuài	adverb	4
fear	怕/怕	pà	verb	7
feel	觉得/覺得	juéde	verb	4
female	女/女	nǚ	adjective	3
fifty	五十/五十	wǔshí	numeral	4
filled	满/滿	mǎn	adjective	5
finally	到底/到底	dàodǐ	adverb	8
find	找到/找到	zhǎodào	verb	1UE
fine	好/好	hǎo	adjective	1
fine arts	美术/美術	měishù	noun	5
finish	完/完	wán	verb	6
finish attending (or teaching) a class	下课/下課	xiàkè	verb	7
five	五/五	wǔ	numeral	2
flower	花/花	huā	noun	4
flower (written language)	英/英	yīng	noun	2

fly	飞/飛	fēi	verb	8
(be) fond of	喜欢/喜歡	xǐhuān	verb	4
food	饭/飯	fàn	noun	4
for	给/給	gěi	preposition	3
for a short while	一下(儿)/一下(兒)	yīxià (r)	expression	2
forever	永远/永遠	yǒngyuǎn	adverb	1UE
forget	忘/忘	wàng	verb	7
forgetful person	马大哈/馬大哈	mǎdàhā	noun	7
forty	四十/四十	sìshí	numeral	3
four	四/四	sì	numeral	2
frequently	常(常)/(常常)	cháng (cháng)	adverb	6
friend	朋友/朋友	péngyou	noun	2
from	从/從	cóng	preposition	8
from now on	从此/從此	cóngcǐ	adverb	1UE
front	前/前	qián	noun	7
full	满/滿	mǎn	adjective	5
fullest extent	尽量/盡量	jìnliàng	adjective	6
fun	乐趣/樂趣	lèqù	noun	2UE

G

Gao	高/高	gāo	proper noun	2
Gao Yingming	高英明/高英明	Gāo Yīngmíng	proper noun	2
garden	园/園	yuán	noun	4
geography	地理/地理	dìlǐ	noun	5
geometry	几何/幾何	jǐhé	noun	5
give	给/給	gěi	verb	3
give a name	起名字/起名字	qǐ míngzi	verb	6
give an examination	考试/考試	kǎoshì	verb	6
go	走/走	zǒu	verb	7
go	去/去	qù	verb	4

go away	走/走	zǒu	verb	7
go out	出门/出門	chūmén	verb	7
go through	过/過	guò	verb	4
go to school	上学/上學	shàngxué	verb	3
God-send	天赐/天賜	tiāncì	proper noun	1UE
God's gift	天赐/天賜	tiāncì	proper noun	1UE
gold	金/金	jīn	noun	1UE
good	好/好	hǎo	adjective	1
goodbye	再见/再見	zàijiàn	expression	4
grace	娜/娜	nà	noun	3
grade	年级/年級	niánjí	noun	6
grammar	语法/語法	yǔfǎ	noun	2
granddaughter	孙女/孫女	sūnnǚ	noun	1UE
grandfather (maternal)	姥爷/姥爺	lǎoye	noun	3
grandfather (paternal)	爷爷/爺爺	yéye	noun	3
grandmother (maternal)	姥姥/姥姥	lǎolao	noun	3
grandmother (paternal)	奶奶/奶奶	nǎinai	noun	3
grandson	孙子/孫子	sūnzi	noun	1UE
great	大/大	dà	adjective	2
Great Wall	长城/長城	chángchéng	proper noun	4
group	群/群	qún	noun	2UE
grow up	长大/長大	zhǎngdà	verb	2UE
guard	守/守	shǒu	verb	2UE

H

half	半/半	bàn	noun	5
hand	手/手	shǒu	noun	7
hand over	交/交	jiāo	verb	7
handle	办/辦	bàn	verb	7
handle business	办公/辦公	bàngōng	verb	7
happy	快乐/快樂	kuàilè	adjective	4

hastily	急忙/急忙	jímáng	adverb	7
have	有/有	yǒu	verb	3
have fun	玩(儿)/玩(兒)	wán (r)	verb	7
have to	得/得	děi	verb	5
have to	只好/祇好	zhǐhǎo	adverb	7
He	何/何	hé	proper noun	5
he	他/他	tā	pronoun	2
hear that	听说/聽説	tīngshuō	verb	4
heart	心/心	xīn	noun	1UE
heaven	天/天	tiān	noun	2
help	帮助/幫助	bāngzhù	verb	1UE
Hemingway	海明威/海明威	Hǎimíngwēi	proper noun	8
her	她/她	tā	pronoun	2
here (informal)	这(儿)/這(兒)	zhè (r)	pronoun	4
here	这里/這裏	zhèlǐ	pronoun	4
hereafter	之后/之後	zhīhòu	preposition	7
hereafter	以后/以後	yǐhòu	preposition	7
high	高/高	gāo	adjective	2
him	他/他	tā	pronoun	2
history	历史/歷史	lìshǐ	noun	5
history	史/史	shǐ	noun	5
hold up	举起/舉起	jǔqǐ	verb	2UE
home	家/家	jiā	noun	3
homework	作业/作業	zuòyè	noun	6
hope	希望/希望	xīwàng	verb	2UE
hope	愿/願	yuàn	verb	1UE
hospital	医院/醫院	yīyuàn	noun	3
household	家庭/家庭	jiātíng	noun	8
how	怎么/怎麽	zěnme	adverb	4
how	怎么样/怎麽樣	zěnmeyàng	adverb	5

how about	怎么样/怎麼樣	zěnmeyàng	adverb	5
how many	几(个)/幾(個)	jǐgè	adjective	3
how old are you (used for elder people)	您多大岁数/您多大歲數	nín duō dà suìshù	expression	3
how old are you (used for young people)	你多大/你多大	nǐ duō dà	expression	3
however	可是/可是	kěshì	conjunction	4
however	不过/不過	bùguò	conjunction	5
Hua	花/花	huā	proper noun	6
hundred	百/百	bǎi	numeral	5
husband	先生/先生	xiānsheng	noun	1

I

I	我/我	wǒ	pronoun	1
ideal	理想/理想	lǐxiǎng	noun	8
if	如果/如果	rúguǒ	conjunction	1UE
if not	不然/不然	bùrán	conjunction	7
immediately	就/就	jiù	adverb	6
in	在/在	zài	preposition	2
in	里/裏	lǐ	preposition	4
(be) in	在/在	zài	verb	2
in addition to	另外/另外	lìngwài	adverb	7
in addition to	除了……(以外),也(or:还)/除了……(以外),也(or:還)	chúle……yǐwài, yě (or: hái)	preposition	6
in a hurry	急忙/急忙	jímáng	adverb	7
inferior	下/下	xià	adjective	4
in other words	也就是说/也就是说	yě jiù shì shuō	expression	6
inside	里/裏	lǐ	preposition	4
instruct	教/教	jiāo	verb	6
intend	打算/打算	dǎsuan	verb	4
interesting	有意思/有意思	yǒu yìsi	adjective	5

English	Chinese	Pinyin	Part of Speech	Lesson
in that case	那(么)/那(麼)	nà (me)	conjunction	4
in the city	城里/城裏	chénglǐ	expression	2UE
in town	城里/城裏	chénglǐ	expression	2UE
introduce	介绍/介紹	jièshào	verb	2
introduction	介绍/介紹	jièshào	noun	2
invariably	总是/總是	zǒngshì	adverb	8
invite	请/請	qǐng	verb	2
Italy	意大利/義大利	Yìdàlì	proper noun	4

J

English	Chinese	Pinyin	Part of Speech	Lesson
Japan	日本/日本	Rìběn	proper noun	4
jar	瓶/瓶	píng	noun	4
jasmine	莉/莉	lì	noun	5
Jenny Bailey	白珍妮/白珍妮	Bái Zhēnnī	proper noun	8
job	工作/工作	gōngzuò	noun	3
journal	日记/日記	rìjì	noun	2UE
journey	路/路	lù	noun	1UE
joyful	快乐/快樂	kuàilè	adjective	4
just now	刚(刚)/剛(剛)	gāng (gāng)	adverb	6
joy	乐趣/樂趣	lèqù	noun	2UE

K

English	Chinese	Pinyin	Part of Speech	Lesson
Kim Maas	马可明/馬可明	Mǎ Kěmíng	proper noun	7
king	王/王	wáng	noun	1UE
know	认识/認識	rènshi	verb	2
know	知道/知道	zhīdào	verb	4
know how	会/會	huì	verb	6

L

English	Chinese	Pinyin	Part of Speech	Lesson
land	地/地	dì	noun	5
language	语/語	yǔ	noun	2
language	语言/語言	yǔyán	noun	6
language	文/文	wén	noun	1

large	大/大	dà	adjective	2
law	法/法	fǎ	noun	2
law firm	律师所/律師所	lùshīsuǒ	noun	3
lawyer	律师/律師	lùshī	noun	3
lead	领/領	lǐng	verb	2UE
learn	学/學	xué	verb	1
leave (a message)	留/留	liú	verd	6
leave something	留下/留下	liúxià	verb	6
lesson	课/課	kè	noun	2
let	让/讓	ràng	verb	7
let go	放/放	fàng	verb	2UE
Li	李/李	Lǐ	proper noun	1
Li Tongwen	李同文/李同文	Lǐ Tóngwén	proper noun	1
library	图书馆/圖書館	túshūguǎn	noun	7
lift	举起/舉起	jǔqǐ	verb	2UE
like	喜欢/喜歡	xǐhuan	verb	4
listen	听/聽	tīng	verb	4
literature	文学/文學	wénxué	noun	8
little	小/小	xiǎo	adjective	1
(a) little while	一会(儿)/一會(兒)	yīhuì (r)	expression	5
Liu	刘/劉	Liú	proper noun	1
Liu Xiaoming	刘小明/劉小明	Liú Xiǎomíng	proper noun	1
live	住/住	zhù	verb	3
look as if	看来/看來	kànlái	verb	5
look at	看/看	kàn	verb	3
look for	寻/尋	xún	verb	1UE
look for	找/找	zhǎo	verb	1UE
long	长/長	cháng	adjective	4
longevity	长寿/長壽	chángshòu	noun	4
lower	下/下	xià	adjective	4

lyrics	歌词/歌詞	gēcí	noun	1UE

M

machine	机/機	jī	noun	7
main	主要/主要	zhǔyào	adjective	1UE
major	主要/主要	zhǔyào	adjective	1UE
make	造/造	zào	verb	8
make	做/做	zuò	verb	3
make an appointment	约/約	yuē	verb	7
make sound	响/響	xiǎng	verb	7
male	男/男	nán	adjective	3
man of letters	文学家/文學家	wénxuéjiā	noun	8
manage	办/辦	bàn	verb	7
manufacture	造/造	zào	verb	8
marry	结婚/結婚	jiéhūn	verb	8
marry (for a man)	成家/成家	chéngjiā	verb	8
material gain	功利/功利	gōnglì	noun	2UE
mathematics	数学/數學	shùxué	noun	5
matter	事(儿)/事(兒)	shì (r)	noun	7
may	可以/可以	kěyǐ	verb	7
may I ask	请问/請問	qǐngwèn	expression	1
me	我/我	wǒ	pronoun	1
meal	饭/飯	fàn	noun	4
meaning	意思/意思	yìsi	noun	5
meet	接/接	jiē	verb	7
metals	金/金	jīn	noun	1UE
method	法/法	fǎ	noun	2
middle	中/中	zhōng	adjective	1
middle school	中学/中學	zhōngxué	noun	2
military officer	军官/軍官	jūnguān	noun	8
minute	分钟/分鐘	fēnzhōng	noun	5

miss	想/想	xiǎng	verb	4
missing person	寻人启示/尋人啓示	xúnrén qǐshì	expression	2UE
mister	先生/先生	xiānsheng	noun	1
mobile phone	手机/手機	shǒujī	noun	7
mom	妈妈/媽媽	māma	noun	3
moment	时候/時候	shíhou	noun	6
mommy	妈妈/媽媽	māma	noun	3
money	钱/錢	qián	noun	2UE
monkey	猴/猴	hóu	noun	1UE
month	月/月	yuè	noun	4
moon	月/月	yuè	noun	4
most	最/最	zuì	adverb	2
mountain	山/山	shān	noun	2UE
mountain village	山村/山村	shāncūn	noun	2UE
move	搬/搬	bān	verb	2UE
movie	电影/電影	diànyǐng	noun	1UE
music	音乐/音樂	yīnyuè	noun	5
mysterious	神秘/神秘	shénmì	adjective	2UE

N

name	名字/名字	míngzi	noun	1
name	名/名	míng	noun	1
name	起名字/起名字	qǐ míngzi	verb	6
(be) named	叫/叫	jiào	verb	1
nation	国/國	guó	noun	2
nearly	差不多/差不多	chàbuduō	adverb	6
nearly	几乎/幾乎	jīhū	adverb	6
nest	巢/巢	cháo	noun	2UE
new	新/新	xīn	adjective	2
new word	生词/生詞	shēngcí	noun	6
newborn animal	娃(娃)/娃(娃)	wá (wa)	noun	1UE

next	下/下	xià	adjective	4
nice	好/好	hǎo	adjective	1
nine	九/九	jiǔ	numeral	2
ninety	九十/九十	jiǔshí	numeral	4
no	不/不	bù	adverb	1
no longer	不再/不再	bùzài	adverb	8
no more	不再/不再	bùzài	adverb	8
nod one's head	点头/點頭	diǎntóu	verb	1UE
noodles	面条/面條	miàntiáo	noun	4
noon	中午/中午	zhōngwǔ	noun	5
normally	平时/平時	píngshí	adverb	6
not	不/不	bù	adverb	1
not	没/没	méi	adverb	3
not long ago	刚(刚)/剛(剛)	gāng (gāng)	adverb	6
not only... but also	不但……而且/不但……而且	bùdàn……érqiě	expression	8
now	现在/現在	xiànzài	adverb	2
number	号码/號碼	hàomǎ	noun	7

O

ocean	海/海	hǎi	noun	8
of course	当然/當然	dāngrán	adverb	8
offer as a tribute	奉献/奉獻	fèngxiàn	verb	2UE
office	办公室/辦公室	bàngōngshì	noun	7
often	常(常)/(常常)	cháng (cháng)	adverb	6
oh	呀/呀	yā (or: ya)	exclamation	1UE
old	老/老	lǎo	adjective	1
on	在/在	zài	preposition	2
on schedule	按时/按時	ànshí	adverb	7
on time	按时/按時	ànshí	adverb	7
one	一/一	yī	numeral	2

one hundred	一百/一百	yībǎi	numeral	5
one thousand	一千/一千	yīqiān	numeral	5
oneself	自己/自己	zìjǐ	pronoun	7
only	只/衹	zhǐ	adverb	3
open	打开/打開	dǎkāi	verb	2
opera	剧/劇	jù	noun	1UE
opera	戏/戲	xì	noun	1UE
or	或(者)/或(者)	huò (zhě)	conjunction	8
or	还是/還是	háishì	conjunction	3
oral	口头/口頭	kǒutóu	adjective	7
ordinal number marker	第/第	dì	particle	2
ordinarily	平时/平時	píngshí	adverb	6
other	别/別	bié	adjective	8
otherwise	不然/不然	bùrán	conjunction	7
ought	应该/應該	yīnggāi	verb	7
outstanding	出色/出色	chūsè	adjective	8

P

packed	满/滿	mǎn	adjective	5
page	页/頁	yè	noun	2
paint	画/畫	huà	verb	8
painting	画(儿)/畫(兒)	huà (r)	noun	8
paper	纸/紙	zhǐ	noun	2UE
park	公园/公園	gōngyuán	noun	4
park	园/園	yuán	noun	4
pass	过/過	guò	verb	4
pearl	珍珠/珍珠	zhēnzhū	noun	8
Pearl S. Buck	赛珍珠/賽珍珠	Sài Zhēnzhū	proper noun	8
Peking University	北京大学/北京大學	Běijīng Dàxué	proper noun	2
people	人/人	rén	noun	2
(a) period of time	期/期	qī	noun	4

person	人/人	rén	noun	2
photograph	照片/照片	zhàopiàn	noun	3
physical education	体育/體育	tǐyù	noun	5
physics	物理/物理	wùlǐ	noun	5
pick up	接/接	jiē	verb	7
picture	照片/照片	zhàopiàn	noun	3
pilot	飞行员/飛行員	fēixíngyuán	noun	8
ping-pong	乒乓球/乒乓球	pīngpāngqiú	noun	7
place	地方/地方	dìfang	noun	1UE
place	所/所	suǒ	noun	3
(a) place for cultural activities	馆/館	guǎn	noun	7
plan	打算/打算	dǎsuan	verb	4
plan	想/想	xiǎng	verb	4
platform	讲台/講臺	jiǎngtái	noun	2UE
play	剧/劇	jù	noun	1UE
play	戲/戲	xì	noun	1UE
play	玩(儿)/玩(兒)	wán (r)	verb	7
please	请/請	qǐng	verb	2
please tell me	请问/請問	qǐngwèn	expression	1
pleasure	乐趣/樂趣	lèqù	noun	2UE
P.M.	下午/下午	xiàwǔ	noun	5
point	点/點	diǎn	noun	5
police	警察/警察	jǐngchá	noun	8
political	政治/政治	zhèngzhì	adjective	5
politics	政治/政治	zhèngzhì	noun	5
poor	穷/窮	qióng	adjective	2UE
postman	邮递员/郵遞員	yóudìyuán	noun	8
power	电/電	diàn	noun	7
practice	练习/練習	liànxí	verb	6
practice	练习/練習	liànxí	noun	6

pretty	漂亮/漂亮	piàoliang	adjective	4
pretty	美/美	měi	adjective	2
principle	道理/道理	dàolǐ	noun	8
prior	之前/之前	zhīqián	preposition	7
prior	以前/以前	yǐqián	adverb	7
probably	可能/可能	kěnéng	adverb	7
problem	题/題	tí	noun	5
pronunciation	发音/發音	fāyīn	noun	6
pronunciation	语音/語音	yǔyīn	noun	6
public	公/公	gōng	adjective	4
public places	院/院	yuàn	noun	3

Q

quarter (of an hour)	刻/刻	kè	noun	5
question	问题/問題	wèntí	noun	7
quickly	一下(儿)/一下(兒)	yīxià (r)	expression	2
quickly	快/快	kuài	adverb	4
quite	很/很	hěn	adverb	4
quiz	测验/測驗	cèyàn	noun	6

R

rainbow	彩虹/彩虹	cǎihóng	noun	2UE
read	读/讀	dú	verb	6
reason	道理/道理	dàolǐ	noun	8
receive	接/接	jiē	verb	7
release	放/放	fàng	verb	2UE
remarkable	出色/出色	chūsè	adjective	8
remember	记住/記住	jìzhù	verb	7
reputation	名/名	míng	noun	1
respond	回答/回答	huídá	verb	7
response	回答/回答	huídá	noun	7
restaurant	餐馆/餐館	cānguǎn	noun	4

review	复习/復習	fùxí	verb	7
review	复习/復習	fùxí	noun	7
right	对/對	duì	adjective	5
right away	就/就	jiù	adverb	6
ring	响/響	xiǎng	verb	7
road	路/路	lù	noun	1UE
room	室/室	shì	noun	7
route	路/路	lù	noun	1UE

S

salute	敬礼/敬禮	jìnglǐ	verb	1UE
same	一样/一樣	yīyàng	adjective	6
say	说/説	shuō	verb	4
schoolmate	同学/同學	tóngxué	noun	1
scientist	科学家/科學家	kēxuéjiā	noun	8
script	文/文	wén	noun	1
sea	海/海	hǎi	noun	8
see you later	回头见/回頭見	huítóujiàn	expression	5
see you soon	回头见/回頭見	huítóujiàn	expression	5
see you soon	一会(儿)见/一會(兒)見	yīhuì (r) jiàn	expression	5
see you tomorrow	明天见/明天見	míngtiān jiàn	expression	4
seek	寻/尋	xún	verb	1UE
seem	看来/看來	kànlái	verb	5
self	自己/自己	zìjǐ	pronoun	7
sell	卖/賣	mài	verb	6
semester	学期/學期	xuéqī	noun	4
semi-	半/半	bàn	noun	5
serious	认真/認真	rènzhēn	adjective	8
serve as	当/當	dāng	verb	8
set free	放/放	fàng	verb	2UE
seven	七/七	qī	numeral	4

seventy	七十/七十	qīshí	numeral	4
shake hands	握手/握手	wòshǒu	verb	1UE
she	她/她	tā	pronoun	2
Shi	史/史	shǐ	proper noun	5
ship	船/船	chuán	noun	1UE
shop	馆/館	guǎn	noun	7
short of	差/差	chà	adjective	5
should	应该/應該	yīnggāi	verb	7
Shuiquan	水泉/水泉	shuǐquán	proper noun	2UE
Sichuan Province	四川/四川	Sìchuān	proper noun	1UE
sick	病/病	bìng	adjective	2UE
since	因为/因爲	yīnwèi	expression	5
sing	唱歌/唱歌	chànggē	verb	6
six	六/六	liù	numeral	2
sixty	六十/六十	liùshí	numeral	4
sky	天/天	tiān	noun	2
sleep	睡觉/睡覺	shuìjiào	verb	2UE
small	小/小	xiǎo	adjective	1
smile	笑/笑	xiào	verb	1UE
so	那(么)/那(麼)	nà (me)	conjunction	4
society	社会/社會	shèhuì	noun	8
soil	地/地	dì	noun	5
solve a problem	解题/解題	jiětí	verb	5
some... some others	有的……有的/有的……有的	yǒude……yǒude	expression	8
sometimes	有时(候)/有時(候)	yǒushí (hou)	adverb	6
song	歌(曲)/歌(曲)	gē (qǔ)	noun	1UE
soon	快/快	kuài	adverb	4
soon	就/就	jiù	adverb	6
sorry	对不起/對不起	duìbuqǐ	expression	5

English	Chinese	Pinyin	Part of Speech	Lesson
sound	声/聲	shēng	noun	6
speak	说/說	shuō	verb	4
speech sounds	语音/語音	yǔyīn	noun	6
spend	花/花	huā	verb	6
spend	过/過	guò	verb	4
spirited	神气/神氣	shénqì	adjective	2UE
sports	体育/體育	tǐyù	noun	5
spray	洒/灑	sǎ	verb	2UE
spring	春(天)/春(天)	chūn (tiān)	noun	1UE
sprinkle	洒/灑	sǎ	verb	2UE
start	开始/開始	kāishǐ	verb	6
start a career	立业/立業	lìyè	verb	8
station manager	台长/臺長	táizhǎng	noun	2UE
stay	留下/留下	liúxià	verb	6
still	还/還	hái	adverb	3
Stoney Joel	周伟石/周偉石	Zhōu Wěishí	proper noun	8
story	故事/故事	gùshi	noun	7
strong	有力/有力	yǒulì	adjective	2UE
study	学/學	xué	verb	1
study	学习/學習	xuéxí	verb	2
student	学生/學生	xuésheng	noun	1
student identification	学生证/學生證	xuésheng zhèng	noun	2UE
substitute an absent teacher	代课/代課	dàikè	verb	2UE
sun	日/日	rì	noun	3
Sunday	星期日/星期日	xīngqīrì	proper noun	4
Sunday	星期天/星期天	xīngqītiān	proper noun	4
surname	姓/姓	xìng	noun	1
surnamed	姓/姓	xìng	verb	1

T

English	Chinese	Pinyin	Part of Speech	Lesson
table tennis	乒乓球/乒乓球	pīngpāngqiú	noun	7

take with	带/帶	dài	verb	7
tale	故事/故事	gùshi	noun	7
tall	高/高	gāo	adjective	2
teach	教/教	jiāo	verb	6
teach a class	上课/上課	shàngkè	verb	2
teacher	老师/老師	lǎoshī	noun	1
team	班/班	bān	noun	6
tear	泪/淚	lèi	noun	2UE
telephone	电话/電話	diànhuà	noun	7
tell	告诉/告訴	gàosu	verb	6
term	期/期	qī	noun	4
ten	十/十	shí	numeral	2
terrible	糟糕/糟糕	zāogāo	adjective	7
terrific	了不起/了不起	liǎo bu qǐ	expression	8
test	考试/考試	kǎoshì	noun	6
test	考试/考試	kǎoshì	verb	6
test	试/試	shì	verb	4
test	测验/測驗	cèyàn	noun	6
text	课文/課文	kèwén	noun	6
thank	谢/謝	xiè	verb	2
thank you	谢谢/謝謝	xièxie	expression	2
thanks	谢谢/謝謝	xièxie	expression	2
that	那/那	nà	pronoun	2
that follows	后面/後面	hòumian	preposition	7
that is	也就是说/也就是説	yě jiù shì shuō	expression	6
them (feminine)	她们/她們	tāmen	pronoun	2
them (masculine)	他们/他們	tāmen	pronoun	2
theme	主题/主題	zhǔtí	noun	1UE
then	那(么)/那(麼)	nà (me)	conjunction	4
there	那里/那裏	nàlǐ	pronoun	4

there (informal)	那(儿)/那(兒)	nà (r)	pronoun	4
therefore	因此/因此	yīncǐ	adverb	8
therefore	所以/所以	suǒyǐ	conjunction	5
these	这些/這些	zhèxiē	pronoun	8
they	她们/她們	tāmen	pronoun	2
they	他们/他們	tāmen	pronoun	2
thing	事(儿)/事(兒)	shì (r)	noun	7
think	觉得/覺得	juéde	verb	4
think	以为/以爲	yǐwéi	verb	2UE
think	想/想	xiǎng	verb	4
thirty	三十/三十	sānshí	numeral	3
this	这/這	zhè	pronoun	2
those	这些/這些	zhèxiē	pronoun	8
thousand	千/千	qiān	numeral	5
three	三/三	sān	numeral	3
thus	所以/所以	suǒyǐ	conjunction	5
time	时间/時間	shíjiān	noun	6
time (recurring instances)	次/次	cì	measure word	4
title	题目/題目	tímù	noun	8
to	对/對	duì	preposition	8
to	给/給	gěi	preposition	3
to	至/至	zhì	preposition	6
today	今天/今天	jīntiān	noun	2
(be) told	听说/聽説	tīngshuō	verb	4
together	一起/一起	yīqǐ	adverb	3
together with	与/與	yǔ	preposition	8
together with...	和……一起/和……一起	hé……yīqǐ	expression	3
tomorrow	明天/明天	míngtiān	noun	4
tone	声/聲	shēng	noun	6
too	也/也	yě	verb	1

too bad	糟糕/糟糕	zāogāo	adjective	7
topic	题目/題目	tímù	noun	8
topic	题/題	tí	noun	5
train or bus ticket	车票/車票	chēpiào	noun	2UE
transform	改变/改變	gǎibiàn	verb	8
truth	真理/真理	zhēnlǐ	noun	2UE
try	试/試	shì	verb	4
turn in	交/交	jiāo	verb	7
turn into	变成/變成	biànchéng	verb	1UE
TV station	电视台/電視臺	diànshìtái	noun	2UE
twenty	二十/二十	èrshí	numeral	3
twenty one	二十一/二十一	èrshíyī	numeral	3
two	二/二	èr	numeral	2

U

understand	明白/明白	míngbai	verb	8
understand	理解/理解	lǐjiě	verb	8
university	大学/大學	dàxué	noun	2
until	至/至	zhì	preposition	6
usage	用法/用法	yòngfǎ	noun	6
use	用法/用法	yòngfǎ	noun	6
use	用/用	yòng	verb	7
useful	有用/有用	yǒuyòng	adjective	8
usually	平时/平時	píngshí	adverb	6

V

vase	瓶/瓶	píng	noun	4
very	很/很	hěn	adverb	4
very soon	一会(儿)/一會(兒)	yīhuì (r)	expression	5
vigorous	神气/神氣	shénqì	adjective	2UE
village	村子/村子	cūnzi	noun	2UE
village head	村长/村長	cūnzhǎng	noun	2UE

vocabulary	生词/生詞	shēngcí	noun	6
vocabulary	词汇/詞匯	cíhuì	noun	7
voice	声/聲	shēng	noun	6

W

wait	等/等	děng	verb	7
wait for	等/等	děng	verb	7
walk	走/走	zǒu	verb	7
want	要/要	yào	verb	4
Wang	王/王	wáng	proper noun	1
watch	看/看	kàn	verb	3
water	水/水	shuǐ	noun	2UE
way	法/法	fǎ	noun	2
way	路/路	lù	noun	1UE
we (dialect)	咱们/咱們	zánmen	pronoun	7
we	我们/我們	wǒmen	pronoun	1
week	星期/星期	xīngqī	noun	4
week	周/周	zhōu	noun	4
Wei Minzhi	魏敏芝/魏敏芝	Wèi Mǐnzhī	proper noun	2UE
well	好/好	hǎo	adverb	1
Wen Xiaoying	文小英/文小英	Wén Xiǎoyīng	proper noun	2
what	什么/什麽	shénme	pronoun	1
what to do	怎么办/怎么辦	zěnmebàn	expression	7
where	哪(儿)/哪(兒)	nǎ (r)	pronoun	3
which	哪个/哪個	nǎgè	pronoun	3
white	白/白	bái	adjective	8
who	谁/誰	shéi (or: shuí)	pronoun	2
who	谁/誰	shuí (or: shéi)	pronoun	2
why	为什么/爲什麽	wèishénme	adverb	5
Willie	威利/威利	Wēilì	proper noun	7
winter	冬/冬	dōng	noun	7

Winter Lamb	蓝冬冬/藍冬冬	Lán Dōngdōng	proper noun	7
wise	英明/英明	yīngmíng	adjective	2
wish	愿/願	yuàn	verb	1UE
wish	祝/祝	zhù	verb	4
with	和/和	hé	conjunction	2
whom	谁/誰	shéi (or: shuí)	pronoun	2
whom	谁/誰	shuí (or: shéi)	pronoun	2
word	字/字	zì	noun	1
work	工作/工作	gōngzuò	noun	3
work	干/干	gàn	verb	6
work	工作/工作	gōngzuò	verb	3
work (artistic and literary)	作品/作品	zuòpǐn	noun	8
work as	当/當	dāng	verb	8
work in an office	办公/辦公	bàngōng	verb	7
work (temporarily)	打工/打工	dǎgōng	verb	2UE
write lyrics	作词/作詞	zuòcí	verb	2UE
write	书写/書寫	shūxiě	verb	6
write	写/寫	xiě	verb	6
writer	作家/作家	zuòjiā	noun	8
writer	文学家/文學家	wénxuéjiā	noun	8
writing	文/文	wén	noun	1
written	笔头/筆頭	bǐtóu	adjective	7
wrong	错/錯	cuò	adjective	4

X

Xie	谢/謝	xiè	proper noun	2
Xie Peng	谢朋/謝朋	Xiè Péng	proper noun	2

Y

Yangtze River	长江/長江	Chángjiāng	proper noun	4
yard	院/院	yuàn	noun	3
year	年/年	nián	noun	3

English	Chinese	Pinyin	Part of Speech	Lesson
year	年级/年級	niánjí	noun	6
year	岁/歲	suì	noun	3
yes	对/對	duì	adjective	5
yesterday	昨天/昨天	zuótiān	noun	7
yet	可是/可是	kěshì	conjunction	4
you (formal)	您/您	nín	pronoun	1
you (plural)	你们/你們	nǐmen	pronoun	1
you (singular)	你/你	nǐ	pronoun	1
you are welcome	不客气/不客氣	bùkèqì	expression	7
young	年轻/年輕	niánqīng	adjective	2UE
younger brother	弟弟/弟弟	dìdi	noun	3
younger sister	妹妹/妹妹	mèimei	noun	3

Z

English	Chinese	Pinyin	Part of Speech	Lesson
zero	零/零	líng	noun	5
Zhao	赵/趙	Zhào	proper noun	4
Zhang	张/張	Zhāng	proper noun	3
Zhang Huike	张慧科/張慧科	Zhāng Huìkē	proper noun	2UE
Zhou	周/周	zhōu	noun	4